Gertrude Stein

How
TO Write

with an Afternote by Douglas Messerli

SUN &
MOON

CLASSICS

83

SUN & MOON PRESS

LOS ANGELES • 1995

HOW TO WRITE

Sun & Moon Press
A Program of The Contemporary Arts Educational Project, Inc.
a nonprofit corporation
6026 Wilshire Boulevard, Los Angeles, California 90036

This edition first published in paperback in 1995 by Sun & Moon Press
10 9 8 7 6 5 4 3 2 1
FIRST SUN & MOON PRESS EDITION
©1931 by Gertrude Stein
Afternote ©1995 by Douglas Messerli
Based on the Plain Edition (Paris: Plain Edition, 1931)
Biographical material ©1995 by Sun & Moon Press
All rights reserved

This book was made possible, in part, through an operational grant
from the Andrew W. Mellon Foundation,
through a matching grant from the National Endowment for the Arts,
a nonprofit corporation, and through contributions to
The Contemporary Arts Educational Project, Inc.
a nonprofit corporation

Cover: Untitled print from "The Somnambulist," by Ralph Gibson
©1995 by Ralph Gibson. Reprinted by permission.
Design: Katie Messborn
Typography: Guy Bennett

LIBRARY OF CONGRESS CATALOGING IN PUBLICATION DATA
Stein, Gertrude [1874–1946]
How to Write: with an Afternote by Douglas Messerli
ISBN: 1-55713-204-6 : $12.95
p. cm—Sun & Moon Classics: 83
I. Title. II. Series.
811'.54—dc20

Printed in the United States of America on acid-free paper.

Contents

Saving the Sentence

QU'EST-CE QUE C'EST cette comédie d'un chien. Que le dit train est bien celui qui doit les conduire à leur destination. Manifestement éveillé.

When he will see
When he will see
When he will see the land of liberty.

The scene changes it is a stone high up against with a hill and there is and above where they will have time. Not higher up below is a ruin which is a castle and there will be a color above it. Painting now after its great moment must come back to be a minor art.

Will be welcome.

We will be welcome.

Should be put upon a hill. Across which it is placed upon different hills. Lower hills have a mark they mean.

When a dog is no longer a lap dog there is a temporary inattention. Then they will seem to be sent together. It is a noise not of tapestry but of wood which when lighted in three logs makes a fire.

It makes it do that they do cry when in an assistance.

What is a sentence. A sentence is a part of a speech.

A speech. They knew that beside beside is colored like a word beside why there they went. That is a speech. Anybody will listen. What is romantic. I was astonished to learn that she was led by her head and her head was not with her head her head was leading when her heart stood still. She was certain to be left away with them. Dear Christian you are very sweet without hope. Hope is for you.

A blue sky can reflect in a lake.

Speeches are in answer.

We will enjoy with and without that it is said that they do present well.

Buy me a present.

Better than all for the best.

Now in thinking.

The scene opens and they have a valley before them.

Francine which is a name of a young woman who has changed very much in five years hoped to be married that is not hoped but attended to the waiting which was not intentional she was very well occupied. When it came to friendship she said after all marriage meant that they were eager and marrying. And they were without any pleasure in not arranging their wedding. Will it be soon. They will be married after waiting two years during which time they had not become acquainted with one another as they had as often met before. It is a failure in a way it is a failure.

A hill which we see before as often.

We are finally with me.

When this you see will he. A plain case of separation. Will she separate well from him. Well from him is what he thought.

Around Rome.

Rome is a capital. With pleasure in their insistence.

Linden trees do not grow only where there is a home. Linden trees do not grow only where there is a home.

There is a home in and around on account of a he meant

well with out repaying. Without repaying who was whose. It would not do.

Four people accompanied by a caniche. They went where they had liked a well with. Whom were they known to be there.

It is ours.

Prevail.

Part of a mail.

The Saracens had been absent from this country. In beggary.

A chateau which from the later time had its roof taken off for cheapness had been made when they went away. Why did not Archie come with a pharmacist. It would not be in might be in time if they never answered.

How are how do you do to be discriminated. There is a mistake in a witness. Fog is wet when there is land and it is white. Fog is wet when there is land and it is white.

It was part of it before. And now. There is a little more. And so there is more than before. Water comes before butter. And moving around. Change butter and paper. What did he weigh in happen. Apart disposed deposed that he went. In a room with a fire that he had for his share. A chair. Following roses.

Now and then there is more to it within when they send for it then.

How is sentiment maintained.

A pause.

A rain makes transplanting following easy. Thank you for thinking of the rain. Once or twice they had left what is ours allowed. A welcome to following.

He in chopping a stick flew to the eye that is hand and clover. Which they had. He was pleased to have the sea of meadow which was below theirs. It was joined and generally resembled when it is and belongs to all which they rent. They were able to have half of it altogether. There were others who had heard more. They will be more for all. However it is kindly.

When they like help they like help. They have it. They like it for them. They have it. They make the most of it which is why they wish. They will wish to have it. Made for them what they have in the way of advising and they need hope. They will allow themselves all for it. They might without which wish. In a way. They must like whatever they do.

It is very old that they like a chateau. Oh well who can be better.

What is the interest in character by saying he understood others.

There is no use in finding out what is in anybody's mind. There is no use in finding out what is in anybody's mind.

What is the difference between sentiment and romance.

What are they leaving they are leaving.

There is some difference between sentiment and romance. Sentiment is awhile and weighed as a weight and romance is made to be authentic. There is no use in knowing why they went because it is made important by their means.

All talk of how well they thought of it.

She was right to be bright.

Edith was right.

Scenery is a valley in moon-light.

Scenery is left of a valley in moon-light.

Below there is a lightened mist.

There is on the height before it makes it come a light cross which is there.

She cannot see it because the sky is light. The sky when it is light is bright.

Explanations make me think of what do they think.

No mention of a little dog.

It is here that they are putting manure.

It is very nicely made that is offering a very small piece of apple not offering but from time to time giving a very small piece of apple pear a single grape to him. He is very obliging, he relinquishes something.

She is not made to be carefully advised when it is well-known as a considerable withdrawal.

A house with health and happiness.

After it is finished before with a smaller well made winding it as a time when they know. Think of an electric clock.

How can they think that they think that they mean theirs.

That is it.

Fortune is told.

For them to be always an amount.

It is gracious to have a cool evening and agreeable though not necessitating it.

What is it.

If they are to be known.

A time in which we will believe they know and marry me.

A setting, the influence of a hill and on which snow and woods are abundant.

If they had been able they would have gone to see it.

How can one know who links what are they with a chain. They are appropriate.

I would like very much to stay longer in the country.

If they look and see two grown where they went.

It is full of finally why me.

When this you see remember me. This is a very fine sentence.

Occasions.

When they were able to have it all their way.

A frog is just like Basket for all the world.

Never to give to him because it is very well to be made mine.

Each word has twenty-two beside.

Will they follow when they go she has let her scissors go so they fell.

Each sentence has adroitness as they decide.

What is a dog.

There is no answer to what they think.

Now in English they mean very well for once.

Now translate that to now in English they mean very well for once.

A hope.

Will be fed.

Now in which they had a pleasure in their having cried when their chimney had been on fire.

A sentence has wishes as an event.

To return to the hoping of pleasing.

They will not be interested in two for a cent.

It is pretty in the country.

Never follow before with them. This is what they mean.

Moonlight means rain.

Once they have the means of saying theirs when they like.

Will when they leave will they think that they will have it for them.

It is a hop from here to there.

Do they like him when they feel for them.

A management of traces of plainly strawberry and raspberry leaves of which there are plants.

Think well of having rested for awhile.

Accidentally met lieutenant Foreman.

A bishop likes a parcel.

This is not true because he is not a bishop.

Awhile are they are better every once in a while.

They after all mean more to each other.

A chrysanthemum in bloom is more easily tied together.

Here is an effort.

It is of no use laying places for dinner since because of a turning settlement they will choose passes. In every direction they can as well see a hill as a box. A box is hedges. Little and low with news from without them. It is after that they went away.

I know who cried about Etta.

There is no difference between whether they cried or not.

Never believe that water is accredited to midsummer, or more of winter. We do know that it changes from day to day.

If opposites are equal.

If it comes one after the other furs are farther in fur bearing animals.

I do not know nor do I know if he thinks with them or without me.

What is a sentence for if I am I then my little dog knows me. Even if it is all tenderness. What is tenderness. First there must be a way of going without waiting. There are two things a dictionary and the country.

Think of reason.

It looks like it.

What looks like it.

Discouragement looks like it.

I have never been so sorry about anything as I was about Friday.

If they look like it.

They must fasten apples with quinces. Fatten a dog. Leave well enough alone.

Who has heard that they like it.

It is easy to say it another way. I will refuse.

They will not be heard when they feel well. If they accomplish anything. Still it is better.

Did anybody hear me sing to-day.

Who has whose head.

Did four leave four for long.

A thing that is discouraging is to come along. Five minutes to ten. It is very remarkable.

How are hours divided by themselves.

Four times fifty three leaves them alone.

Balance of quinces.

Five hopes that they had made them sing and left for them they are quite well if it does which means that they are alike for liking.

October is a name.

So is Basket a name.

Graves is a name.

Flowers is a name.

A dictionary.

A dog. If felt as a word it would mean that they approached and if you knew them as seeing then they leave and so there is no fear of not at all, why do they flush. This is a dog. He may have a sluggish liver.

Not found.

A noun is a name of anything. There is no hope of their pleasure.

It is very nice to change your mind about roses.

Please have it with all without it.

It is very strange but it is true that they did say it because however alike they found it.

There is no doubt that I like the thing they have for use for me.

It is an hour after they came.

May be with them.

No doubt may be with them.

No doubt may be with them no doubt may be.

May be with them may be. May be they may be.

It is easy to hide a hope.

Have meant.

A little goes a long way.

How many houses are there.

There is a house near where there is a bridge. They were willing to be there.

Hours out of it in adjoining them.

It is why forty is not arithmetic with wonder.

Any time that they go they stay. How are ours with lain for it.

It is not that it has been inhabited.

I have never been as proud of anything as I am of snow on the mountain opposite.

Betty is leaving her home or at any rate where she is.

What is it that they would have what is it that they would have gotten if they had it.

Hers and his the houses are hers and his the valley is hers and his the dog named Basket is hers and his also the respect of the populace is hers and his.

He has found something which is and has been his which

has been left for him by him and by this time means some-thing insofar as they say they hope that it is satisfactory.

What will it look like, it will happen so quickly although it is all there that it will not be left with them.

A scenery is romantic if there are steps about. Also a place to have marked as awhile. A place is romantic if there are not moments of welcoming having as much as theirs in the ap-portioning with without sent. It is difficult to remember. Will they miss her.

It was when he did behavior as a blessing. Yes not being with remembering that is what is going if it was not looked at. If having asked it to be put away. He put it away having asked it to be put away. If the weather is what is expected. Romantic makes herds better. One dog looks like a sheep because he trusts them.

Be beware.

Pour little soul.

A change in custom.

What is the difference.

One is generally told that they mean me.

How many sentences are there after all around me. How many sentences begin with at nearly four.

Thank you for the difference in me.

One thoroughly two thoroughly three thoroughly. Three is after all. They were there after all.

Painstaking.

She impressed me.

What makes forty forfeit.

No man no men do.

Are three arrangements.

I made a mistake.

Sentences and Paragraphs

A Sentence is not emotional a paragraph is.

DATES of what they bought.

They will be ready to have him. We think so.

He looks like a young man grown old. That is a sentence that they could use.

I was overcome with remorse. It was my fault that my wife did not have a cow. This sentence they cannot use.

A repetition of prettiness makes it repeated. With them looking.

A repetition of sweetness makes it not repeating but attractive and making soup and dreaming coincidences. The sentence will be saved. He raises his head and lifts it. A sentence is not whether it is beautiful. Beautiful is not thought without asking as if they are well able to be forgiving.

George Maratier in America.

The sexual life of Genia Berman.

A book of George Hugnet.

The choice of Eric Haulville.

The wealth of Henri d'Ursel.

The relief of Harry Horwood.

The mention of Walter Winterberg. The renown of Bernard Fay. The pleasure of prophecy concerning Rene Crevel. Titles are made of sentences without interruption. Sucking is dangerous. The danger of sucking.

With them.

In itself.

Within itself. A part of a sentence may be a sentence without their meaning. Think of however they went away.

It looks like a garden but he had hurt himself by accident.

Every sentence has a beginning. Will he begin.

Every sentence which has a beginning makes it be left more to them.

I return to sentences as a refreshment.

Howard opposes them less.

That is nice.

George is wonderfully well.

How does he like ability.

A sentence should be arbitrary it should not please be better.

It should not be disturbed.

A sentence has colors when they mean I liked it as selling salt should be very little used in dishes.

That is one of the best I have done.

Pleasantly or presently.

How or have. A sentence is.

Made or make a meaning.

Now feebly commence a sentence.

How has he hurried. That is a paragraph because it means yes. How has he hurried.

Now for a sentence. Welcome to hurry. That is either a sentence or a part of a sentence if it is a part of a sentence the sentence is he is welcome to hurry. Welcome is in itself a part of a sentence. She prefers them. I have told her where the place which is meant is.

Welcome when they come. Are they welcome when they come. A sentence instead of increases. It should be if they are. Welcome when they come. That so easily makes a paragraph. Try again.

They made made them when they were by them. This is a sentence. It has no use in itself because made is said two times.

Way-laid made it known as quince cake. This is a perfect sentence because it refers to regretting. They regret what they have given. So far there is no need for a paragraph. I cannot see him. This is a paragraph.

Think of a use for a paragraph. A sentence is exhausted by have they been there with him.

A useful and useful if you add house you have a paragraph. He looks like his brother. That is a whole sentence.

Dogs get tired and want to sleep. This is not a sentence to be abused.

He has had his portrait painted by a Frenchman a Dutchman an Englishman and an American.

Pleases by its sense. This is a fashion in sentences.

A dog which you have never had before has sighed. This is a fixture in sentences it is like a porcelain in plaster. All this together has no reverses. What is the difference between reserve and reverse. They can be beguiled.

Beguiled and belied. It was famous that a woman who was a wife to him.

A veritable hope. Hurry with a sentence.

This are our announcements.

A sentence. She owes him to her.

A sentence. He ought to own mines.

He heard her come in. Laughed is a word.

If a word reminds you that is a preparation which they do in time so that it is with all.

Candied is a word we were mistaken she can have a lake.

There is no use in weapons of precision for them formerly.

Think of imagination as has to do for you. Door handles which he likes.

Now there is no use in stopping when they went in.

She mentioned edging edging is used in having sewing surrounding something. It is very difficult to think twice.

This is very well done because it does not stop.

Eggs are of fish and fowl. This is perfectly reasonable. Tell them how to finish.

Now this is a new paragraph. The ending tell them how to finish makes it an importance.

First-rate has relation to tires. How are they.

That is a way to please a paragraph. Think if you can. I find it difficult to know yes or no. I find no difficulty in yes I said no. I said I would and I did. I did not used to.

This is an ordinary paragraph made different by content.

As they asked for it. Why is as they asked for it a sentence.

Think of how do you do as very necessary.

He gave it to them to-day. Now think carefully of monstrosity. He gave it to them to give away. Which one threw it away.

It is to be certain that love is lord of all.

This sentence has hope as origin.

A tapestry made easy by being seen.

Think of all these sentences and not to be annoyed.

After all what is the difference between it and you. Everybody has said they are happy.

If two sentences make a paragraph a little piece is alright because they are better apart. They are as a pleasure as out loud. Now think.

A paragraph such as silly.

That is alright.

So there we are just as all the same.

No not out loud never accrue as allowed.

What does he mean by eating.

There you are. There are marks where he went away.

What does he do by himself. There you are. Left left left right left he had a good job and he left.

Buy a pair and with them do this for them which they like as well.

It is very necessary to be held by Fanny.

Now all this is still sentences. Paragraphs are still why you were selfish.

Shell fish are what they eat. This is neither a paragraph nor a sentence.

When it is there it is out there. This is a sentiment not a sentence.

Now that is something not to think but to link. A little there. I lost a piece of my cuff button and I found it. This is not a sentence because they remain behind.

Now that is it. I have it. They do not leave it because they do send it. Now the minute you do more you make a subject of a severance. A sentence has been heard. Now listen. Have it made for me. That is a request. A sentence is proper if they have more than they could. They could. Without leaving it. A sentence makes not it told but it hold. A hold is where they put things. Now what is a sentence. A sentence hopes that you are very well and happy. It is very selfish. They like to be taken away. A sentence can be taken care of. The minute you disperse a crowd you have a sentence. They were witnesses to it even if you did not stop. There there is no paragraph. If it had a different father it would have.

I heard how they liked everybody and I said so too.

That is not a sentence and you see just why it is not why it should be.

Once when they were nearly ready they had ordered it to close.

This is a perfect example and it is not because it is a finish it is not ended nor is it continued it is not fastened and they will not neglect. There you are they will not neglect and yet once again they have mustaches. Think well do they grow any taller after they have a beard. They do although all experience is to the contrary.

Once when they were nearly ready they had ordered it to close.

This is one of the series of saving the sentence.

Remarks are made.

The courtiers make witty remarks.

They payed where they went.

Habits of which they are the owners are those they have without it being to them of any aid.

It is February.

They add it up.

He does not sound like me.

Nor do I sound like him.

Think that a sentence has been made.

I am very miserable about sentences. I can cry about sentences but not about hair cloth.

Now this is one way of relenting.

Think of a sentence. A whole sentence. Who is kind. We have known one who is kind. That is a very good sentence.

A separate cushion is not as comfortable.

This is a sentence that comes in the midst not in the midst of other things but in the midst of the same thing.

They have that as flourishes.

That is a sentence that comes by obedience to intermittence.

That is the cruelest thing I ever heard is the favorite phrase of Gilbert.

Saving the sentence volume one.

Or three

The difference between a short story and a paragraph. There is none.

They come and go. It is the cruelest thing I ever heard is the favorite phrase of Gilbert. And he is right. He has heard many cruel things and it is the cruelest thing that he has heard.

It is very hard to save the sentence.

Part of it is explained.

I like evidence of it.

He is to get away as usual.

Music is nondescript.

This is a sentence. They have taken exception to this statement because there will be exceptions when words are harbingers of means, by which they made names. He accompanied words by musical tunes.

How are houses crowded. A crowd contemplate moving. This is a commonplace sentence facing they will object.

It is a pleasure to play with a dog.

Bower is a secluded place where they had names. Find their names. All this meets the objection.

A little bit of way and she comes to say that he is the best taken care of anyway.

This is a light sentence with positive joy and so they have it. Do understand and to understand. This is so light it is an emotion and so a paragraph. Yes so a paragraph.

A man. One man. Of interest to one man. They say they will find it interesting.

How are ours received. That is a question which they make. Now think of a sentence. All these are parts. One man makes four children. He is not taught without care.

This sentence comes to the same place as all they said.

Now what is the difference between a sentence and I mean.

The difference is a sentence is that they will wish women.

Do you all see.

Now here is a sentence.

Are they coming back. That is not a sentence.

A sentence is from this time I will make up my mind.

Then they have hurried.

A sentence can be three things they can use. A sentence can be three things made with hurry.

Come and see me.

Come Thursday and you will see them.

Wait for what you are waiting for.

By the time that it is here they have had it and it is what they selected.

I like what they give me. Now all these sentences have been made with their assistance.

Now make a sentence all alone.

They remember a walk. They remember a part of it. Which they took with them.

Now who eases a pleasure.

I ought to be a very happy woman.

Premeditated meditation concerns analysis. Now this is a sentence but it might not be.

Premeditated. That is meditated before meditation.

Meditation. Means reserved the right to meditate.

Concerns. This cannot be a word in a sentence. Because it is not of use in itself.

Analysis is a womanly word. It means that they discover there are laws.

It means that she cannot work as long as this.

It is hard not to while away the time.

It is hard not to remember what it is.

With them they accord in the circumstances.

Sentences make one sigh.

There were three kinds of sentences are there. Do sentences follow the three. There are three kinds of sentences. Are there three kinds of sentences that follow the three.

If his ear is back is it drying. One says there are three kinds of sentences and every other one is just alike. Butter spreads thinly.

They made it be away as they went or were sent. This is a mixture of a memory and a reproduction. This is never noisy.

Nothing is noisy.

How are a sentence is the same.

If it is very well done they make it with butter. I prefer it not with butter.

What is a sentence with tears. Is she using red in her tapestry red in her tapestry. All these sentences are so full of with glass, glass is held it can make coffee so too. Now then what is it.

A sentence is Humbert with him.

There are so few kings. He was so funny.

He was so funny. That is a sentence.

She resembled him. Now that you see is because of it it is not so, she was exactly like her. Exactly alike her. If you forget a paragraph.

Hop in hope for.

Neglecting.

I will write to Christian Berard.

It is alright.

Once or twice it does not make any difference.

Does not make any difference.

Let us meditate.

Does not make any difference.

They fasten that they are not by noticing.

He would not hurt even if it does bother his teeth by it. Now think carefully whether they say it.

I would use a sentence if I could.

Why does it not please me to be sitting here.

Who likes to hear her hear of them. See how bad that is.

A sentence is saved not any sentence no not any sentence at all not yet.

It is not very easy to save a sentence. The sentence that is the one they are saving if they are lucky which has been predicted to them.

Never ask any one what a sentence is or what it has been.

It is of no interest if you know what it has to do with it.

Come back to complacency.

What is a sentence.

If he has wished. Wild and while.

A sentence says that the end of it is that they send in order to better themselves in order to sentence. A sentence is that they will have will they be well as well. What is a sentence. A sentence is tardily with them at a glance as an advance. Listen to this. It does make any difference if his voice is welling they will be well if they receive their welcome with as without as well with it.

It is all a relief.

Everything is worth while with a pudding an angel made of pudding.

Do you see why I am happy.

Happy is to find what it does. What is it it does.

What is the difference between a question and answer. There is no question and no answer. There is an announcement. There is at the outset.

Have never had the outset.

We feel that if we say we we will go.

This a simple meaning. A sentence that is simple in a cross with a meaning.

A sentence says you know what I mean. Dear do I well I guess I do.

Keep away from that door and go back there, that has not a meaning that has an association does he do so he does but not by guess work or difference there is no difference.

I think there which I wish here.

For no movement.

It does make any difference if a sentence is not in two.

We change from Saturday to to-day.

She thinks that she can wish that she can have it be there.

What is a sentence. A sentence is not a fair. A fair is followed by partake. This does make a sentence.

Think how everybody follows me.

A sentence makes them all not an avoidance of difficulty. A sentence is this. They never think before hand if they do they lay carpets. Lay carpets is never a command. You can see that a sentence has no mystery. A mystery would be a reception. They receive nothing. In this way if it finishes. This is so obviously what they will do. Obviously what they will do is no mistake because we did not know it. We did not know it is not a mistake either. Leave it alone is not theirs as a mistake. Artificially is what they call when they call out. Who knows how many have been careful. Sentences are made wonderfully one at a time. Who makes them. Nobody can make them because nobody can what ever they do see.

All this makes sentences so clear I know how I like them.

What is a sentence mostly what is a sentence. With them a sentence is with us about us all about us we will be willing with what a sentence is. A sentence is that they cannot be carefully there is a doubt about it.

The great question is can you think a sentence. What is a sentence. He thought a sentence. Who calls him to come which he did.

The Earles parlor was a parlor in a house in Lynn. Does it make any difference if a sentence is balanced it does and it does not.

The balancing of a sentence is mound and round. They will thank you anywhere. What is a sentence. A sentence is a duplicate. An exact duplicate is depreciated. Why is a duplicated sentence not depreciated. Because it is a witness. No witnesses are without value. Even which it may be they do not know that their right hand is their right hand nor their left hand which is their left hand.

A sentence then can easily make a mistake. A sentence must be used. Who has had a sentence read for him. He will be pleased with what he has and has heard. This is an exceedingly pretty sentence which has been changed.

I did not expect to be interested but I am. Now the whole question of questions and not answer is very interesting. The whole thing about all day is not at all when they were owned. What is a question. To thank for a question is no mistake.

We change from Saturday to to-day.

Arthur A Grammar

Successions of words are so agreeable.

It is about this.

Arthur angelic angelica did spend the time.

Escape calling battles.

Fire plans do rather exercise individually make left to temper never call rely matter this in a call to be meant share that it is a relative make in out of sound out of sound. If repeat repeat exactly and pansies perpetually planted upon it.

Camille Marsin as an exercise in paragraphs.

Upper half to make much have a seemingly bewailing out included march plain carry account in rope for the not which rested alike. Remember it just. Wire is it.

Couple cut into.

As to risk.

Howard has held.

Might which is folded.

Always there there are always an hour for their being resting.

Disturb seemly.

Raise which does demean apply in disposition fanned in entirely that a pre-appointment makes nack arouse preventable security of in approach call penalty by ingrain fasten copy for the considerable within usual declaration with vicissitude plainly coupled of announcement they can pry with a coupled for the attachment in a peculiar disturb in a checking of a particular remained that they fairly come with a calling around for land shatter just a point with all might in fairly distaste just with a bettering of likely as well in effect to be doubtfully remark what is a tomato to the capture do be blindly in ignominy pertain fasten finally in cohesion comply their gross of a tendency polite in recourse of the clambering deny for like in the complying of a jeopardy so soon does interrelate the way meant comply in this not a day called restively complaisant definite just whether it is melodious for the shut of practice that it is made a with apply dear have it is a couple of their having it make leave about so much better after a minute. It is not of any importance that they like to be very well. A grammar means positively no prayer for a decline of pressure.

Begin pay many a ring.

Anything that is why then may give them a share. Of feeling like it.

Now now have at a forget a formally planned discomfort in a clamber thin in alike come at a close choose a practice of why interminable left a calamity of a console to be shut in on account of without violent past of the capacity in quiet disconcert remained to be the proferred joined in diminish comply district of a ground without an estrangement covered in a notably letting notion repetition dictate divine that it is why a sharpener comes to a table in pieces for the demeanor of a made away corrosion of a willing plainly taught accompany with festoon in carpeting a competition to be thought fully now that it is time to go when it is a difference between coming or in inviting can ship a tree so that it is thought better of.

Apply able to be shutting the door to afterwards which is taken to be an article inclined for the pleasure of their

subsistence in around the contentment presented in an assistance behind the mainly with them just as when ever fairly
it is partly made to be so that it is introduced in a particular
referring in an amount particularly with the fancy for the
round about where it is a considerable undertaking as a
granted for the trouble it has taken recommenced for instance
in allowed whenever it is appointed just as well not to do so
considerably in respect to about knowing it is likely to have a
point as much as respected in return for the nearly where
they come should without more pleasing for a time made for
it to arouse lain this to be half with a chance appointed clearly
in a part now fairly anticipated interrupted account of winding a reign of their plants just there which is how they see to
it about it with a playful does when it matters at all at call
liked it for that might however do they not do it for them
which is why they were left to the part of it simultaneously
having the best of it for the time in which it is always any way
come to be a custom for they have to gather what they like to
do which is however it is arranged in spite of liking it very
much left to them always as a part of a trying it for the time in
which they are always having it for them and it has to be
heard alike to handle it as an occasional in reference to always does it come to be afterwards finally not a point of just
as it can they like to see whatever it is by the time that it is all
done as afterward made away nicely in the joining of it around
the mountain how many couple of hours is it.

And is told just what to do.

They must like it in order to be pleased.

It is partly for their having it that makes it plan it as a part
of their pleasing just like it. Every time they apologise.

How long is there to be once after a while just as they like
to know about it which is why they come and stay because

now and then where they do sound very often as if they were possibly going not to go around more nearly to be shown.

A place is very near there.

It looks like it.

A sentence may be learned by them in their way which is why they have thought of it. It is not without them as a blame of which it is why they could never ask. In their way they must be close to it which is why they are alike and have to have a finish without being sure. It is always just what ever they do not resume for this cordially.

Why should it be always in their way.

Independent of stretches of does it permit them to needless interference around there will never have in entirety allowing reconsider holding partly residue article known about where they were. It is not.

Eight eighty eight happen for the reestablishment of individual to a blending by a chance for the opposite likeness of planning involved rejoin when a fancy theirs a glance of behind the last at for the example returning practical amount in profusion come to this chance which is it that their amount forms while more easily in a middle nearly place a credit for the nicely become prevailing desirable in change found known appoint there in member of willing this integrally difference between rose in proven cinnamon that which is closely too soon send plain at most once to the have it a coincident matter of ways by nearly all which are be shattered in couple of rain remain all bought so with then not in private theirs as apart with a chance pleas with a loose covered bent to lately which in partly of their wherever whatever it is armistice lain and with while worth at pliable restitution around a by light blissful to be joined for a considerable restful a whither most of it a variety of their distress well able reconsider considerable considerate a glowing reversal unified point in pillows lain as pistache very welcome in our time blame by a having exchanged one tree for about with a call for it now at a plainly indicated in diatribe do for well in it a preclusion of fastener ladle with seen this is occasion for not having let it alone.

Deception.

Aggregate.

A narrowly bestirred mistaken federation presumed differ in a plaster that denial present well dense meant differ in commonality their problem of resemblance of effectual not a distance.

How.

Do you know.

May a while ago.

Disillusion.

It is very well a date which makes each separate in a leaf in a dismissal.

Very grammatical.

How many do go.

Heard how many have gone.

While buttoned done.

Made maidenly.

A house on and a wire to differ between a rosary and roses which are a screen forlorn they may be to take an account of betaken next to choosing at a passably withstand outlet a considerable region.

Why awhile every once in a while.

Now know what to do for a change.

Are allow discover over cover an over coat. This is not a grammar. Grammar is made whether there has been a better whether it is alike are to be hand in hand which is stitches a polite that is a dollar ball carried a mainly for only timely bother in only begs legacy preponderate with a called so as a weight behavior unknown come as the same rather applied formerly around wounded to do there in enchant poorly fix an employment persist repercussion in suddenly and extract it for them that it may be mainly all will do requite all day certainly hour glass but whether amount of it is irresistible always may day come to the indicate whether a renewable makes it daily when weaken there is a tendency to parry what they pay for it.

As approachable payed eradicate a plenty of chagrin. Arthur are the interval appoint anticipate emendation partly dubiously controversy denote inculcate settle signify utter invalidate cohesion regain firm famously betide disrespect whichever do they just in willing and if are seen does matter lion like disentangle whichever ribbon for the fairly does make it a radical this allowance which is a state none insight tightly lament in does endeavor in complement do gather able maintain prejudge verge tarry town with wielding coupling inter and do needless leave public pair of betterment in intermediate do be gone for nearly rash must it is apology for thought too have idle placate thrown they call dislike place meant shut has shapen a fan's run angle tonnage with wending powerfully lapsed too much theirs which is what they thought it is now an earned glowing gently shown for the predicament indubitable dispense are for matter lain join it pollen not a grate their will prevent gallop or do a never at a believed they do see rushed as turning made a plan very much known softener theirs allow did amount recognisable mean plates of estrange from then in stretching in behind theirs known does as much with a count near welcome kneels heels knee three forged with a news plenty pun persuaded or there or there a

graphic went to go mend sing to central stated a joint mentioned with when it is winding of wool.

Burned paper made not a hole inferred from the habit of
their had been very tender to a partly joined disturb well positively disconcerting patiently for next appointing justly with
an apple come to the do not accustomed made fairly in a
stand with all gotten interpolating wresting daintily mining
framed pointless shown occupation disappointedly not notably with whom as to come let in colliding dismay nodding
coupled for instance tell a managing singling far more does
it without widening they to blanketing more formerly indubitable partially festive just as main with inclined refuse pall
marketed privately lest as then do they fell are just does by
this as likely where for the mealing without nameless come
harvesting just joined ten made in does to more this aground
having it is as call called right about divesting rhododendron
made once forty as have nets other thought for lightly angle
may be at a call comestible will well or need be time there
when freight is dated articles might do.

At attracted meadow meadows bearing add lined a couple
tearing a little more duty parted in a choice whichever mar-
shalling not which fasten remade remind not in case mocca-
sin sudden dated precarious marguerite fast in a case there is
unit do for at all peculiar for a polite with all a classing dove-
tail in totality this is interval does dozen providentially af-
fected placate wounding does as much early pay master to
the educating partly doubting foremost coupled clearly and
can. Very does a polite really readily vainly charming doubled
shall detained mar rest when name this towering they dismay
ten all ways cause however amount not to know how do you
do do love me. Applicable did state faction as arrange lain

mended distrained there account when checking notably committed do Kate remind with a waged knots communed reaffirm drags irresolute committed by an article goes finely made a stain which is like their account of when a hurricane caught it.

Might amount stating disconcert whatever is most whom fairly picking attributable prevailing restitution admirably with widening however declare call a wall wallow bust mentor back for watching it is cooling displacing formidably into.

Have Howard has forgotten. Edgar shows known dismay mailed steadily encroachment.

Not to say forty.

Are taught.

An episode in unpracticed.

Refuse resistance.

Arthur object.

Who knows draws.

Acclaim.

Dismay disturb history attest fortune ably apply why merit absolutely it is prettily a criterion of preconception fished with amount more far with a vim record of abstraction why not a nestle that they come by does it do whatever it is desirable Claribel ducking amounts to that in priding have lain disturb shorn appoint.

Next how in favor it makes planks for be like taken do join reigned for as likely plating donkey minded it for meaning dominant reflected gust of training in being liking does a chance they will keep not to a house in fatigue that is what aimed antagonistic platter for the annulment of delicately rationing demarcation restitution lumped meant mainly light for them marked in pieces reflect theirs wondered in appetite tuned roused very well in chosen mentioned rapt leaving alike made have it reached followed in stretching ardent amendment little pause with wind mentions agreeably to make it much of it went where in veiling acutely.

Why is Arthur grammatical. Arthur is grammatical because in usage felt in do other dainties point less considerable remain this in finely identified longingly rested comestible formed theirs half in harboring loan.

Intrusion.

Gardening compel.

Lain.

Comfortable.

It is predict.

When this.

Is so.

A very easy source of income.

Very old in starting.

How old.

In starting.

Ralph Church.

Arthur Raffel.

Does.

Whenever.

I land.

Narrowly.

Need but.

All.

Whose too does take them.

Let us think of sitting.

A grammar.

He recounted unified.

Back to Arthur.

Again found might with a pleasure restitution.

Again ours of it.

Melodious.

Tranquil invite patient needless considerable despicable investigation hurry in considering partially if went tall by and need her likely in avoidance denominator in reaching this in clarifying demean theirs praises just win not mainly lest perfect as strewn may we for just with plan lain mess in casing this with may many leave as ours without where leaves make it do for formerly relinquish plans without rest of the credit that makes it do whatever more than without an appointment let it make it merry for their winding do not nearly precaution with as plainly theirs with them with the known an interest in right and when ever they were incisive to now liking armature because with a peculiarity just making finally furnish dismantle the peculiar with arrangement restitution in climb with a prevalent disjoint in callousness as is without a presently deforming need letting privately just with a differing as there make it my allow disarming come to be just what ever they had with only ours exactly to be with a welcome to the train as yet which is whenever a fastening does amount rained for the last quietly. A lost discourtesy for a wonder that after fifty they are not the same. A little amount of how they bow. It is idle to be afraid of mother and son when they are cousins and very obliging to be in between as well when it is a fragrant amount of penciling because it is too true. How often through theirs with a willing.

Not with a curtain indestructible comfortable table and chair made a disappoint with meant aslant in unification this distance amassing considerable that it is foremost where they make as soon indubitable rain lake main are chosen this in amount. He objects very much. Cousins can be married to their brother with guessing that it is their variety in as it went for more a pleasure.

Grammar is the art of reckoning that it is by themselves that they are one and two. To please this in displeasing they are gracious in rebounding to their mastery of employing it again in difference comfort alone theirs made having been taught to look like their just as room. A grammar makes it very much fifty to one which is the same as fifty-fifty do you not think so. They were wider widening widen in remainder in coupled that it is best who makes a door handle matter. If it is a matter. Like like a pencil. To learn to hear it right it is delightful to matter which is when it is inherited alike alone. Grammar grammatical grammatical fickle fickle in an instance with a doubt a day. This is to be on account of grammatical every day. After fifty how can they be indifferent to along. It is easy to change marguerites pointedly. Ever and even ever mainly. Every little Arthur. The dears with accusation of drawing up. Make it a repetition and find them. In sewn grammar. How do you do. Grammar make with James James with names names called couple of identations referring does with discolor demur once below so as sought seek copied inclined to amount name near.

The difference between is a stable. Just call.

Plainly does inept remount have an able to pay call.

Now I want not to manage half land marvelous.

Are there part close.

There are three vacations.

Dislike.

In frame known case argue meant couple charges did meet mastering reference have it unable how are too may firm interest collection reconsider considerable notions of collapse.

Considerable fastener they will beguile faults in around wherever complacently very likely having interested not allowed the becoming why my and likely. Arthur be changed obliged heartily lain reduced flowered in patiently do nor to began mind whether it is choosing chosen own it polite. Not again dilated pink in custom do flattery tenderly night find a sense in glorification wandering presumably with a leaning of hindrance in Jane and Janet for a premature dismal dismay come to erasure precious close to nearly alike by the coupling to be caught with demand demands done without here in before done drastically does further agglomeration in predicament namely a spoon.

If an inference appointed so that not by and wide hitherto does legacy coincidence a convince add toned it is knocked and plead or orthograph told provide he calls does take. If fifty makes thirty and eighty who is helped to hold distaste tremble in intelligence double disconcert leave oak alone and be sorry that it was a credit accredited be like a pear bloom customary hospitality nearly considerably in organ perused inclose cows and glance do and origin.

Howard is forgotten.

He has held.

In a state to be likewise out and aloud.

Anger or angry.

Forget accountably raining this is do make a fanned it looking best love to be similar to face it the does mellow matter to them business of course.

Hopping in at all conspicuous in a trained horn.

Grammar is the same as relative.

Grand in well tell how means and mast.

Grammar felt in telling that not telling in stories.

Can be angry that with all he did not need to care need care careful apple appear justifiable capable. Grammatical whimsies one two cured fruit.

Why do some things that are darned in medicament pensively demanded.

Grammar is drained with by and to.

Rose water and glycerine.

Could think.

As soon as it does was worried hours aloud.

Read call.

Hour our last hour glass.

Grammar recondite.

A little thought.

That he was glad.

Of it.

Part and pet.

Grammar an angel an angel made of pudding a pudding made of angels pudding angel pudding at a thought so.

Once a week three times accumulate deft cotton at stake. Why did we never hear about it.

Grammar in appointment.

Does dancing pay. Yes if they call it for it.

Call for it however whatever identify more than have a satisfactory be alike this is what ever they plan as they make which makes it be more often a coldly and deceived done with it as if ever after a pansy at her attract deploying deploring the event which makes it do fortunately their devotion to indicate in abundance like and whatever it will in dotting theirs in difficulty which is generous in once in a while attributed decline for and to be not without an acquaintance as chanced a gaining of where it was more than a very little all that they could it would do. They like best to have all of it walked in a literal diagonal prevailing in a carefulness that may make does it and dozens claim mine with a permission it is very often thought full of declaration as called a part of

in her chance come with it to be forth coming gone further
which is might just as well in for plenty of privately theirs
that is where they very well know hours of it.

Right.

Right right right right left.

Right left right left I had a good job and I left.

Right left right left right I had a good job and I left.

Told grammar.

Grammar.

What is it. Who was it.

Artichokes.

Articles.

A version.

He merely feels.

Does he.

Does it.

He merely feels does it.

He merely feels does he.

Makes.

In prints it.

Prints prints it.

Forgotten.

He has forgotten to count.

He has forgotten how to count.

Aid and alike.

Of account.

Howard Howard.

Arthur Arthur.

Rene Crevel.

Grammar.

Our account.

On our account.

Pause.

Pressed.

Rebate.

House and Howard.

Howard has a house. He has absolutely ours.

Grammar will.

Maintained authorise colored postals make macadamised roads never the less in unification extraordinary believed relayed plainly coupled entirely antelope with our precaution pardonably raised intercourse administer heard negatively how outer below candid meant interposition faintly have it opposite lain customary blooms conceive having Ellen inlain to be aroused that it was trained relation remainder consign preeminent caused causasus yes no How are Arthur Arthur's aim aimed cause pleas placate presently dominated having used close however may we stare to saw sell heaving a grass.

May shift them.

Pretty adopted pay pained loved right about cast integral precious a flood that is out seating guessed in not a very longed estrangement this is how hourly.

Leaves are occupied regained an eclipse does challenge indubitable long in crowded escape founded a cup of separated display coat.

He hurried out.

Arthur Raffel Howard Gans named across beware of the cuckoos of France. Because if wish alarm he is not fairly assorted in provinces do fork a glassing of predicating the run prize. Annoyance. A grammar of Arthur is a noon grammar. Behind a belating. It is not so. Howard is the one who did not covered a polite with having happen a bold after consider play foster and fallow. Divide a banana in three called a resemble. Hand handy handy handily handily handed handed bundled bundled cropping out prevailing integral conclusion restraint unpaid this hands out loved his money they made crated a passively told parcelling mock a mark who had crowed as if necks next to compare comparatively coupling are natural regaled for a loser are which defame legatee with withstood shamble come mixed Knots say hurry willing as cried out a very sad mistake mistaken hoped appetite are there climbing parties which are nervously reported different laid up leave high mire mired are a page does was warped definite rebuttal a changed man new to may waited are forfeit fortify double distress.

Howard hurried grammar.

Happy to hold a topic which is out lasting possibly making fortunately theirs as they do this with it as to call the nascent provender massed hem stitched in allusion portable in clad maintenance coming perfectible as a nucleus comes understated comfort to them surely for at all cut it out as a hummed aground into tune coupled coupling could fellow in distress ratiocination woods a benevolence for them as shore shore line argued in two reckoned and remainder put shut averaging actively ditto center let an alloy resist in chicken for the reign to-day they call however how are are there distaste depredation do blown very fairly dubiety constrained inkling regained as a cherishing primarily for theirs in case it is better to be best main a mandoline do help a joint lacking this is a did go for the opposition in a pride.

A come to tears with all with well without amass two name it gentle very gentle gently.

Are Arthurs hurried.

Continuity combined.

Lack lakes.

Undoubted reference able flagrantly does double to

jacobean have a doubt in Illinois and aim habit of intrusion careless of carelessly ingrained are sent a patently crowded in rejection of a due distress that is my mind.

A grammar hurry.

So good so beautiful but is it a grammar in chief.

From here to here in from there to there.

From here.

From here from here to from here to there.

Frown.

First time.

Add obeyed to·here.

From here to here. Add obeyed to from here to from here to here.

Add obeyed to from here. Add obeyed to from here to from here.

Add obeyed to from here.

In sleep.

Howard is not in mummery.

Howard curtained.

Octagon amused octagonal.

Second none.

Succumb.

Second.

Success.

Section.

Succor.

Sugar.

Succession.

Seen.

Savory.

Are bathing.

No words in grammar.

Resistance in happily.
A visitor does not ring.
Abused.
Actual.
Cut it.
Do be cut.
Apart applied Bertie Applegarth.
Thrown grammar grammar in claim just.
Hanford and lily.
Obtained have disturbed inversion.
Found about.
Are whether.
Grammarian.
Inch banished barred precarious.
One flowered.
How appreciable.
Cup up.

Has as desirable did carried amiable hurricane calendar dribble exaggerate how our estate dump it or call.

World would be worried.

It would be word went welcomed prevailing as signed confidence does commission incontestable remnant did display. Plainly careless.

It was a pleasure that there was a handle.

It is aghast without whether fair is it provender collided offered present.

Ate a cake.
Pity a poor blind man.
However have a habit.
In intervene dumb dastardly.
Grammar in use.
How rain is sent.

Went away to stay.

Combine lists with paint.

Letters follow.

Did double.

With trouble.

Edwin Dodge.

Grammar prepared.

Good-night in gaining.

However lilies of the valley.

Who cantered dozens in chose as aided petal meat sorrowful dull articled main yet.

Start Startle Startled abundance.

How are Howard and Arthur.

Not very well.

Grammar.

Wept up on marches.

Distinctly a precarious distance.

Have had.

Kindly heard.

Hidden Stretches.

Means of retreat.

Marriage is at once admitted.

Grammar is a conditional expanse. Supposing there is a word let us say predicted and include beyond that color and coloring, prepared to help it will be rapidly dispersed in as many ways that they finally do relish harpoons in a mixed implication that have curtains faults. This is ideally ever ever as well as they can in courage and in a fresh endeavor to be advised. A grammar consists in their reminding appointment to have its effect. A consequence of a sigh, they will be meant to have it be attested as a plunder in place of on their account in especial recall of application depending letting handled be mainly there as askance. It is easy that they have this softness to be clothed in rapidity.

A blame for calling.

Grammar if complicated is widened and there is a descent to be repelled in attitude do main in pressure coupled have make a present there as cares in are place consent prescription into two that main in mainly. Called enough. Why in veiling nun's veiling nun's creep and china in to do covered coughed carpeted a recline intermediary balance cages of passed in mine. Grammar includes excuse felicity. Very seldom a plentiful to be sure coupled alone as excited their make. Assume in origin.

Grammar has pause pause pauses paused partly perfectly does stitch have meant. Is there any fear. Not a cuckoo singing in a cuckoo tree singing to me oh singing to me. Estranged by a new moon which can be imitated. A grammar in collection. At a bird eglantine and Kleber. This how sounds sound. A grammar has melody and disunion and there occasion in branch come flattering a maddened imbroglio. A grammar in continuity. A grammar in disassociation find does well and tangle. An indicted description meant to be coupled. Withdrew.

Display is display that a quarter felt jumped regain in began a plenty of in to do declare a pointless rest when demand intention come plaintively rescind in floral walk. Are hearty caught made printing a calendar.

Are best.

Let her press.

Does day daintily dictate deploy rammed with a better folly leaves lie. Does die. Did display a meant couple with a stretch a pressure.

What is the difference between talkative and grammar

grammar makes a parlor a nun's affair also an hour a preceding theirs after all however it well and not found column in integer of required stall. The difference between vocabulary and amounting they will sell however one a day one a day without exactly counting.

Walter if he did know he was older than his grand father twenty-six his cousin seven ate a berry cup a faintly did disengage exceedingly that same sent Simon. Having a hotel. This is pretty well grammar. Walter a grammar repeat a name and call it Danny that is if he was called Sarah Amelia and there was callousness. Start again. Sort. Soft. Sofa or pigeon which if turned around is in memory. A grammar of grammatical phrases.

A grammar has been called a grammar of diagram. This is not to be selfish. A grammar has been called a list of what is to be done with it. Also it can be certainly different that individuals are usual that is supposing a man is apt to be definitely dissuaded who can be thought that when he was a baby he did sigh. A grammar hours of announce of details which is coupled with perfectly discolor absolutely theirs as in distance coupled with why in where comfortably justify placing lain account of plainly this in praise doubled nearly rapidly knocking slenderly in place of resting in shouldering refrain offer conditional about is this true.

A grammar relates to not liking to see again those you used to know. A grammar relates fostering dismal if handled definitely is to be used to again resemble not a choice having after it about the intention of planned come casually however in determination theirs concretely rested for the aim of account. A grammar displays never of which it is possibly acting without foresight. A grammar of appointment.

Disunion.

Double doubling.

Howard acting as dividend.

Harold justification.

Arthur unearned grammar.

How is Howard.

How is Howard and how are Arthur and Harold.

How are Arthur and Harold and have, and having meeting understood.

Ability subjoined deliberately recollected particularly reconsidered confident appoint reference however disappointing amiably hardly opposition sumptuous doubling induce rapidly lain about.

Grammar makes dates. Dates are a fruit that may be pressed together or may be lain in a box regularly still attached to a stem. In this way they think. Grammar may be reconstituted. A blame.

Grammar.

Howard.

Howard and Arthur.

Howard and Arthur and not Harold and Governor.

Howard divided makes it no different.

Arthur.

Arthur is an author.

Howard is a declaration.

Harold integrally.

Governor to be divorced.

Grammar who hesitates.

Apply supply.

Supply apply.

Ease tease tease ease.

Cake makes pudding. Pudding does make cake.

Grammar aroused.

Return a pigeon seated.

A seated pigeon turned makes sculpture.

Force horses not to care.

Cared for horses are either up or down.

Who hung it up on a wall instead of standing it on a table.

A seated pigeon turned makes sculpture is the best example of not being harassed.

Grammar is not grown.

God given ducks did disappoint.

A grammar if to bid to say so.

Hear owned is a pale made panting collusion remainder fonder have a pinch.

Arbuthnot.

Bertie Arbuthnot.

Rearouse.

A word in season.

Wish he would not come.

Howard is out.

Following.

He called following.

Grammar may be serially hampered.

Alone in London.

Ask have been hit.

May be serially hampered.

Supposing she was ready.

Supposing she was ready before I was.

Supposing she was ready before I was before they came.

Supposing she was ready after they came.

Supposing she was ready before I was after they came.

Supposing she was ready before I was before they came after they came.

Supposing she was ready before I was before they came.

Grammar before announcement.

Foliage is in the trees.

Grammar.

Thought far out.

What is the difference between resemblance and grammar. Think. What is the difference between resemblance and grammar.

Resemblance is not a thing to feel. Nor is grammar.

Resemblance to charging charging up hill but if there is plenty of time they will coarsen. There is no need of a hill in a flat country a city is a flat country there is no need of a hill in a city a city is a habit a habit of hyacinths wild hyacinths and a city all wild hyacinths have the same color and cannot have the same odor. To be disappointed in whatever is said although a great deal of it pleases.

What is the difference between resemblance and grammar. There is none. Grammar is at best an oval ostrich egg and grammar is far better.

Grammar and resemblance.

Grammar and agreeableness.

Grammar is resemblance and with proper preparation is certain of dividing half and half.

Grammar makes a plate.

Grammar a noun grammar a resemblance grammar agreeableness grammar going to be sweetly circumscribed in a division of cake made of butter. There should be no butter with flower no milk with cups no mining with have a day. There is a sound fertile. Fertility.

Grammar and resemblance could any one forget how to be told. How is however. Allow for how.

Grammar is resemblance. They can be indifferent.

Grammar resemblance.

Way cause dust helping themselves.

Hardy bay invites titles.

Repeat in ahead.

Now and man.

Turnover.

Way cause dust helping themselves hardy bay invites titles repeat in ahead now and man turnover parts in speech there very welcome having it pointedly afire with gentle fairly displace did it can feel a dance.

Canfield, a dance.

Grammar is restless and earned.

Walking in can field a dance grammar is restless and earned.

Surprise attacks.

Surprise attacks may not surprise and if they do can change their mind.

Is simplicity conviction or grammar and is simplicity more than put in.

How whatever.

Grammar is intense in dried again there and then.

The question is if you have a vocabulary have you any need of grammar except for explanation that is the question, communication and direction repetition and intuition that is the question. Returned for grammar.

Candied or candied potatoes.

Very sadly grammar.

How have they dismissal.

Irrigation somnolent undefined remittance planned cake from in justice dumbfounded eluded better messed in mistaken in undeniable rapid hourly a grass polish mistaken for the finish extra mischance fashioned opposite alone theirs in eradication does amount plainly to be divested in collusion

indefatigable radiant piled committed to theirs tens in reference to just as well privately does permission even allow a
rent before double leaves out pass it can very well pass in
between fine which is colored silly are there argument announce establish rubber with it post around mingled possibly to be come whether well around alone it is called how or
endowed mainly fished theirs with name called very upper
and resist appoint there which fairly is it in a token come to
come at a table top.

It is hours around when green is tea tea torn color.

Our hour too too makes nine twenty this is coupled con-
trite.

Needles in grammar.

Needles in grammar plain can place careful just as pleasure is come with a bundle comfort with appoint. Thinks in
grammar.

It is easier to know that a vocabulary can say so.

House.

This is a curtain it can also be a place for which there is a
preference.

Consider a house.

In an address consider a house in an address.

A vocabulary is not an annoyance when they see lilies
over roses.

A grammar has nothing to win her as foliage is priceless.

Consider.

Hours in a house.

A house held ours.

How has a house made a distinct impression.

Come with and when.

Leave grammar alone with feeling.

A ruling says that after is always round as a round as the shield of my fathers.

A rain drop can be heard.

Begin again lightly to begin again and go like a making hay if it is what is thought.

Grammar in continuity.

If it is allowed it does not make any difference who can insult first.

Have hover in the and for the sake.

A pigeon cut cooed.

It is always me.

If it is older is it Harriet.

Arthur a grammar he could not write rightly.

Therefor he hesitated to write.

Helped to matter.

Elliot Paul over all.

This arouses grammar.

Not this in kind.

Bravig Imbs wishes.

A penalty of slain.

Disturb.

Apart.

Once after.

All these kind grammar.

Like a kind.

Grammar matter.

Grammar is useless because there is nothing to say.

PART II

Arthur a grammar.

Questionaire in question.

What is a question.

Twenty questions.

A grammar is an astrakhan coat in black and other colors it is an obliging management of their requesting in indulgence made mainly as if in predicament as in occasion made plainly as if in serviceable does it shine.

A question and answer.

How do you like it.

Grammar can be contained on account of their providing medaling in a ground of allowing with or without meant because which made coupled become blanketed with a candidly increased just as if in predicting example of which without meant and coupled inclined as much without meant to be thought as if it were as ably rested too. Considerable as it counted heavily in part.

What is grammar when they make it round and round. As round as they are called.

Did they guess whether they wished. A politely definitely detailed blame of when they go.

What is a grammar ordinarily. A grammar is question and answer answer undoubted however how and about.

What is Arthur a grammar.

Arthur is a grammar.

Arthur a grammar.

What can there be in a difficulty.

Seriously in grammar.

Thinking that a little baby sigh can sigh.

That is so much.

Sayn can say only he is dead that he is interested in what is said.

That is another in consequence.

Better and flutter must and man can beam.

Now think of seams.

Embroidery consists in remembering that it is but what she meant.

There an instance of grammar.

Suppose embroidery is two and two. There can be reflected that it is as if it were having red about.

This is an instance of having settled it.

Grammar uses twenty in a predicament. Include hyacinths and mosses which grow in abundance.

Grammar. In picking hyacinths quickly they suit admirably this makes grammar a preparation. Grammar unites parts and praises. In just this way.

Grammar untiringly.

Grammar perhaps grammar.

Saying why are cabbages what I have not seen because they are one in having been returned as painted. Think of the difference between reality and what happened. This includes curiously. There is no change whatever.

Vocabulary is made of words which have been come to be like when after it is before that they sighed. In the same way grammar amounts to not be plainly so pleased with prettily figuring as approaching and reproaching half after noon. They are preoccupied with practically suppressing dismay with advantage this is why why bother. Tell the old gentleman not to bother.

Grammar made mustered in and out count twenty. That is the beginning. After that they amount to it. It is very helpful to be with a habit of with all included. Grammar grammatical. Help helped help reunited.

Grammar makes it doubtful.

To begin with women. Women and men. Men and elaboration. Elaboration and octave. Octave and the name of sentencing.

This makes a grammar partly.

Think of sighing.

A baby sighs.

Think of sighing.

Think of sighing a baby sighs.

Think of sighing a baby sighs. Think of sighing.

Think of sighing a baby sighs think of sighing.

This is how Howard Howard is forgiving. Not for forgiving but for coming. Everything in grammar a baby sighs sighs before thinking.

Thinking how is coming and sitting a better name for everything that makes a complete haversack make plunges in perpetuation.

Suppose a grammar uses invention.

Apply thousand to seen at once.

Again agate.

There is no grammar in opposition but there is if there is omnipresent successful intermediation. Best and most in interplay. So many count flowers and are very pleased to have it be as they like.

A grammar in appointment.

Arthur a grammar.

Is there grammar in a title. There is grammar in a title. Thank you.

Grammar a title.

Apart from a positively in a friend in time.

Arrangement of grammar.

A bay of say may Tuesday.

Incline.

Incline bears a relation to resemblance passes a brief and otherwise having it at their peril. Think of grammar if he ceases to behave as he did.

Grammar opposite have harboring all particles of inevitable to be a change in ringing a bell with whether it is partaken of inexactitude modeled at mainly their forty precaution in adjoining meant a piece with however a standing pearl of which close it about which in a plan come with about guessed why. With a jumped away.

Daisy a grammar.

Three daisies as a way to say love to pay everything away.

Daisy a grammar.

He has left all to Paul who has gone away to ask it to be given away not a point in connection.

Grammar added spender.

Arthur a grammar in announcements.

What is grammar. Simply this that they call places faces this way.

Arthur a grammar.

It is a bath in luxury.

Announcement never means straw-berries have bellies.

Able to abide by time in which to try.

Grammar makes a little boy explain that it was by the time he could not remember.

Grammar pitiful in doubles.

Grammar find which is stretches.

Supposing they thought that he was hurt and they were upset.

It all happened to be that they were all did double have as lost.

Grammar bound.

Bound as abound as a closed as a puddle with delineated covering after all goes to be appointed as a wall at a wall at or orange lined into tame nettled considered as giving.

He felt well.

A grammar with.

He sat there.

He changed to having remembered smiling they call which is applying with customs in panting.

A grammar whines.

Arthur a grammar.

Ivanhoe bore a relation to which wishes.

Arthur a grammar.

Give it to them.

They gave it to me.

When this you see you are all to me.

Arthur a grammar.

Makes it do is not what is said.

What is said is attuned.

It is what when at a positively come up and see about it but now there is no use because we are delayed.

Read grammar.

The difference is opposite opposed upper hour about.

Read an end.

Read to an end.

Be very careful of having had a little longer in obliging whichever it was for.

Forbidden.

Arrange add take.

Sound as grammar is when ways are approachable. They do matter matter to whom.

A grammar lender or love her.

A grammar with a wedding.

What is a grammar when there are eight taken.

How easily does everybody believe in Arthur a grammar.

Arthur a grammar or two and two.

A grammar loads hay on to a wagon.

Whenever words come before the mind there is a mistake.

This makes instant grammar.

Little letter kiss me makes house have a spouse little letter kiss me a house have a spouse.

Dear me grammar. Supposing grammar made diagram have felicity never dependent clauses. Jumped up again.

Did deliberate with a doilly.

A pigeon withstands porcelain.

Dove tail in outlandish public.

Distribute might mightily deem.

An obstacle primarily in collusion.

Did he leave it.

A grammar is united by having diagraming making it usual.

Fastens beside monogram.

Undated predict distaste more.

Numbers with a fan.

Precocity in union.

Love hearing in the center there able called well what of it.

Grammar undated Ellen has wells.

Grammar just allowed aided materially in finely discharge exits. In a minute.

Grammar. Do they converse.

Grammar. Do they proceed to have a little delicacy in dark blue this makes it a tenderness incident to magnificently define.

Grammar. In main might attendance did appointment assure in joint better next with privilege. Privileges.

Grammar. Find faintly.

Grammar. A thousand and six might mean sixteen hundred or it might mean a thousand and sixty or it might a thousand and six. In any case it was stolen in a sense.

Grammar. Distant does disentangle might lean native without concern.

Grammar. Heated with pouring it in with plenty of care.

Grammar. Could they be nervous apart.

Grammar. Hourly against with wedding.

Grammar. Find faintly a regional investigation blinded incautiously be stationed in expressing without a pearl of reconciliation.

Grammar. Make midwinter plays fancifully that it is advantageously to develop with investigation does replace demean with a clarity refrain just appointment does with chancing a colliding between dust and dustless in dusters. This is a grammar intermedially.

Grammar. It is very strange when the attention is very definitely designed the dropping of scissors is noisy.

Grammar. With or without windows.

Grammar. Leave projects to be known by having plainly disturbed with it a profusion.

Grammar. Lets be all well.

Grammar. Different differently doubled in excuse.

Grammar. They may be found being amused and not aware of impersonation to be a trifle more listless when the first minute they will come shut within in case left more can faint.

Grammar. Having known that this is whatever they can leave.

Grammar. A couple of remaining whether they go.

Grammar. Let it be elaborated by continued use of pansies.

Grammar. Obliged.

Grammar. Pedestal comments relation within account positively denote indicate preference lain within precaution for their amount that it is lined with more enameled to truly very really particularly in reclamation.

Grammar. Delighted to have known about it.

Grammar. With all of it too.

Grammar. Better be left to be more with out of lately dozens confidently change apart.

Grammar. In the time of nearly fairly where is it that this comes couple consider why in kindly nodded come coming in a planted for them extremity needles delight do camera camera bedewed in darting come to call for the change beneath with open upper door to be known Jenny.

Grammar. How many eggs are there in it. None to-night because carrots and peas are used without a count count countess.

Grammar. Ladies may be at stake.

One two three four five six seven.

May may be Mary. Mary may be at stake. Mary may be Mabel Mabel may be may fairly May Mary.

Grammar returned for instance.

Account for it.

Grammar. Spindles audacious a reading desk copies an obstacle to interesting him here.

Leaving a sentence.

Handles becoming influence made readily in return in deliberation may accountably refer markedly in presently offer a displacing come to genuine in arouse lain fairly matter in contest to an appointing them newly in tempter for noon Claire makes a noise does point little oblige composing in infringement can declare meant in parlor as announce beneficial imply readjustable differ in requite best measure amiable let it do for the part of the time in about that they may make solving and about with just may marry carry in do do whichever clouded in hurled about made mechanic a lock with oblong in acute named which muster apply deference in place come without care of tell may doubt in fasten they extermish in a balance lengthen notable needless link comply in due extra plainly as well matter for a tie when between Christian a Christian and Paul adieu. This is might with picture.

Grammar. In a breath.

1. What is the doubt when after all.
2. Oblige a taken get well finally double parted in case remainder loan a boat about.
3. With a withdraw finding two more mend matter meanwhile applied in opportunity tell and tell.
4. Four five six seven all good children go to heaven some are good and some are bad one two three four five six seven.

Grammar. In seduced.

Grammar. Remain.

Grammar. Out and about.

Grammar. He will have had doubt.

Grammar. Enemies deter partners from leaning advisably to in relation then remarkably lately north with tableing in fern with aground theirs in redistribution does prefer lain to take.

Grammar. How are Howards held out. Howard means nothing nothing at all in adding in in in English. She has sneezed.

Grammar. How many hours are there in asking for mats.

Grammar. Leave lain about.

Grammar. He may have shells at will.

Grammar. Leave layers out.

Grammar. Does presence with a famish make dark in carrots with an allowance for pigeons perching which they do perch. It is very kind of them to disturb them and they will be always about always not as lain intact.

How come, a treatise in sound and sense and not correlated to grammar.

Mrs. Edwards who is Mrs. Taylor but Mr. Taylor is not Mr. Taylor. Literalness is not deceptive it destroys similarity.

They are accounted a perceptive and productive and inclusive and receptive and related and defeated and delayed and maintained and reminded and prevailed upon in out of doubt which made a matter with in calculated remembering faulty with purchasable entertained might have made when confidential that it is won with a war left ounce of recall. He and a voice three voices. Make a day three any way done Sunday. How are hands called. It will and can do softly. Soften in shown. Made a barrel barrel sewn. Sewing is what she has to do.

Narrative is it for one. Narrative conceived and developed really only filling and so not connected with for grammar.

Narrative a connected narrative which is narrative makes it choose. Is it for me then if it is give it to me or rather let me have it as I will have to be going soon. Letting it alone. Connect narrative. A narrative makes twenty placate twenty one and one and one. A narrative need never relieve honey suckle. A grammar is underestimated to newly found admirably gainsaid.

Grammar not to be deterred by Arthur a grammar.

How come. Made in whether spoon in countless plaids in pleasure.

Grammar. In enterprise without with whether revise

prevision post when they bake. Grammar is not furtive. Round and about but they are cloudless. Grammar have useful blushes which are flushes. Have honey suckle which is of various colors, have rose daisies have orchids called Monsieur which is a name fame rename from interested them for her. How can grammar be nevertheless. What is grammar. Grammar is indwelling without a premonition of accomplishment but there is succor.

Think about grammar and a nightingale. It is very beneficent to hear four nightingales. This makes remarkably Arthur a grammar not at night but in the afternoon. Arthur a grammar, lady fingers and infusions and bother with apples.

A grammar consists in having more made maiden in eclipse. A tail of a comet is a memory. Grammar may be fortunately within a call. Consider grammar.

One two all out but you. This is a retreat.

Three four shut the door.

This is dotted.

Five six fairly fix it to be as if it were coupled.

Made necessary by excitement.

Consider grammar grammar may fairly be said to be not explicative. Grammar. One two three completely. It is impossible to avoid meaning and if there is meaning and it says what it does there is grammar. Arthur a grammar.

A sentence means that there is a future. In a sentence one two three regularly. They may reconsider a sentence and collect it for then. A sentence if it is established does not collaborate. A sentence infer confidently that this which management reference in amount makes which is recalled in establishment. A sentence does not offer three one two three all out but three a sentence used to have the connection and is without withal when it consists of coupling in examiners. Pointed differentiates pointedly in serving that ten baskets outnumbers six hats.

A sentence indicates that there is no failure. There could be no doubt that they should be in account with halting which makes it unnecessary to come which is by in fact and fanciful made to be in around comply this is a noon felt. Like this now the supplies come to be supplied.

A sentence refers to wedding weddings.

There is a difference between grammar and a sentence this is grammar in a sentence I will agree to no map with which you may be dissatisfied and therefore beg you to point out what you regard as incorrect in the positions of the troops in my two sketches.

Grammar may deface the portrait of a member of a family better with making a defined oxen with a tasselated covering which will not annoy in gathering beauty. It is very old in a rain-fall with preparation in flushing by winding plain carry for will stand in clarity retain in added just meant. There and there hear by when they will decry flatter made into amount.

Arthur a grammar.

Should in undertaken for double amiable with pottery in called rest without a plain condition need complete let in call the more come by.

How to come how to how to numb with heat and numb with are branches.

Grammar how come whose is a battle of behave in a doubtful way away.

The oldest country is the United States of America. The oldest country that is observed is the United States of America. In the oldest country the United States of America there is the oldest arrangement of lines and words which make bake relate to after soon make cake which is why it is as if when it is bringing there they may say day canter in canter cantering is reunion fitness is carry all. She sleeps by day.

It is not well to doubt the reason why fortuitous is colored in that way not to think again. Thank you.

Enigma makes Susan do. Separately fall follow thorough antagonistic.

What is a grammar to a hare in running. A grammar is in need of little words. There can be no grammar without and and if if you are prevailed upon to be very well and thank you. Grammar is meant to have fairly soften fairly often it is alight in white and makes a goat have a mother and a sister two are mother and daughter when the days are long there is more necessity for distraction and walks are pleasant. Arthur a grammar or manner.

A grammar is not painstaking begin by not singing, around a coat. Plan around a coat. If with all wind in summer and spring. Grammar is not restitution it comes easily. Think a thing. If it is said that the days being longer diversions are more necessary this is because after twilight they have dinner and this they are weaker as ever. Understand that grammar. Authority in afternoon and after grammar. Grammar is in our power.

PART II

Just grammar.
Bar Harbor.
Into take an ask.
Take and ask.
Go only.
Preventive.

Patents applied apply for.

Make birds measure.

Harbor hot houses.

Not grammar but sewed change.

About Otho about about whine about about tremble about with about about where they went.

Grammar inundated.

A little river which is not watered is not a calamity if they had had arrangements plainly in repose.

Grammar.

Lain.

And elder.

Putting soldiers where there optical in an ideally maintained scrupulous partly in at stake.

A grammar makes an attack.

What is grammar.

Back a ground.

What is an answer.

Thickening.

Never look to see what they are doing.

What is an answer.

What is a grammar.

Grammatical when the sun is sunday.

Grammar is the breaking of forests in the coming of the extra sun and the existence principally of which it was. Grammar readily begins.

Grammar is occupied allowances.

Grammar made making of grain grain is put about and at a splendid eagle eglantine and a circle of preventing wishes.

Imagine in grammar.

Out and outer.

She was inherited.

A bending in close.

A grammar is our allowance.

What is grammar. What is an answer in favor of whether in the way of only go.

Call his happiness mine.

Grammar is unawaiting.

Meaning clouds tears.

Prizes for smiles and suspicion.

Grammar in rather.

Grammar which just as well.

Portions in farther.

Grammar.

Either is about melted.

Went fanned in hour trust with lain recuperation.

Attack attach grammar.

Why is grammar not dull.

Because it is a diagram.

PART III

A for watches.

B for below

m for mountain

d for does it

k for alright.

This is went in haste.

A diagram means that called is called for, they man the ropes they will be lost they undertake to overthrow their undertaking.

That is about aloud.

Grammar comfort indelible and needless be wondering in widening lain and lane.

A grammar is certainly that poplars in the moonlight are in the landscape which is the favorite if it is shown and if it is matter of unlike upper.

Think of grammar a prize for encouragement is grammar.

A prize for tractability is grammar and well thought of that is to say if there is difficulty in recapturing the word.

Allow an allowance of wheat and blinding butter.

Grammar feel what is behind be agitated.

Grammar makes a mother.

A mother and trumpets.

Lines of corner of premonitory do the dispersal of just with gainsay pearls did and prevent.

Grammar. Grammar is and and did do day deign divide.

Listen.

Grammar with the green trees has summer off the wood and rocks employment.

Grammar does dictate diminish that it is considerable loyal read royal tiny concert concerted in rebate.

Consider grammar.

Grammar makes merry related.

Mr. William Jewett naturally preferred a chateau.

Mr. Bravig Imbs does not repine.

Mr. Fred Genevray has a familiar use of a bicycle.

Mrs. Arthur Hope is surely moderately pleased that there are changes made in the reception of their being rather repressed.

This is all one way.

Now account for it.

A little boy is afraid in general if he is to be a general he is not to be dangerous and so he would be in command in general of a general.

This comes out concretely.

She is not afraid of anything except having swum and this makes it be said that they are in perfect accord and yet it has been stretched to a division not of avoidance but of pretention.

Arthur a grammar was named Arthur a grammar because he could read but not write. Also because he was fluent articulate and necessarily paid slowly. Arthur a grammar is adventurous, they may be pontifically and this is never in presently red renowned. Imagine grammar. If a claxon is heard that means it. It is all all Paul.

Poplar trees give shade but there is no permanent shade in the day-time.

Grammar if to be known that they smile in return for having thanked then it is pretty to be employed in their employ in watching a river. In watching a river it is not necessary that it can be used.

A grammar reasonably.

Arthur a grammar.

His brother Gilbert.

Gilbert is ahead.

Arthur a grammar.

His brother Daniel.

Arthur a grammar.

What is a grammar. A grammar is a collection of observations on the necessity of their having been nothing modulated.

Consider how she hears me. I am content disappointed and reluctant quick and announced very top-heavy and obliged and she is present when there is poverty and positively a renown and this is the way they amount to it.

This is grammar in retrospect.

Grammar is awfully dependent upon persistence of not having been a which of them they take.

Take nothing.

Taken it too.

Arthur a grammar.

Arthur a grammar can lose permanence.

A grammar may might make.

Relief in willing that they appoint symptoms.

What is grammar.

Walking up and down.

She got up sat down walked around and embroidered.

When clouds resemble a horse.

A leaf and a bird.

Grammar is outlined.

Resembles swinging.

A grammar in out loud.

Painted hot weather.

A grammar this at have hatted right this at sight this at right this at light why are might and night refused. Curiously. A butter burden.

Grammar in case.

Incased is in the marsh with a large tree.

Doubtfully grammar if they make watches which have grounds.

About placing widows and children.

Pointed stretches of articles imitated.

Distaste turned which a dismay of finding.

Grammar may never.

Never may grammar.

A house may be ruined.

Not Arthur or grammar.

Grammar fair lay.

Arouse grasped really feeling.

Examples are rare.

Grammar is fellow to fought it rather than so much as much a seated in a softer sailing in a crash with a won a wind can be hot hot what hot water. Fairly a mistake to prefer one bush to another.

Grammar how are eight.

Grammar has nothing to do with distance. Thank you.

Grammar Philadelphia.

That is a sound equal to their value.

Grammar might be courageous.

Grammar and heather.

Meyer makes antiquity.

Antiquity is not grammar.

Charles is assured of it.

They cannot recall grammar.

Arthur a grammar because if it is not grammar it is nothing he does not hear and he does not destroy he does fasten the left to right in without doubt but not always.

Division.

A white is a white mountain.

Relate that to grammar.

A white is a white mountain.

A white is a white mountain nearly. Nearly means less use of. A white is a white mountain nearly means less use of. A white is a white mountain nearly means less use of more of it with a recount of the non use of it. A white is a white mountain means nearly less use of it by nearly.

This is out of allowed grammar.

Arthur a grammar. After all.

Opposite or doubt.

A grammar in possession of obsequies. Distance does never mingle grammar with sound.

Howard out right.

Distance does never mingle grammar with sound.

How are Howards half with recess.

Plaudits in remain acts rename cause of reach waned a previously dozens.

Grammar is undated.

Grammar is undated because furlows and furrows are avaricious with hunting hares in partial referring to enable utter with renown come distaste unable.

How can beginning and end beginning with white in iron end whom with lent.

A grammar colors reddened.

Withal may joining be with played reading. It is daily reddening. Be played full of grant it. A grammar is a cause of poplars wire. By this I mean an island of whether green with attached whether finally knotted carried all reachable by after at a distance. Now let us know distance is grammar by after at a plain is description. Dealing is description detained is grammar. Appointed is grammar at and when is description.

Arthur a grammar can be both.

Once in a while may carry. Carry me across. A locomotive may plan that they are so pleased. This needs it. As a place. Grammar are stages very nearly slender goats. This is both.

Arthur a grammar irremediably having thought first.

She was photographed with earrings.

She was photographed with trees.

Arthur.

Made mention of their difficulties.

Theirs made handsomely mine.

All this is premature.

Arthur a grammar.

In preference.

The detail of the house is very sweet.

Replenish.

It is nice.

Arthur a grammar.

On meaning one.

Are pages meaning one.

Lend satisfy meaning one.

Passably well meaning one.

On meaning one is a beginning.

Hurried after is a frame for a marsh willow.

Missing alike when they are trying this can count are right.

And prevailed on them to have display discover that it is passed with all dozens. This is grammar consecutively.

Evening light is yellow or green.

That is why they are very much back of that left of it.

These are all examples of concentrating discursive grammar.

Arthur is in no relation with Henry.

They have not the same interest in not at all about candied and candid because it is fatiguing.

How Arthur differs from him.

Arthur as a grammar is nicely married before their return which is a surprise to not anything.

They were the daughter for a part of a day and an hour and let her letting let it leant easily not to known know and.

The grammar of chosen.

Definition made a hand.

They do not hurry at all.

Leaves which are left and cones which are burned later.

Grammar amounts to all who call about it being left here.

Grammar does redouble horses which if it is difficult are more used than whether in leaving their employment.

That is nearly perfectly ready remain in demarcation of excellence in how about it.

A grammar in never round about in substance. They are with it all.

Remain for grammar.

To remain for grammar.

Dismay lend may send it finer than all about it.

Does not do this.

There is a whenever they had angled for in the same.

Grammar which not with or whether they are recurred does allowed.

This makes reliable deliberate.

Think cousin think.

However how about how it is entering.

Can any one leave it to her and changing them to in at last where merriment come to in attractive. That is what grammar is not now Arthur a grammar.

Grammar fund feel it partly cause of beneath they blamed a little on them.

Not grammar.

Distance, not grammar.

Out with their well as you.

With without you.

Very difficult very difficult.

With this with as you.

With as.

Well as you.

Very often they are flurried. As now.

With with as with well as in their well with as you.

Forget that everybody knows what they owe.

That is all at once.

Went indent agreed angered they feel never with added bread as yet.

Grammar makes no mistakes.

Grammar uses indisposes in that way. There can be a name for riches.

Grammar has a measure for poplars. They are for near and for far.

Grammar also has a place for prizes.

Grammar also makes one branch shake before another. So it does.

Grammar does not need a balustrade to be broken so much so that separate parts of it are far apart and in that way are recognised and very pretty. It is partly there as earns. Very well.

Grammar may not be counted.

Make it changes.

To-morrow is grammar. Allow.

Partly they wait for fruit which is grapes and peaches. If peaches are called peaches do they grow where they grow that is where grapes grow. To study a desire to continue.

Josephine a grammar.

Joseph a difference between their allowing four in eight or four in five.

A grammar does not trouble theirs with the use of their placing it before a hanging well entitled riding covering.

Josephine a grammar.

She kisses an acquaintance.

That is if there has been a sufficiently long interval of absence.

They remain indefinite in reappointing.

Arthur a grammar.

They are rewarded by their ways in case of realisable with drawing.

A grammar.

He would continue.

Now and look if seen they must have had a habit of it there.

That is alright.

Went about made with blithe in mention theirs named as without there.

It is called a tunnel in a wall.

This is all felt and well in reliability.

Does such as amount to remake.

What is it without that.

Grammar is understood in amount.

Arthur Hannibal a grammar which has been a disappointment.

Very extraordinary that they should never remind the rest of their pressure with their precaution to be surely circumstance in which can be found netting in around the composed with have out with allow.

Does grammar flatter. If he is not used to flattery does it seem just.

He and with it.

Little liable to be invaded in the middle of plenty of their making.

This is preparation.

It is very well to welcome rain.

Any hour of these with.

Plates and plans and carry it in as they must be with without prevail in a couple of which when it is approved lain with waste make just as remain limit recalled in places that in fasten however as a call.

Grammar is made in two.

Why they went as they said.

It is wetter in the marshes than they were.

Sometimes they have grapes.

Hours fellow below sprained in abrupt with a rounded. Now think of grammar.

Justly how are Arthur and Howard.

Justly wind has been in time to come.

Amassed in a ride without mentioning whether it was a train or otherwise.

In case of herd heard he used useful.

This is grammar in credence.

Think though with though they were.

Try it again happen.

Trying it again happen.

What is the difference between came and went.

How are Howards not Arthur a grammar.

How are Howards.

Wild and willowed.

A poplar has a place for not before by an occasion for principally.

This has started as in this winter.

How is it made is an answer. Always make allowances for ships.

There is a difference between ahead and a shed. In how many days.

What is wanted to make them come back.

Think of their not minding it at all.

Are different is grammar.

Hold and ready.

They have been seen slowly if they waited.

It is very much as comprise.

How does it sound if it is different.

Joseph Geronimo can always change his name.

Within August may be called grammar.

What is grammar grammar is an allowance with withdrew poplars and varieties it is chosen. Think awhile, grammar is an indifference to apply that that theirs secondarily consents to sign. Grammar.

He hears everything in waiting for them.

He might forget and overlook his pocket book.

Not to say pocket book because it is a pocketbook.

Grammar grammar is undated.

It has without presently in there by then that they were too in use.

That is migrating.

Festoon does make dearly rested.

She said she often smelled wood burning.

Arthur or Ferdinand a grammar.

The lay of the land of course it was refrained from mentioning. They included rapidly and vegetation.

Hour and hours away from between the rest of it.

Grammar may not be mistaken.

Grammar may not be mistaken for winding along presently this is just as it is or has become.

Grammar is mistaken at times.

Grammar is mistaken at times for fondly yours. Grammar is mistaken at times for burnt ivy with a piece of glass.

Grammar is mistaken at times.

Grammar can with by free carriage in an automobile in an accident which may way lay their liking.

Grammar is very well. Grammar is all very well.

Grammar is mistaken for burnt ivy in an out of door oven.

Grammar is mistaken for ivy burnt by an out of door oven.

Grammar may may be to withdrew.

Grammar may not be likeness.

Grammar may be indifference in deciding that very likely there is enough as not very much all of it has been just as if it is when called completed while they like by comparison because and with as ardent. Burnt by the flame of an out of door oven which has a chimney and used it as well once.

Grammar may does and better than for them this is made while completely and understood.

Grammar while they do not delay as they rest.

Rested.

Arthur whether craves a word of love.

By restraint they had settled that they were anxious.

Partly by foresight made integrally useful.

Are Arthur's plans what could it be more like if with what it was that it could be for their wishes.

Try again.

Time table is not an hour glass.

They have seen them.

A fur coat is made for her.

Plainly in welcome and partly their all. There is grammar in verification. Plainly, plainly with and without them their in allowance harbored. Well within welcome. And around in Arundel which is an Arundel county. This is the one instance where association is not misused but familiarly a family makes a presence not necessary as it would and was. Partly more than occurred, if it is possible to have said they were the same it is of no importance. Their is an older brother who has been never left as an appointment of porcelain. All, be called a history of whiter than seen with in wherein bestowed deem.

Does seeing others remind one of that or is it bewildering.

She has heard that they were excited.

In plenty of time there has been heard that they have been excited

One at a time they left it to them to decide.

By the time that they were careful it is about all of matter of course.

Plantagenant may be a name for a saw mill and ditches.

What is it.

A grammar fairly may decline to be bothered.

A grammar. Indicate that she is pointing and explaining. A gesture is not in motion. If she is not talking have the name-sake alike with them. Beginning avoidance. If she is rather angry they may. Grammar. If he is not forward and back it does not count. Grammar. With allowance.

To be mainly there at hand. Grammar. They will walk. Not forward and back.

Grammar. Hours do not count.

Grammar. If it is said aloud before waiting do they defer it.

Grammar. Dismantle a prevailing shawl or pleasure.

Grammar. That is a case of peculiar because not often but did they mean it when they said it.

Grammar. Recount.

She knew of him.

They differ in color and they without choice.

It is easy to recognise that it is not a house still it is in case that it is still that it is and easy to recognise it is not a house on that hill.

It is easy to still recognise that it is not a house on that hill.

No omen that it is not a man and not a house on a heavy hill.

Planned grammar. At first at a movement. Separated grammar from under crowds. Supply the pleasure of under clouds. Grammar in resistance. If a gypsy threatens to hit his wife he is off without meaning it forward and back. In this way grammar is not restless. It is very easy.

Grammar is not restless if there is sun at a distance.

Grammar may carry opportunities.

Living by seasons by years or by now might make grammars. It might make grammars.

Grammar. It might make grammars.

I like the sun. So do they.

I like branches. They like branches.

Grammar is before them.

Winifred a grammar.

They mind looking.

It is best not to wait till five o'clock to bring the oxen. It is best to bring them sooner.

Grammar. Laying it squarer they make whatever they had do.

Grammar. Well covered.

Come back to movement at a distance.

Louis. A grammar.

It might be why they were their own.

Louisa a grammar.

Fails to be beneficent in interrupting their decline it fails in being beneficent in interrupting their decline.

Partly in pickets pickets are without then.

Archie a grammar.

Announce makes it be a party to an origin.

Ernest William a grammar. They might strew straw about in that way have thrown straw about in that way.

Coming to it in stretches. Timothy a grammar. There is no resemblance without a grammar.

A thousand and out.

There is more than ever that it occurred.

A grammar makes it seem like water wells which have no

mown hay because after all it was put by when they went too soon.

Herbert is a name.

There are hours of excitement.

They are never to notice their difference in trees.

They are not to have in mind that they are to have a difference in trees.

Annie Swan a grammar.

She made it left that her wish was meant.

Fred Chester a grammar.

They meant to be loosened from their seeing that soon some in politeness fought it at once.

Bent to their wishes

Partly a grammar.

Annie Swan bent to their wishes.

Annie Swan is sure that a dog can bark at a cow.

Susan a grammar sustained in wishes.

Germaine greeted the half mother of her brother when she brought her child and liked it.

Germaine and grammar. She rests and remains away for a not very long time.

Germaine lets it be what they had intentionally went about to do.

Follow out loud.

Francine a grammar.

He having been used to it mistakes it for it.

A smoke does not always mean a train it means a field.

As signature a grammar.

Passed a little way without sending in that with them for there anticipating with as best in their account.

What did it do.

Painted white with paint.

Advancing.

Household a grammar.

Not to have alike a gardener.

Joseph under son a grammar.

A grammar makes it easy to change from a factory to a garden.

From working in a factory to working in a garden without distress.

A grammar without distress.

Not very often, a grammar.

Very slowly. A grammar.

Why do they say that they go as slowly with or without it and why do they go as slowly with or without it.

Katherine Tardy which is a narne.

Josephine Geronimo and Virgilia Tardy were present at the planting of poplars in the marshes.

There might be by taking a piece out of the hill side a place to plant walnut trees which would give walnuts and be forgotten having been heard of one at a time.

If it is incredible that it is as near as that this is that part of the hill opposite which when it was a nearly fairly placed creditably current ending they might be lending known without a claimant. In this way every bit of it is owned.

Windows a grammar.

With and about reminding that it is fairly with and without most in conclusion.

Willows a grammar.

Before they are welcome they may defer that.

Willows a grammar. A hillside was burnt.

Edith Geronimo is without a witness.

When there is no more grass to be found pink dahlias can take its place.

When there is no more grass to be found pink dahlias can

take its place and when the pink dahlias are gone a yellow dahlia can take their place slowly. In spite of a hesitation a yellow dahlia can be consumed after pink dahlias have been absorbed after they have replaced the grass which is no longer a delight.

Partly a grammar.

How many times can they be indifferent to a distant sound.

Grammar of intermittence.

If a sound is made which grows louder and then stops how many times may it be repeated.

Hills a grammar.

A hill slopes and there is a long length when there is not a deception.

Hills a grammar.

Battles become hills. Hills a grammar.

Hills give names to battles.

Hills a grammar.

Battles are named because there have been hills which have made a hill in a battle.

Hills a grammar.

A bay and hills hills are surrounded by their having their distance very near.

Hills a grammar.

What is the difference between a description and grammar.

Hills a grammar.

Very nearly hills.

There are hills which are very well known very well known hills.

Poplars. Poplars may be they certainly will be cut down and sawn up.

Poplars may be indeed they will be cut down and used as wood.

Indeed, a grammar.

Poplars indeed will be and may be indeed will be cut down and will be sawn up and indeed will be used as wood and may be used for wood.

Indeed a grammar.

Finally will be and indeed may be cut down and having grown tall poplars are very easily sawn into boards and used as wood.

The difference between eighteen and eighteen other things being taken into account because if it is ending in plenty of intermediate begun beginning it would be hot in bearing it as eighteen was if it could caught with an in difference in replied.

Left allowed her.

Winifred went with Vincent and Virgil Geronimo to prepare a letter to their mother.

Has happen to handle curtains roughly.

Vincent and a space in grammar.

With why and wire. How many things can be called upside down. Answer. Cyclamen, liver patty, long large white open widening, turning pages which is disturbing.

Critically. Good flour can make good bread is not the same as good flour does make good bread.

Good flour does make good bread is not the same as good flour can make good bread.

Eighteen if when it is arisen is not befriended with eighteen when it is in decimal with contrast.

How can you say not to have understood that it is cold when it is just as warm.

Finally compare this and not their mend on the mend.

Begin for the use of instant grammar.

How can they be that they are that it is cold and was will be warm just as the same.

Grammar relieve leaf regain leaf or leaves.

Grammar, regain leaves.

There are their leaves or their leaves.

Grammar which when in the main has to do with the fact that the same heat is the same cold or do so.

Grammar which is the same as heat when which is the same for cold.

Grammar which is in a forsaken with pinks nannies and carnations that it is the same with cold which with warm.

Once again.

A grammar once again.

Once again.

Mrs. Penfold said and it was true that Vincent Geronimo was just then with them.

Which was true.

Grammar. They made a plan to think of them.

Vincent Geronimo feels the absence of Mary Louise not that it is of any importance as her place has been taken.

Grammar. They without doubt. They will without doubt they will do without it without doubt. They will do without doubt they will do without it without doubt they will do without it without doubt they will do without it.

Left alone. A grammar.

Display that is it coupled by an introductory copy.

An is in dismay.

Display that it is coupled by an introductory copy.

A grammar should never be wreathed easily.

Win sent, a grammar.

In sent, a grammar.

A grammar is in went and in went, in sent, win sent.

A grammar is very long or else unsatisfactory.

Grammar in pronounces.

Hours follow.

Grammar meant most.

A grammar is why they made their own in the way they were after they had not liked where they went.

A grammar in fought.

Resemblance. A grammar.

There is no resemblance, it is not what they remind them to be an interval like it.

Mary. A grammar.

Mary Rose. A grammar.

Would it be awhile.

Laying it down makes it that it might do.

Laying it down makes it that it might do.

Before it would have been wasted.

It would have been wasted before laying it down makes it that it might do.

She can be left to it very next to the acceptance of in line as it is asked.

If they were selling would they go or stay.

Walter a grammar.

There is an attraction in out of their leaving.

Can he refer to the ladling it in a bundle. While in there for a day.

It is a disappointment not to reach it to them it is to them a disappointment that they did not reach it to them. Thanking them for everything.

She is to consent.

Florence a grammar.

She is to consent.

Grammar is meant that they will leave with delicacy that they will have to do that which they did expect to do.

Antoinette a grammar.

Shelves are made of glass not in houses which have the most of all to be responsible that they have accounted for it.

A grammar they may like Tuesday.

Grammar is not at all that they had not decided that they could leave that to them who had been told that if they came they could be informed.

Grammar is an item that blames carpets which have lily as their distributing.

This is the way they may.

Grammar correctly leads Ada to have been either or there. Hesitation destroys grammar.

What is the meaning of grammar. Grammar arouses without doubt that invitation. Supposing that there is a building at each corner is there one in the middle and if there is one in the middle and it is a shrine all three are in use. This can be seen from many distances although there cannot be any certainty that in the whole there are four or five. It has not been decided but it is known, that it is alike.

Grammar may be what they will give with it.

Louise a grammar omelet and carrot carrot and omelet.

Louise a grammar.

Wood which is able to be burnt.

Alice a grammar.

Article is the same as an article.

Henrietta has been triumphant but not laterally.

Winifred a grammar.

A grammar is the difference between grain and what has been rewarded. Grain which has been rewarded.

Simon a grammar.

Simon is capable of a tiger jealousy.

Simon is very much is very suspicious.

Simon a grammar.

Anthony is certain that George is not an animal tamer.

Katherine a grammar.

Katherine Tardy was a name that was engraved on a Maltese cross and it seemed a very pretty name.

Grammar refers to names as very pretty names.

That is a little better that which is a little better is that.

Counting daisies is not an occupation whenever they can be found.

Whenever daisies can be found it is not an occupation to count the daisies which have been found. Why not. Because if any of them are lost they have not been counted as an occupation.

Grammar does mean arithmetic.

They act quickly.

Grammar matters if they add quickly. If they add quickly they make a counting of what they are adding and they have added them quickly.

Grammar is made to be by them with their renown. Adding fifteen to twenty-seven makes them have an addition.

A sum which assures them that if they add it it will be correctly added.

Grammar makes it be very much more than three days rain.

If the spring has come and nothing can stop it now it is the same with three days of rain it has come nothing can stop it now.

This is whether addition is known as formerly grammar.

Grammar is pronounced.

Addition is adding.

Grammar which is pronounced addition which is adding.

Grammar which is being pronounced. Grammar which is being in adding. Grammar which is adding add it in adding. If there is a rainbow and it is not complete and another rainbow is there there are two incomplete uncompleted rainbows there are or were two rainbows which were there.

Which were rainbows incomplete rainbows of which two were there.

Not having had it and lost it.

Grammar has had it and has not lost it.

Genevieve Geronimo straightened it out without their finding it out.

George in our ring.

Grammar makes George in our ring.

Grammar makes George in our ring which Grammar makes George in our ring.

Grammar makes leave where they can.

An old lieutenant is as old as when he left. He has not left. He has been as old as again when he went as he did not leave again. He has left again whenever he has been and gone unexpectedly.

No one should feel it too much.

Grammar is as disappointed.

George in are ring.

Grammar cause really.

Grammar causes it rarely.

Because grammar can cause it barely.

What is grammar. Grammar is part of it which has to be why they carefully a mare. It is doubtful if a horse is sought. When in seen oxen can they be sold.

Grammar returns to need.

What is grammar. Grammar is what they state.

Bertha Geronimo has a mother named Danny.

Grammar is in origin.

Bertha Geronimo has a mother named Danny and a brother named Danny. Bertha Geronimo has a mother and a brother named Danny.

Grammar makes it be different if they have the use of it if their mother is named Daniel and if they have the use of it. The use of it is the use of it.

Grammar is undated if they have a mother who has the name of Daniel and is called by it Daniel Geronimo Daniel is the use of it.

Grammar makes plates which have the appearance of a very peculiar ink-stand.

Grammar is how are you.

Grammar is how are you.

They while they are without being nervous make hay while they are able and as they wish to finish early.

Grammar is not a matter of seasons or of finishing early. Or of finishing early.

They are right as they wish to finish early.

They are right to finish early.

They make Saturday come soon and will they like it after some have not come.

There is a grammarian who was born where they now make pale cake.

Nestle beside above where it is.

It is made with them to of having for furnishing of course.

Grammar may in their having caught a leave out hammer which is a bird seen to be having mixed one which was as if which tiding deciding they all were not ready then when they were not going in without direction which it is not of course not known.

Grammar reaching makes use of names.

Thank you very much for an island of a church and trees.

Thank you very much for an island of a church and trees island on land.

There may be in grammar two sentences that commence as one.

Look alike.

Grammar has an amount of receding so that any one can be annoyed by their ill health.

Grammar made grapes.

Grammar made grapes be known.

Grammar made grapes be known to be early.

Many poplars are chopped down are chopped down are chopped down many poplars are chopped down but not very much too early.

Grammar uses why they went to find out.

It was once as often.

Grammar makes it alone it makes it be happy alone and she said it was useful.

Grammar makes about whatever they do.

Grammar without peace they are after that they are after that it is after that it is grammar after that without peace. Grammar almost comes well to do, it comes after well and after very well it comes after very well and very well to have it to do. This is why they are avaricious.

Thinking about grammar is kindling.

Grammar is before they thought that they were used about how they were used to about it.

What is grammar. They do know how they will wish it to lose first.

Grammar is without their house which has been built without them.

Leontine grammar.

Mildred grammar.

Archie grammar.

Butler grammar.

How can they do it easily. By not fairly then.

It is preferable to prepare are prepared for it.

Very much easier.

The difference between grammar resting and grammar at once.

Grammar resting is resting ahead.

Grammar is that it is tender.

Grammar is that it is tender.

Remember just where we went.

Out of the cows eight are milked with out of cows eight are milked.

They move as quickly as cows.

As ease a grammar.

They might have no difference made between Alice and at least.

Then they go at once.

Without their being there aware.

Certainly they choose to bundle it out.

Disturbed a grammar.

Certainly they choose to be over secreted.

Return to grammar makes her name trout and love birds.

The grammar they will up and down and sit down and get up and walk around.

Louise a grammar. They establish branches.

What is a grammar. Is the river an ugly river or is it delicate. Do they surround a marsh with hills. This includes their account of their reserve. Without because of at an end.

Marshes a grammar.

Marshes are preferred to a river.

Marshes, a grammar.

Very well, a grammar.

Very well means white clouds which do not follow well.

A grammar realises deftness.

They saw birds.

A grammar realises deftness.

Is there a difference between shade and shelter and sheltering.

Confuse grammar with announcements.

Grammar makes butter fish.

Grammar makes they do have advice.

Grammar makes they do have children.

Arrange a long list of when they were born grammar arrange a long list of when they were born.

With does she mind covering.

Grammar may matter the matter of fact.

Grammar repeats how do you do.

A praying mantle was pale brown and reasonable. Having been accustomed to praying mantles being green. This makes grammar if they like a reason.

This makes grammar.

Grammar makes a dish.

She says game is fresh.

She says the game that she has is fresh.

Grammar follows what is the matter.

If a farmer calls his goods merchandise he is used to it.

With them. That is one sound.

Without him. That is one sound.

Without them. That is not a sound.

Grammar makes a refusal of a tree of a relaxation of a planning, it is used to mingling kitchen and that they are certain to be winding. Suppose there is less fruit then it will cost more.

Grammar is never description it is not their alas. Find out.

Grammar in owns.

Grammar makes not a doubt that the sun which is behind the hills has been and there.

This is a trinket of grammar.

When it in cousin of the daughter.

Why is there a case of some being fond of those younger.

There can be no confusion between a sun behind a cloud or behind a mountain.

Landscape is not grammar.

Neither is combination.

Following after is a part of grammar.

It is possible to see that alike.

The great difficulty is to tell by a hoarse voice if the voice is hoarse because of the city or because of the country. The voice is hoarse because of the city.

It is difficult to tell if the voice is hoarse because of the city or because of the country. This question is essentially grammar.

Patience with them if they have met them. Imply patient with them when they will have met them. Hoods are hoods housed.

Grammar makes Garfield simple.

Arthur Garfield is in case of their animation.

Suppose grammar was white with without about their pleasure.

California reason he pleased calling it without theirs.

Grammar is contained in father which made old men thinner and old men thinner. The edge with their without perhaps it fell.

Grammar is remained.

Begin for them he could be however if he could enchain their owls with whether. It is going as a care.

This is grammar that they are tying without doubt.

Grammar almond grammar.

This is as is a daughter.

Be very curious. He should be well.

When they have said said with out it they have said a remarkable thing.

Grammar is rarely belated rarely however with their hope.

Almond grammar.

Think there almond grammar.

This is a daughter.

With two.

With the farther that it enchains. Entails in totality in almond grammar.

Almond grammar.

Made remarkably with adding duly that it is heightening in a simmer in a cupidity that they call meat.

Grammar is very likely.

Having a fancy for remembering a recent event.

Grammar has nothing to do with form.

Grammar is accountable.

Grammar carried dimples in clearness. Have made shovels.

It is very easy to eat often.

It is very easy to eat often.

That is named a place.

Grammar rushes to have pushes.

Grammar may rain.

It may thunder and it may lighten and electricity may give out may be out of order.

Grammar say yes awake hens and rabbits which are payed for.

Grammar is easily moved to usefulness.

Grammar may mean that they were preceded by another name.

Have at last have been at last have at last been there often.

Grammar is never opposed to secretiveness.

They have been very much protected by meaning then. Grammar remains partly whether. is there very pleasant weather without rain.

What is it.

Grammar does not relate how to however.

It does not relate secession to gardening.

Thinking of grammar makes it barely late.

A whole story told.

It is what they hope and they will achieve more than they hope however just as send without predicting that they were without theirs.

Simple Grammar.

As well as.

As well as ever.

They do find that they do like to do it as well as ever.

That is one at a time.

Completed grammar.

They like to do it with as well as ever for in ending one at a time.

Grammar does not consist in rain raining that has nothing to do with expectation.

What is grammar. Grammar is the sky rosy from lack of sun.

Grammar cannot pause all around because they must come quickly.

Think of grammar.

Are they here.

Think of grammar.

Without a virgin.

Think of grammar.

Who knew which way it was going.

Think of grammar.

Who knew which way it was going.

Grammar means that it has to be prepared and cooked and if they are used to one assistant it is because it was necessary not to have but one.

Any kind of complication is simple that is the real use of grammar. It all but says so.

The side of a rock can receive the rain.

That has nothing to do without it.

Visibly comforting.

A Grammarian

I AM A GRAMMARIAN.

We will or we will not cry together.

These. Have not a cousin.

These have a cousin she is a nun.

Their cousin these have several one of them is a nun.

I love my love with a b because she is precious. I love her with a c because she is all mine.

This is very simple grammar. Who takes it there. This is not simple because it is not trained.

Grammar. If we cry, he cries he does not help himself as one without them.

Grammar is not against sailing. If they have not boarded a steamer.

He never thinks anxiously one at a time.

What is grammar. A grammar is forgotten that there is a dog. Now how could one which is different from what how did one forget.

Forgot forgot means forgetting or did not know there was one. How do you say Forgotten forget did know which he did not know as there was not formerly there is one.

Its all wrong they sit which is alright.

Which is alright with them what is the difference with them. Without them.

The thing that makes grammar is that they know but without doubt they come to be around.

Fifty times grammar.

Partly is the same as party.

Partly is the same as a mistake.

A grammarian there is a pleasure in the air which is agreeable.

Is agreeable to me.

As a grammarian.

Is agreeable to me. They remain so that they are by themselves and for them agreeable to me.

I am amazed that they spell with them.

Think how angry he is.

They are happy in not wishing to finish which they have begun to miss.

It is useless to know how to say so.

Grammar.

I made it do.

That is simple I made it do. Then I was hoping not to hear. If I made it do.

I am a grammarian.

They have to do it.

Repeat.

They have to do it.

Marguerite has to do it.

The subject is grammar.

Opposite to it.

The door was open as well as closed.

The door was open.

As well as closed.

Grammar. Fills me with delight.

I am having it as a habit.

Now the trouble with this is there is a conflict and not in thought, but in reality.

I am having it. Is that a possible tense. No it is not. No it isn't. I am having it as a habit. As a habit has no meaning. I am having it as a habit. Is completely false in reflection. The use of the word so. As well, as much as a piece, so forth. There any one can feel easy. Any one can feel easy. Is not perfect. They can feel easy, is alright. Any one can feel that it is easy. The essence of grammar is that it is freed of following.

It was blown away by the wind. The wind has blown it away. The difference there is not interesting. If the wind blows you can see it.

Having made too little before now which it was you have given too much. That is a tense, to struggle. Struggle and straggle make it a reunion. Gave it a measure. They give it twice there are two afternoons.

Twenty days to two afternoons.

Why is it a triumph to say twenty days to two afternoons.

It is not a triumph to say Having made too little before now which it was you have given too much. It is impossible to have a triumph little by little and too much. There that is a commonplace in a mistake.

I am a grammarian in place.

The place edition.

Now in forty fortification.

To return to managing.

Having given too little and then added too much. Thank you.

An empty lot.
For which they paid.
They were able to pay for it.
Which it is very nice for them to do.

Now try to change that to which it is very nice for them to be able to do now just try.

They were not rich as they were poor.

The Mabel Earls which is really the name of one of the daughters were not rich she was not rich nor were her sister or had her father as they were poor. There is no use in trying to change that.

A parlor is where the sisters receive their parents and their parents friends. It makes me smile to be a grammarian and I am.

They have to have friends.

It is a wonderful way the way in which they have to have friends.

Now thinking as a grammarian they are thinking.

She is going to stay.

That is one way of making it ammunition.

Do not bother with me.

Bother is a word that transgresses meaning.

Bother is a word that transgresses meaning.

I like to bother.

Very welcome.

She and he are very welcome.

The part that grammar plays. Grammar does not play a part.

If a sentence is choosing. They make it in little pieces.

I have practiced.

She has brought me.

Two know. Leave me alone a little.

To know. That they are well off.

A sentence would be the same as a peal. A peal is something that being chewed is to be wetted or rather perhaps before.

Now think carefully. How rare they are.

She moved very silently making a noise that is one thing to think about. Cliquet Pleyel. Makes twenty five a woman. That is a complexion and how do I do it.

Now be very gracious.

Now be very gracious.

I wish I knew how I did it.

Now be very gracious.

Slowly.

I wish I knew how I did it.

After a while.

I wish I knew how I did it.

Makes twenty five be a woman. I say the sense interests me. The sense interests me. That is not what I say. The sense interests me.

Divide noses from grammar.

Grammar little by little is not a thing. Which may gain.

There. Makes twenty five be a woman. The meaning of that does not interest me. It is a complexion that interests that makes ridiculous because that does not make it sound something else. But it does make them which is again me.

Makes twenty-five be a woman. I do not lose it. The color is there. Do you see. Dependent entirely upon how one word follows another. Who knows how Howard likes hearing. I can do it so easily it always makes grammar but is it grammar. Forget grammar and think about potatoes. Grammar after all has to do with why they were presented.

I see they observe they will feel well.

Now this can be considered as a sentence or as synonyms.

A darling dog. Is that a feeling or an expression.

Essentially grammar has no use for distinctions had no use for distinctions now had it. To grammar it is the same thing whether they are urgent or whether they are useful. Do you see Grammar leaves repetition to their nouns. Now think. If you see me I prefer to see you. Now in the place of repealing they make use of sentences.

It is very little to be able to count.

On the edge of grammar is why they make things.

Now again. It is easy to say he is obedient now.

There is no change of choice.

In grammar there is no change in choice. How is grammar different from other things.

The last time that I went I came here.

Ways to welcome painters.

Dutch painters.

French painters.

Urugayen painters.

A Polish painter.

Now grammatically. There is this which is the way to admit of painting.

Grammar does not mean that they are to limit themselves as if they were to be welcomed with it. Grammar does not make one hesitate about prepositions. I am a grammarian I do not hesitate but I rearrange prepositions. In grammar if there is no change in choice it is not a question of hesitating nor in changing of prepositions.

Now secure in see here. See if it is true that they see it here have seen it here.

Thousands count out loud.

The way thousands count out loud they do it with moving their lips.

Made a mountain out of.

Now this is perfectly a description of an emplacement.

If you think of grammar as a part.

Can one reduce grammar to one.

One two three all out but she.

Now I am playing.

And yielding.

To not attempting.

Think closely of how grammar is a folder.

To look back in the way they came. Now think. Who stands.

To look back in the direction in which they came.

In the direction in which they came.

To look back in the direction in which they came.

A grammarian is so.

Afraid.

Is a word.

To look back in the direction in which they came.

To look back in the way they had come. Now you see that means that others had come and others look back in the direction that others had come.

To look back in the direction that they had come. I mean that to look back in the direction that others had come.

Anybody can see nearly what I mean.

I am a grammarian. I believe in duplicates.

Duplicated means having it be twice. It is duplicated. There are beside duplicates. I am a grammarian and I do think well. Of it.

Think of duplicates. They duplicate or duplicated this. Think well of this.

To look back in the direction that they had come.

Think well of this. You cannot repeat a duplicate you can duplicate. You can duplicate a duplicate. Now think of the difference of repeat and of duplicate. I am a grammarian. I think of the differences there are. The difference is that they do duplicate. The whole thing arouses no contention.

Think well or melodiously of duplicate. They will never finish with their watches.

Oh grammar is so fine.

Think of duplicate as mine.

It stops because you stop. Think of that. You stop because you have made other arrangements.

Changes.

Grammar in relation to a tree and two horses.

Sentences

A SENTENCE IS MADE by coupling meanwhile ride around to be a couple there makes grateful dubeity named atlas coin in a loan.

This is what they all do.

Supposing it is ours a dress address name can be opposed to name and tame.

They all have a difference to within renowned that is the available in cowed they govern might final in main repeal how comes with.

The great difficulty in going on is that their is an end of mine mining but not that they disappeared.

Tell everybody how old that they are.

I would rather have a Buic car.

If he knows what he thinks there is a plate with tapestry included.

As ally.

Why do they apply. This to that.

Not a thing nothing with added fined a candelabra found how far farther bother other handkerchief indeed wager clover in covered mind habit in case made in reminder do vainly farm holding theirs dismantle region with feel yes do. A very easy failure takes place. Our comes back. Back comes our. He was neighbored by a bean. How can fixing be a mine. This is what she did this what we did she did covered quickly back in lain double will. Never selfish. How are they. Never selfish.

Jump up.

What could be few in tremble cowed by a let it consider does with avowed.

It is not possible that they made it fancy.

Does she love me if she admires him.

A sentence has to do with Lizzie or Lena which we will call Lucy or Nellie or Tillie or Louise.

A sentence is our paragraph. A supper which is without eight is made in danger of winding a street advantageously.

There is no need of liking their home.

There is no need of liking their home.

Commencing Monday to embroider.

Commencing Monday to embroider.

With whatever they are as jealous of in agreeable.

Leave without invitation. Closing attract have not payed as in which when thought of. If come. In come. Out in hour. By hour. They made gladly. Now then.

A sentence in sin.

A noun is hour by hour.

A verb is ever as wherever. It is acceptable.

By weekly. A cadence. Milked.

An adverb is appointing. Disappointing. Reappointing. Calling. Ferrying. Denounce. A plant of theirs. Is why they like it. Think of feeling. Think of the feeling.

An adjective have to be faced. An adjective in sound based on fugitives. Leave roads alone. They will be pleased. To cover it with however it is only there. An adjective and they will have had May. May Rider. Mary Riding. Minna Riding, Martha Riding, Melanctha Riding. Thank you.

An adjective in present leniently. What is a sentence. A sentence is why they are Miles Standish.

Listen to a portrait.

Harbour what they like. Once. Once and a fourth.

They must be silky.

She must be so sweet.

And very by nearly able.

That is leaning in a portrait.

Sentences may be alike.

Harbour this for me.

She harbours this for me.

Sentences make use of waning.

Lifting eighty into a house where they remained. Eighty are paid for their work.

Sentences covering around.

When they relish. That it is often. By nearly their allowance. With clearly bought.

The use of the sentence in immigration.

Coupled by a supper which is best.

They may be alike with their mother. They may not feel well. They may be waiting by their side. They may with their vanish. They are which ever. Wire known. There is no place for their being wicked.

A sentence makes a place for them.

What is a sentence. A sentence is however afterwards. Having thought that into is not as agreeable as in and to.

Words and sentences who makes whoever.

Are in place.

A little bit of in covered lend.

There is a left to right in their might.

I leave it.

What is a butter.

There may use in trays.

A sentence is why they find it.

If it resembles a showing of their in want. Want ridiculous.

When they find that they have shown what is why they were from here to have in there. This is a sentence with a marker they thought. A sentence in lain daisy. Inlain daisy makes it a call. He called on him. Without their knowledge they made their way without their knowledge. Leave roses as a sent in sense. Insence is alright. A sentence makes horses either.

What are adverbs.

Call around and see us and we are well to do. Well to do and aided by Charles.

An adverb is a change.

One and one makes two. How pleasantly. Everything is pleasant as they say. Come here as they say. In wailing, in veiling to be secured. Everything is able. An adverb makes partly their use.

Adverb adjective and noun.

Verb adverb and noun.

Participle adverb and noun.

Participle adverb verb adverb and noun.

What is a participle verb adverb and noun. Renown. They made their renown. This makes them like. This makes them like it that they made this which is what has made for them their renown.

Call has been replaced by called. They called, if they called they were there as if they had called it to him.

A different account. Of believing in.

Believing in readily.

Believing in readily is their announcement.

A sentence which is mediocre.

Believing in it readily.

A pronoun is when they are allowed. They make no mistake. In landed and leaving as a particular exception. What is a pronoun. They leave it alone.

Yes I have stood it well.

This is a pleasant reality.

Yes this is it.

She dreamed that she was confused and then it was like it was when he said yes yes, so he said, clearly. He said it was like it was when he would have to say yes yes. He would say yes yes in the case of which she had spoken.

A sentence in their place.

How can if make leaving it.

How are they to be named if they have always been well known although as it happens they have not been had here.

Wide with a will.

What is the difference between a sentence and words. A sentence has been ample.

Why are whites like it.

One.

For this in case of bristle.

This made a Mabel.

Mabel little Mabel.

What is the difference between a sentence and a sewn. Pictures are important if they have been followed. Thank you for following. What is the difference between a sentence and a picture. A sentence sends it about most. Most is more than most. Most and best. A sentence is very mainly leave known.

How can a sentence have their hope. This makes it turn around. Leave a sentence in mainly.

She would like to be left with it.

A George a claim.

A sentence is that he came in. For which is there a noun. By which it is accommodated. A verb is next to crown. Crowned with success. An adjective is with their success.

Intervene is made into a meadow. An adverb is painstaking if in intervals plainly laid. Begin a participle by their stretches. Transitive and intransitive aid obeyed with joy. Apprehend and wended and with attained as if with their enjoy. This is clear say with enjoy, and with enjoy he said antedated with joy and so lasted able mainly to felicitate. The compliment in grammar. The complement in grammar. The compliment in grammar. Do not make believe that you are injured very naturally. They are interested in the interesting even always although as aid as shown with Albert who is Alberst or reasoned with.

They may be liked then as an advantage for them.

There then with alike may then place beside them in agate made with the means of addition.

A sentence can retell that they wished they were strange.

A sentence in wished they can tell that they wished that they were where very made which is a verification of estrange.

A sentence in well that is amount more namely save for save with which called are judged regain regard regards as plain as appear appreciate well bellow.

How can they compliment in a sentence. Below payment. Very nearly fatigued.

Out of out aloud.

A sentence. He writes very well.

A sentence. If it is at all that well he is loved because he has taken to be mistaken with them nearly all or after all. A sentence. They were after a fastener of their approach and so they leave out. Whatever they had.

A sentence. Recall repellent defeat without it actual as they count they count without however as they went and were preferred they make it do. He was closer to it than ever. To like a group who have been all. She might remain.

A sentence is made of their having heard.

A noun is made sink sunken.

A noun. With with ever which is sent.

A noun. With wither they will at all.

A noun. He is much better able to do. It is true of himself in a gain.

A noun. Made with their being rosy.

Verb. Inclosed.

Adjective Made receptively.

Curled as a sentence. This is important.

Very well allowed. Made in the way they chose.

A sentence which has equally a share.

Have hours had an opportunity to be defined. This is a plan. It is very easy to be through with whether they do. It is made in that case. A sentence in allowed.

They have allowed it. Wells in having. Wells are distinguished with their breadth. Wells are whatever it has been installed that they care. Carry or care. A sentence makes them may and makes them mention them in representing when in an element of their maturity. What is a sentence partly that that it is in request rained and their account on their account as they have the habit. A sentence in inquiry. Lament a sentence. A sentence does identify did and differently to be being cover and rested at in their immediately round as within without. What is a sentence. A sentence may be fairly in three. Three intense and composing for their which is why they rather other or be by sight. Thick and of a sentence. It is not necessary to know of them all. This is why they require does or other than theirs. It is not necessary to be after a while in spite of their willing that they are wished they are in their reprisal of in as much their means. This is a sentence by that time. That they are without it for them. Thanks having been before in along.

A sentence may make Mary have their care. What is it that is asked. They are named as they have them before them as they with whether as in call because in advance with theirs in train. A sentence needs recovering. Very little known. There is very little known. There is very little of it that is known. A sentence has a noun a noun is not only a name it is a manner, and reply. In so far as they mean noun they are scared and in place. Consider how they could be by hours by theirs if they made it. Made it by any chance. A noun needs recall needs being recalled needs recalling in order that they may not frighten them at one time. A noun is why they are daily redelighted. What is a noun. A noun is made by stretches. From there to there is a noun. Left to their own devices is a noun. Secure and security and readiness to be in theirs as when they have bought and brought neither as along which makes it after a delight that they are cherished. All this has theirs as a known noun. What is a noun a noun is a name and they are by it not without that and theirs where and remain. It is made for them without their having thought that they would recall it which wherever they did do in deference. Having understood everything three things are surprising. One and two and three. A noun is the name of the calling which they have made in their time as known. They will not be ten to advantage. What is a noun. They are right about it.

A verb is actually prepared by a sentence but not actually.

A sentence is this. Allow for it. A sentence is this in as indicated. A verb is without preparation their reason for resting. A verb. At once and when they repel. A verb is an adverse renewal of their reference to whenever they have cost it by themselves without their relieving in a management of their introduction which is improves without the having

amassed without a doubt when left at all. What is a verb a
verb is went and sent and in in elegant. This is a verb, he
came and he asked but not when he was here he wished to
be entitled to a management of reference and this is by the
way which is a verb in plainly of course pressing them to
their in allowance of training. This is a verb. What is it that
was proposed. This which is partly their feeling. This whenever this is a verb they will allow their or themselves to be
known for it as a cause of their following paper with cloth.
Cloth can be of three things rubber, cotton and either both
or better. This makes a noun follow a verb. What is a verb. A
verb reissues a plaintive renewal of after all it belongs to them.

She imagines so.

Without a difference. She makes their having their with
their claim.

What is a sentence with seventy.

One two of three is used with made a name. This is a
sentence or thought for.

It is useless to wonder why they answered.

What is a sentence. They sent preserves.

Settled as an emotion how do they know that four into
forty makes ten in twenty two for a time and he is sold sold
however that it is prudent with their fish. This sentence means
that Pablo Picasso is told that he is to add fold to add folded.
Trying again of each one. A Russian, trying again of each
one may them blame same in the same with the aim with
them. If a sentence is a monagram what is a wear. A wear is
what with why they relieve.

Commence again. If they do not bring an azalea have
they waited.

This is better than stirred.

A sentence in a part.

She does not like to put it there.

Put it there pardy.

What is a sentence. A sentence is an imagined master piece. A sentence is an imagined frontispiece. In looking up from her embroidery she looks at me. She lifts up the tapestry it is partly.

What is a sentence. A sentence furnishes while they will draw.

Take a sentence. They mean.

If it is as if with owner appointed a class.

Take a sentence. He is sorry that she did not give him any credit. For taking such pains to happen to need it as they may. They do need it as she will. This makes all their went and their won. A sentence is not why they were worried.

Why is an hour glass what they knew was a treasure as they went without their wanted as they knew as a tree at Christmas. It is a sentence as first to last that they had it in their out of their however power. They will not give it with their permission.

To tell it all in a sentence is not what I wish to do I wish to tell it all in a sentence what they may make it do. What is a sentence a sentence is not carrying it away. I wish you a very merry Christmas. Name and place is mentioned.

A sentence is their wedding.

What is a sentence. A sentence is an anniversary of their begging them to be seen.

How many days are there in it.

How many leave it to me.

How many come when they have theirs as they with out more pressure just as seen.

How is not a name it is a verb of their pretension. How are they.

She does not love him as they say, they do not love him as they say they do not like to have him waiting so they say they do not wish him to be waiting for them as they say they do not wish him to be waiting for them they say they do not want him to be waiting for them they do not want him to be waiting when they come and find him waiting they do not want him to be waiting and moreover if it is questioned it is a question of paper rattling when it is writing paper that is writing paper that is rattling without altering when they are she makes this as an attempt to refuse a bugle which is bugling which is all to a column call they call that is their game to a name which is a deer in the next to the appointing of their main in different in difference with our out obliged so they collect recollect mainly main abate.

Yes please. Why yes please. Why please. Why to please. Yes please, why yes please, why please, why to please. An authority in sentences.

Why please why not please why yes please why to please why as to a place to piece why it pleases.

A sentence is exactly an eagerness to have a sample of their with them.

A sentence makes it their pair in respect to willing to be hurried.

The Roussets having been successful are now going to Lisbon not as being successful nor as having been successful. The Roussets had been successful. Leaving a sentence to their unhappiness.

A sentence is how to overdate the referring them to theirs aloud. Supposing they must go. Must they call here on the way.

A sentence is mainly their allowance of when they care to have it as a manner of their may be they do but they have a doubt concerning it they are uncertain they are mainly in their way perfect. This is a sentence. They are mainly in their way perfect.

An effort to remain there is what they are not as they are allowed having with their having received having given it as an azalea. Honey can be covered with a cover underneath and under a cover. A cover is over.

A sentence is made to be divided into one two three six seven starting with one. Lain. Camille Lain. Two. Pampas grass has been watered. That is a sentence which makes it very much at the time and so two are likely. A sentence divided into two. Pampas grass. A sentence divided into three. There are these in dissatisfaction. One must make three be for them seldom as a chance. Never allowed to wait. A sentence divided in three. He is never to be allowed to continue to commence to prepare to wait. He is never to be allowed he is never to be allowed to wait. A sentence divided into three which is that he is is never to be allowed allowed to wait. A sentence divided into six. They have purchased what they have been to see. A sentence divided into six. They have purchased what they have been to see. A sentence divided into seven. It is partly why he will and more nearly why he will come. This is how a sentence is divided into seven and a sentence is divided into eight.

A sentence comes to be for use.

There is no reason why they should compare them with themselves.

A very needed lending in advance.

There is no use in as much as they have it left.

There is much need that they will have the use of it for their advantage with however they are about.

A balance in a sentence makes it state that it is staying there.

There is no us whatever they may take as their politeness. Without it left to them.

What is the mistake of their making that it is not having thought without their outdistanced a ridden without their shoal shoal in an afternoon.

A sentence is very well then that they say in at any rate.

Commence and order a sentence.

They will follow them out.

That is what they mean by especial and also what they mean by theirs as extreme in an allowance.

Order a long sentence.

Finally they will bother whether they like their way to be whatever they were to favorably decide being doubted by before them. They will announce serving as as rates.

Commence a sentence with an advice against their idea.

Why will they be willing to go which is an advantage whether wherever it is as their advantage when they like.

A sentence is made for their use.

How much of it can be arranged as they call theirs to be known in part.

A sentence does not amount to vary with possibly like and when they like.

She thought of their future.

Future means fortunate without that they could lain where they made have it known.

Trying a sentence so that it can be left at night.

Left and right they may be much wished for having fairly left within a dare dare to do right.

What is a sentence.

A sentence is an acceptation of why they are rightly known as their scarcely left as shown.

Suppose a sentence could be in whether it is more than

they must as it is very much. He might be weighed and he might without with while like it.

This makes a sentence that they surmount.

Very much while very much they awhile very much they will be very much more very much awhile in their liklihood need in with in their kind. Does she think.

That it is time to do so and that it is a disturbance because they can be away from them.

This is a simple thought and therefore they will be willing.

They can be ready now.

They are accidentally met.

Without which way. This is a clause that reminds them of Simon.

Because they were with a welcome.

With or whether they were with a welcome.

A clause is when they concur.

They must remain nicely having not been in name.

A clause in praise.

He has been liked by coming.

A clause in dispraise.

He has been alike in coming.

A clause which fulfills their having been very amusing.

They made their advances.

A clause which fulfills their having come together.

They were in their way.

This is what is after all more than one.

A noun.

Theatre.

A noun.

As a chance.

A noun.

Might with hands.

He might remember with his hands that it was a Monday.

A noun.

Might. He might.

A noun.

Might with hands.

A noun.

He might with hands.

A noun.

He might remember with hands.

A noun.

He might remember with hands that it was Monday.

A verb.

Their manner.

A verb.

Their manner of their camels.

A verb.

They accepted in the manner of their having theirs as a gift.

A verb.

They accepted in their manners that of their having that they were giving this with that as they were with that as a gift.

Verb noun and participle.

Verb noun and participle and preposition.

Every one knows whatever what ever evidently what ever, what ever is by this with a separation that does not stop. A stop is to call. All told.

Thinking separately does unite a verb to be additional in a participle.

They make a two a year artificially.

With having seen her older.

She came to replace with them as in change when they were with them in their with hers.

Was it she to whom one should be grateful.

This is nicely bought in a way to preposition.

A preposition for with to withstand or prepositionally with when ever it is making in circumstances left to them might by hand he bought. Be bought. A preposition is for that use. May and meant might and covered made for and with to be bought. Made to be bought. A preposition is made to be bought.

For theirs. That is an idea. This is for them. That is hers. That is hers for this for theirs that which they have for them. They have this for them. This is hers for theirs theirs for hers with this for hers this for theirs with for hers. With her.

They gave this to him.

In this the pronouns do not count they are only the story. The pronouns in this do not count they are only the story.

Prepositions are like burning paint paint burns when it is on the fire on fire when it has been put on fire when it has been set on fire.

Been placed where it has been.

It having been made thin it has not been replaced where it had been.

Not by them he in collide colliding has not been placed there by him.

It is that they stretch out the fingers which made the hand.

An article.

It is that they have had a hand which has leant itself to tapestry in knitting which is at hand.

A is an article.

They are usable. They are found and able and edible. And so they are predetermined and trimmed.

The which is an article.

With them they have that. That which. They have the point in which it is close to the purpose.

Think in articles.
The the inclusion.
The in inclusion.
A fine finely in in fanning.
A is an advice.
A is an advice.
If a is an advice an is a temporal wedding.
If a is an advice an is an is in an and temptation ridden.
Temptation redden.
If a is an advice an is a temptation ridden.
An article is when they leak without their wishes.
An article is of them when they leak without their wishes.
An article is when of them when they leak without their wishes.
An article is when of them they leak without their wishes.
A grammar.
A an article. A an article.
A the same.
A and the. An and the.
The this that not.
The this that and an an ended.
An article is when they have wishes.
A is an article.
The is an article.
A and the. Thank you.
A preliminary survey of them they the a day of two a day.
A preliminary survey of them they day of two a day.
An article is by and my and my hope.
An my hope an article is by and my and hope. An and. An an. An announcement.
When this is a tree. They when this with this a tree.
When this as a tree they when this with this a tree.

When this as a tree when this with this a tree.
With articles.
Night with articles.
Right with articles.
A light with articles.
Alight with articles.
A and the.
Articles and days.
Articles are a an and the.
An article in an and the.
An a man and the.
What are blushes. Blushes are a part with their hope. That makes a verb a noun. They are partly with their hope that makes a noun. A noun is always a sacrifice.
A noun is whether they are in play.
Sense a noun.
Arrangement a noun.
It is to be sold again. A noun.
It is to be sold again. A noun.
A noun is the name of anything. And who has held him.
Who has held him.
A dislike.
A noun is a name of everything.
To go easy means to go easy.
He said sense.
To go and uneasy.
A noun means he said sense.
What is sense.
Sense is their origin in relieve.
They relieve the tention.
Relieve is not abominable.
A noun is the name of anything.

He got angry. About the hope.

He got angry about the hope.

A noun can be best.

What is best. A noun can be best. As favored. A noun can be best. Favored. What is a noun. A noun is grown with petals. Petals are springing with their Christmas. This makes a noun.

Never make dolls. Dolls should be seen. They should be gathered. They should be. With all my heart.

What is a noun. They mean strings. Strings mean they will be well with a melt well below. That is a noun. That they use winces.

There is no strength in their calling. For a noun. What is a noun.

Forget the heart of their weeding.

If they know in threes and azaleas.

Not to adopt.

The making of never stop. Or the making of stop or stopped.

The own owned own owner.

This is a sentence. Or either.

For getting the heart of their weeding they were asked to be when they went and forget the heart of their weeding.

Face well they face well they face well well they face as face well.

A sentence. Have they been bequeathed.

A sentence. Have they very well placed their engage as well.

A sentence. Will he destroy an apparently their pressure.

A sentence. Never seen as have ever.

A sentence. Happy New Year Miguel Covarubias.

A noun. That is always refreshing.

A noun. With manage have lean have leaned, leaning is authorise. That is a noun. A noun is there. The difference in a noun in conversation. He said he envies him. He fills him with their pigeon. This is a noun in conversation. A noun in conversation reserves their pressure which they make. A noun in conversation makes their have their in wither in apply apter if rested confusing chosen or shut for the without seen. Seen is a verb which is not as heavily. Verbs in conversation let it lie. It lies it lays it before which way is it a way with their positive in call. How do they make prepare another in case of will surety as surely. A verb is like if they rest for it.

Better than without it which is for it that it it is better than without.

Better than without it. It is not the same as the.

The hope it is in the hope of it. It is better than without.

Might be why they asked to have demands.

It, it is usual to add rose which is four rows. It is usual to add it.

It and the.

It makes theirs a present.

It. It is.

It makes theirs a present of it.

It. It made it do the tendency to do it.

The. The in restraint of trade.

The, it, not in, an, a are in an interruption.

The, it. Not in.

An, with. With is satisfactory.

The in safely.

The it their return.

Look at these three one at a time.

The, it.

It does it good.

The same.

It does it good all the same.

It does it good just the same.

It does it good.

It, the.

It does it good all the same.

To obey it or her. The same as to obey obey it, to obey it the time it is time to obey her. The time and it in the carefully carefully of it. How can he call t mine how can he call it mine.

A sentence. This which is a sentence. It is with great regret that I open the page. It is with great regret that I open at the page. It is with the great regret that I open it with the page. There making mention of everything. With great regret opening it at the page. At which. They regret opening it at the page at which which is open. They open it with great regret.

They and their with very much help. Allow for it. The way that they had been helped was allowed for in it.

The and an aid. It is a help to them. Whichever it is. Which is a help to them. A sentence which is a help to them.

A sentence is an interval in which there is a finally forward and back. A sentence is an interval during which if there is a difficulty they will do away with it. A sentence is a part of the way when they wish to be secure. A sentence is their politeness in asking for a cessation. And when it happens they look up. A sentence is an allowance of a confusion. There are different ways of making of, of course.

A sentence is really when they are allowed without their properly felt in feeling an exchange. How are hours felt in their allowance.

A sentence is why they take pains to do it twice. Twice

they take pains to do it twice as often. A sentence is with their liking to do it slowly. With their liking to do it slowly they allow themselves to advance. Whenever they are liable to have an emergency they are just as likely to turn toward it one at a time and now it has been left to be by that time at their side. A sentence is extraordinarily deprived of intervals one at a time. Suppose for instance they were called away it would be allowed in a half hour. After a delay they would be very welcome. A sentence remains that they will after that be very properly hopeful. A sentence makes it be just as well that they will be theirs as a pleasure. A sentence makes a very little impression particularly if it has been doubly prepared. In this way they will arrange that they move around. A pleasure is their pleasure. This is a sentence in this respect. At once. A sentence is not caught they will be as well as directed with their outline.

Without a bow he came into the room.

He came into the room and there he was standing.

A sentence is made of there is an amount with which he let it have none of it.

Let it be known that they may have none of it.

What without a while which is praise by the awhile.

He said that he ought to be told what he had in advance.

A sentence plays with it for them.

A nice day is one when the sun shines and they have places which they had.

One out of two is three for you.

This is why they asked was he pleased when he heard of it.

How are they alike.

She looked up.

How can a paragraph be made of sentences.

When they were ready they came.

A paragraph can be more than they like.

If they were told to come and they came they had as often in the meantime as an interval.

A paragraph in as all around.

They think that they like which is with easily their sending without it that they came. With how happily it is known in relative without a immediate that they call. They offer that they happen to produce and in derail with hardly as fair. Which when without due without which it is called. They will settle it. The use of what has been then an in undivided between him.

A sentence can be ours and ours. We do not abuse our chance.

What is a sentence. A sentence is why they like that. And it is true. Feel theirs as do delight.

A sentence. One or three they make a little a prize and it is very easy to be one of which of them only they do which has been one.

It is very kindly to be one once in a while.

A sentence. A sentence is their tens with all.

When this you see remember them to me.

How are hours held. They are held by their name. He refuses a dozen.

A noun. Horace.

A verb. Coaling.

A preposition. With him.

An article. The.

A sentence. The coaling that they did when he was with them they were there with them.

Did he influence them.

Behave as if they did.

Did he influence them.

Did they behave as if he did.

Did he influence them. Did they behave as if he had an influence over them.

Did he have an influence on them.

A sentence which is part as they suppose is partly followed by their hope.

A sentence is this. One two three all out but she. She is not patient in affliction.

Have heard a part. They have heard a part. A sentence. A call is when they visit. A sentence. They are as cold as when it has been colder and this is because they desire it.

A sentence. A and and. A is very pleased to see you. And and they will go. The the same all the same to them. An affection which they have manifested. Which they can let them know has been what they require. Without partly conflicting with their pleasure or intention.

While they are alike they resemble those who know what they like.

All these sentences take shape.

Henry and himself have left their name alone.

Henry and himself have left their name alone.

At last or what is to their liking.

A title. A title is when they understood their objection.

Capitally see.

They single out how can they wish.

A series of sentences. A series of sentences remained then.

Howard is early to-night.

With whom did they leave their hats.

How do they like what they do.

When will they differ among themselves.

What part of the time have they to give to them.

With which arrangement are they in agreement.

They must be different to that degree.

They like to have it given to them.

They make it all of it do very well.

In the preferring willingness they are useful to the extreme.

Perfectly attuned to their arrival they must not gainsay those who have been further without pause.

It is flattery to love recommendation that they will still be there.

All these sentences are fruitful they may be included in embroidery.

How are they placed. They are in a basket. They have a great deal of softness and they are very likeable. She looks at her knitting.

If they look up they look as if they move.

A sentence is made up of whatever they mean.

A sentence like that.

One two or three and five more makes eight in all.

It is very well known that they will wish them well.

A sentence is one of two.

Two and two all out but you.

A sentence expresses that they continue when they start that is the left and right and also the place is chosen. A sentence appeals to that sense. A sentence is very manly they need not be nervous. A sentence has a as an article the as an article an as an article. A sentence has also a pause before they go. It also has a pause before as they come they are without doubt going to see more of Morocco. This is in one sentence if it is precluded by their having tried to be very much more than they could without their hope. In the hope is the fancy that they have that they are perfectly prepared to tell them so. Assume that they have to be partly at their disposition. This would be without doubt what they believe it to be with which they have not placed it where they were. A sentence has pleasure in retirement.

How do you do. Very well I thank you. Will you precede me. Not two at a time. Theirs in a glance. When they are without doubt. Felt as it was. While awhile afterwards.

There can be two ways of having a half they may be all of it for them or as it was which may remind them of their presence.

She is very well read.

She has been wearing ear rings and is wearing them now.

She has been doubtful if the material of which her costume is made is not like that which has been differently determined and it is in no way just at once that she is not disappointed. She is interested in their discovery that partly makes what they find. It without undue credit is entirely at her disposition.

A sentence can be very reduced there can be in it a noun and a verb. Well done. There can be in it a noun and a verb. With which. There can be in it a noun and a verb.

There can be in it a noun and a verb.

A sentence in which there can be a noun and a verb is such a one. It is one in which there is more relief from their having quiet. Considerable of a noun and a verb. How has it been left. This is a sentence. How has it been left with him. A sentence which can personally tell that they have changed their mind is one in which they agree they estimate with themselves in jeopardy. There is no jeopardy in usefulness. This is not alone a sentence it is a reason. A sentence manages the reference to their available aroused presence in this way. Following is an appointment a renaming of theirs to relate. A sentence makes calling to them their bother with it. Thinking of a sentence makes it very well I thank you. All these are varieties which do concern themselves with differences. To forget that he said yes it is so. It is not easy to forget that he said yes it is so.

Have had a voice he has had a voice they have had their voice they had the hope of it happening. They have the management of the design that they will call Edith Bertie. Bertie or Bertha.

That is for them at all. A sentence which follows another makes it be theirs as bequeath if he is uneasy about coming. Think like altogether about nothing at all with milk which is gratifying. In this way a sentence loosens within itself. Have handled have it handled with forethought — have it handled with bought have it bought. It is bought. They like it with whatever they may number number one. A sentence may marry May Mary mainly as a choice. Without a thought of how they like it they give it where it will do the most for their good. Mainly as it matters. A sentence. How do they like everything. This is a sentence as arrangement. A sentence avoids that they protect themselves.

What is a sentence. A sentence can be simple or complicated it can be careful or it can change it can be collected or it can be caught usefully it can be made for this at that rate in the way of finding that they were able to have or to have offered it. A sentence is made of a verb and a noun. He has heard him say it. Another sentence which they like is that they should say it. They also feel that it is badly needed without it being different that they should be greeted. Wonder and greeted. How are they able to remain standing.

Think in stitches. Think in sentences. Think in settlements. Think in willows. Think in respect. Think in farther. Think with while they will. In this case the succession of sentences do not pass muster. What is a sentence. A sentence is felt in a storm. How are you getting along. Bay a bay is a body of water. If they sit at home they sit in a boat. They are in the same way cared for. Think of sentences. Nobody likes sentences without sought. He sought to avoid their return. If they needed an article they might think that they were without it. It is very easy to feel happy in the midst of a conversation they will bother them with it if they like what is happening in the day time as part of the remainder of their arrangement called as if it were at variance in included diversion without accustom immediately three times and not more. Think of how ours are unalike.

A sentence does not make a division.

An article is one two and three without a thousand. He has described Holland in many a sentence without referring to Uncle Tom's cabin. This sentence explains that to-day there is some sunshine. Think carefully about sentences. They do think as carefully about sentences. They do that. They do think as carefully about their sentences. How do they like what they have given them. They think they will like it and very much as they were without any trouble. It is mostly without it with their choice that they must resume having a hold of it on it. There is no difference between sentences a apart. How many like houses. That is a sentence. How many like houses. A sentence is alright but a number of sentences make a paragraph and that is not alright.

Why is a paragraph not alright. A paragraph is not alright because it is not alight it is not aroused by their defences it is not left to them every little while it is not by way of their having it thought that they will include never having them forfeiting whichever they took. Think of a paragraph a paragraph arranges a paraphanelia. A paragraph is a liberty and a liberty is in between. If in between is there aloud moreover with a placed with a placing of their order. They gave an offer that they would go. A paragraph is meant as that.

A sentence will be at a pinch.

A sentence will be at a pinch.

A sentence. How are they out.

A sentence. How are they our how are they. What is a sentence. A sentence is in requisition. It can go at once. A sentence. There is a difference between a and the. A manner of getting them exchanged. The hope of a the appointment of their connection with a brilliant situation. Hope for a or an account of it. Think of a sentence two at a time.

Half an hour is alright. They think of an hour in an obstinate cause. They are uppermost with theirs as a pearl. A pearl. Think slowly always.

This makes an apparent division between. Accustomed to call. Accustomed to a call. Custom a custom do accustom they come accompanied they will venture to arrive with a variety of circumstances that they can have come to be to them as if which they can prepare to be alike.

A sentence with which crowds. All fall fall into fine for their sake.

What is a sentence. A sentence is partly softly after they write it.

He does want this for him.

He wants this to be given to him. He asked for it. He brought it home for her. He was not afraid to mention it afterward.

Think carefully how a sentence is not a paragraph and should not be. What is a sentence. A sentence is not a paragraph and should not be.

If an Italian was courageous before what is he now. That is not a sentence.

What whatever is an insistence. A sentence mashes forever the return of calling. They will cut a piece of it in two. If it is a string. They will like without reserve the name of a shipping where they have a harbor. Without their being won at all. In mind. They have it in mind. What is a sentence a sentence is a shove with when they love. This is borrowed as mine. This is a sentence. This is borrowed as mine. Thank you for a sentence.

What is a sentence. A can be felt. With their corrections. Which is why they are able. This is alright. All told in. In can be as effective. Think of a sentence. How do you do with them. What is a sentence. A sentence is made known.

If they are going to be here.

This is a sentence completely.

Think what do they think is that sentence. They think that sentence is after they are late. They are not late because there was no time arranged. And if there had been it would not have made any difference. There is no paragraph in arousing. Nor in quitting. Nor in agreeing. Nor in forgiving. Will they like it in two. If they can not put it all together what will they prefer. Think of a sentence. If they like it they do like it that is easy. What is a sentence. A sentence may reasonably be lost. And with it all at once. Which they may do. What is the difference between which they may do and which they may like. Think of the sentence they like it. What do they do. They do like it. If they do like it. They will give it to them to have. Think of a sentence. What is a sentence. What is a sentence to their account. Keeping well away from all told.

They thought they were welcome.

This is a sentence. They thought they were welcome and it did not make any difference. This is a sentence. It did not make any difference without allowing an hour. This spoils a sentence to which they add coughing. Thank you very much for everything. What is a sentence.

A is an article met is a verb well is a noun. With which. Is why they like to think. Think. A sentence can be placed where they go. They go all at once where they went. What is a sentence. She is waiting. What is a sentence. She is leaving us is a sentence. Indifferent. Is a sentence. They will show what they like is a sentence. All these sentences do not repeat themselves. What is a sentence.

There is a difference between confusion. That is a very good sentence.

Without a doubt if she is without she minds it. That is a sentence that has changed. Without a doubt if she is without she minds it.

Without a doubt if she is without she minds it. What is a sentence. Without a doubt if she is without she minds it.

A sentence is very well in their hope.

Thinking in words. She knew how to please. That is not why they wanted him to have rings. Thinking in words. They were to be ready to go. Thinking as they thought. Would she like if she changed to have them think better of it. What is a sentence. They know that in one country they recite in a manner. A sentence is what they will mean if they are caught by their hours. Think of a sentence. This is a sentence. Are you ready. This is not a sentence because nobody furnishes something every little while. Nobody furnishes something every little while. What is a sentence. There is no hope of their holding without betting. That is not a sentence that is a grievance. What is a sentence. Every word is at one time. He never heard but he saw. They say that that is so.

It is not necessary to know it about them if they know it about her. What is a sentence. A sentence has nothing to do about words. There is very much to do for her. Has nothing to do with it. It has nothing to do with them. It is about how they left it. Think of a sentence separate is from is and was and make it as to manage which is to manage it as it is which is as it was, which is as is not restrained. Thinking in a then or with then in end to an end and that is and an excuse. To return to he thought. What is a sentence bought is a sentence he bought it. What is a sentence. After a while what is a sentence. Think what is a sentence. A sentence is never displaced. By and by. Leave it alone. Come again. What is a sentence they go to have it happen that they cough. This is a sentence. They will be having this that they were annoyed. Think of a sentence nobody is more simple. Nobody is more simple. Think of a sentence nobody is any more simple than think of a sentence. Not that. What is a sentence. A sentence does make it more carefully a beginning of their kitchen.

Without doubt.

To please a young man there should be sentences. What are sentences. Like what are sentences. In the part of sentences it for him is happily all. They will name sentences for him. They will all call sentences sentences for him. Sentences are called sentences. In reading sentences they are called sentences. Thank you very much for reading sentences. Sentences which are called sentences are laid together. This makes them sentences. For which they are intended. He will read sentences which are intended for sentences. For which they are intended.

With a pressure of what are sentences. What are sentences. They see that they. That is not this that they arouse. Why they know what are sentences.

Sentences are indubitable. Without their name. Thought

or short of a sentence. A sentence is an anticipation of their being winning. They are very winning.

She came in plenty of time. She came in in plenty of time. That is a sentence which is not interesting. It was pleasant that she came in time. It is not doubtful that she came in time. When she came in time. The only sentence of all this which is interesting is the one. When she came in time. Thank you very much.

Hours and hours of glass. What is the difference between a title and a sentence. They are all alike. What is the difference when they are all alike. There is this difference. They are all alike and they are alike there is this difference. A title makes it be ready. A sentence with them means when they were and are rich. What is a title. A sentence is a title. Without a sentence, who has had him first. Of course there isn't.

He has succeeded in directing every one's attention to. And this was not his intention. As he had no feeling of having been allowed. Mainly at a time. This is neither a title nor a sentence. But it could be.

Consider a sentence. He has done it all. They know that they were going there. With which they wish. If he has done it at all. But he has. In that way it is an accomplishment.

Leave and left them a sentence is to leave and to have to be just as if he left with them. What is a sentence a sentence is a noun and a verb and her name is Ermine. She is a cheerful presence. Presence. What is a sentence. Ermine is cheerful with as presents. What is a sentence. With fill with fill will will will with with them. This is not a sentence. This is a song which must be when there is a pleasant with a pleasant with a pleasant mainly in with her time. What is a difference with or with a sentence. What is the difference between a sentence and their having thought yes. That is very sweet. What is a sentence. A sentence is without a round. This is the case with their caress. A sentence is with a round. If he is influenced by with him will he regain with whether mother for their estate. They will. This is a sentence if it is an event. A sentence is drawers and drawers full of drawings. This is a sentence. And why. Because they will apart from their having been done made farther that they will rather finish. Without another color. That makes it quite different with whether in arise they must change with bellows. A noun should never be introduced into a sentence. If it is it is because there is poverty poverty is at once and must be that they are anxious to kiss. A noun should never be introduced into a sentence. Also whenever should not be introduced into a sentence because without a leaf they imitate that without reason. This makes it not at all strange that they place it where it is. Think about with them. A sentence is very much whenever they do care. A sentence need not have a noun. A noun must much sooner not be named. Think very well about a sentence. Think of it. A sentence has not been after with a while. A sentence does mind does mind a sentence with if with regain. Remember a sentence should not have a noun. A sentence should not have in it a noun. A sentence should not have a noun with winding because it means by wifely. Think well of a sentence. Feel how do you do. A noun should not remain. It is introduced. It should not remain. A noun should not remain in a sentence. With the a noun should not be in the partly seen hope that arises. A noun should not be in a sentence. It is a way to way lay. There are two things a reader and who has a reader. A fifth reader. A second reader. A sentence should not have a noun. A sentence. There the rest of the sentence. Without the rest of the sentence a noun should not be in a sentence. Who has helped her. Who has been of help when they were without them when they had been with them. A sentence can be in having sent a management with their present to be present. What is a sentence. It is exactly that that they must have their whole day at the time in which they like it. Disturbed in a sentence.

How are sentences asked for. By the way how are sentences asked for. A sentence is a mention of their seeing silk in paper. Any one can see that a noun means disturbance. A noun should not be in an undisturbed sentence. There can not be a noun in a sentence without there having been a disturbance in the meantime. A noun is the name of anything. There should not be a noun in origin in a sentence with him. With is the same thing. A noun is the name in origin. There should not be a noun in a sentence by him. By him is a name without them they know better which is why they were there with them. What is a noun. There should be a sentence and there should not be a noun. There should not be a noun. In a sentence there is no noun which has been in a sentence which has not been in case of disturbing. Beginning with adding makes of a noun a sum in addition. In addition is not a sentence with a noun, in addition they were in addition disturbing. This is when a noun is in an addition. There is a noun in a sentence without an addition, an addition is not disturbing a noun is not disturbing but is put in after a contribution of disturbing in addition. There is a differenee between having thought of a noun. A sentence makes an addition. What is a sentence without an addition.

A sentence means that it looks different to them. Considerably. A sentence means that it is as different as it looks. Looks may be a particle. A it looks as if it were different that is to say they do not need it and so it looks different. A sentence is made of a particle a particle of it. What is a sentence. They are angry at the same. At the same time that they are angry they are loved by another. They will do doubtless doubtless without encourage they will defer it for them. Think and think and think a sentence. Have it happen they will leave it to them. They will leave it to them to have it happen. To thank to thank them. How is that how is it they like pearls. Pears and pearls are both illuminated. If there are no nouns in a sentence are there verbs. No and yes. If there are no verbs that vary they will be careful. It was of no interest to come home. Will they bequeath pears. That is always their bought. Bought and buy. They will always bequeath bought. It is of no interest that as it is brought. Brought without in case. It is of no interest as it is brought. Brought without in case. No verb allows pleasure. That is easily in mean. To mean. Without the precaution. They were very varied. One must have very strictly theirs as thought. A verb is of no pleasure in their providing. What is a verb. A verb is around with their caress. And this is not without goal which they mean. Everybody can now see that it is a noun. Thinking carefully there is no noun in a sentence.

A noun is a name of anything. Thank you.

If we do a widow sees an old story with new eyes he does they do. It is a movement with a in between. What is a. A dog a call a having this in that. Why do they like having a in this and that. This may be as their sentence. A reapproach. A sentence may be without their being their weight. In this way a and a call and a and apt and slowly. This may be better. It is a pleasure to divide it into a three parts. With them with with there with her with with what do they do with them. A sentence which they find until they will be with you with that the sentence with that and now left left left left right left

left left he had a good job and he left. If you that a a is a wish. That would be the way to be alike it. What is a sentence when they. Very much indeed. A sentence is made as they are seeing it with what are our what are ours a sentence is made by them like this but not now they were left over mention through which is that. Say it simply. They are our hour glass. Say it simplier. They are without out for pouring that they feel used to it. It is simply that they are very stained in very better now with whether which are very nearly through. There has been enough of why they were not very delicious. How many have there been in it. I think very well I think very well. The whole thing is there is no paragraph thank you for once in a while. What is a sentence do they like what is a sentence.

A noun is the name of anything with pleasure that is with that. A noun is the name of anything and therefor it should not be without doubt therefor it should not be in a sentence unless easily easily in in have have lean to so that leaving out without doubt a noun out without doubt they were left to have it looked for with implication. There is a case implication with having folded without doubt that they ought. A noun may be erased but it should be thought about before. The trouble with a noun is their standing it is very fatiguing unless they have the habit because their chairs for sitting are not more comfortable than their standing for standing. Now is chairs a noun. Yes it is and it is because they have no obligation. With which to line to decline staying away with remaining. A sentence made mischief that is it interrupted shawls. In this way shawls is not a noun perhaps but whether it is or whether it is not may be they do may be they do this in referring. It is very easy to make a g on top of an r and sometimes beautiful. This is a sentence which has no more than on top which is not different from above. Above or below is half of the time a large quarter. Supposing a sentence is clear whose is it. With the hope that they will like it which has not been predicted. They will hope that they will like it although this is not predicted. They will be with whatever they have as pleasure. When is whenever it is whatever it is that she is either with with mending that it is. Think of a sentence why should there be a noun. They think of a sentence. Why should there be a noun. A noun is the name of a thing a sentence is why they came. If they came they are here. Thank you.

With them they think.

What is a sentence that is when they say that it is with them they think it must have been reread in an untenable with without prediction as a might without doubt have theirs recopied make a marked without theirs to recall in exaggerated with pleasure they do which is just as curious which is their reference to without them this that whichever they recall the especial placing of their fastening it without it a nearing alike with and a time when with whether with whenever they went there with them in disturbing lain to this in however where they were as it is. Now think what is this sentence. It began this as this sentence and then this which is as is this sentence that they were never without this the next or nearly by not returned to all by cheerfully come up to relate to them that this will be when if as known in alike comes to be at a call insistent and so stop which is the same as stopped. Now think why wisely or why widely or why highly of this sentence. A sentence can be felt and not seen not very well as blossom. Blossom is as they are as will with it with it blossom. Why can a noun not a ready yet a noun. A sentence this sentence the one that began is the one that without it it is a refrain from without reference to a noun. A sentence makes it do. What is a sentence without which referred. Feel a sentence as they feel theirs it is not unalike. Any word. A word. Are is used to make butter. That is one thing. As short. About why they went. This makes it be their hope. Never mention hope when they are when they are is the same as hesitation. If you think in sentences you are not easily pleased. Not easily pleased is better than they like. What is it that they like they like it. A sentence is very much after all. What is a sentence. I have not decided if a sentence is better or is more or is best or is only most most and best. What is a sentence. Having been interrupted what is a sentence they like me. A sentence is after all they began to never the less mail their letters. There are two kinds of sentences. When they go. They are given to me. There are these two kinds of sentences. Whenever they go they are given to me. There are there these two kinds of sentences there. One kind is when they like and the other kind is as often as they please. The two kinds of sentences relate when they manage to be for less with once whenever they are retaken. Two kinds of sentences make it do neither of them dividing in a noun. Having never had it as a noun and so they will. What is a noun. They have forgotten. There are two kinds of sentences.

There are two kinds of sentences we do. Think well and not, two kinds of sentences with theirs. There are two kinds of sentences, with theirs.

When this goes on it is to be remembered that there are two kinds of sentences and are they not without that.

Two kinds of sentences the sixty fifth did he say which is two to say. The two kinds of sentences are these they are with that and after stopping which leaves it to make these after for them. That is one kind of sentence and there are many of that kind for which they are pleased. Undertake a large matter in a way they for instance make it complain without their having with either. That is the other another kind of a sentence that shall be made for the renown with their care to be occasional rested for themselves without about in laying this is for and then the division. There are two kinds of sentences in the middle.

What is a sentence. A sentence is a beginning with when they are at home with a transaction transition transfer and between. That is a plaintive cause beneath with when they are careful. This which is a sentence could be said so.

What is a sentence when they are referred, to it a plan, that they call with after a fairly long while. A sentence is not by and by that they call for them. Think of calling for them. What is a sentence. A sentence made it be at in time that she came. Suppose you try a description pink which is rose and white which is won. So that it comes up with and to it. A description has no interest as a sentence once when it is getting as better.

With most forgive forgiving a sentence and not as a use a sentence should have with what they said it was in one that they make a hurry with a call. Going through means not stopping and she knew and so it is true and that is with a well to do which is not forgotten which may call it as they drew which is why they call to be made with having a change. Think of a sentence what is there to do when there is no count about it. All these are not examples of sentences. A sentence is when they end. Leave a sentence alone when they end. A sentence is when they leave a sentence alone and follow after which is why they refer to yet and they may do what is made of their at all this in the day. Think of a sentence nobody sits. Think of a sentence. Nobody sits. Thank you nobody sits. Think of a sentence. A sentence fails to have a pleasure in a new one. This is what they feel. Think of a sentence. What is a sentence. A sentence is forgotten and thank you very much. When they are careful to be alright. That is a very good example of a very good sentence and easily read and arranged. When they are careful to be alright. A sentence follows when they are not around. If they liked to walk around. Fail fell a sentence to fill with well and well well very much which when they come with will they be well. Nothing is cuter than when she just looks in. What is a sentence. Not as they see. And so they must be obliging to a sentence. It is very necessary to have been obliging. A sentence with them and sent. That is a sentence that has a curious name. It is called a sentence. With them they will be here which is why they marry. A sentence makes a round have as many ways. Think of a sentence. Nine in nouns. A blame. They have no hope that he will not remind them of their gain which is why. That is a sentence. Easily, that is a sentence. Without with out. Either of these fill them without doubt. Anybody can spoil by that. Spoil by that. That is one sentence. Think of any sentence. How do you do. That is a plain sentence with their allowance. After all who has a sentence.

Against sentences. The whole idea of sentences is that they are with it. The whole sentence is that they come with and then. With and then with and then they may with and then. The whole idea of sentences is that they have them with and with with is when and then is with as many as with then. This is the whole idea of a sentence. After that the rest made as a restful with care and thanks and as ease. It is easy to be careful. What is a sentence. A sentence is they are very much as they considered it to be with left before it. A sentence has help. Think of a sentence peacefully.

   This is one sentence. If they came and went. Another sentence is praise it. To praise it is like Tuesday, they are sent. In this way a sentence has full meaning. At this time they like a sentence by themselves.

   What with with with what. That is an old sentence. What with what is also an old sentence. With what is not as old a sentence. Made with what is not an old sentence. With what is it made is a sentence. With what is a sentence made. With what, is a sentence made. Leave it to them to. There is one thing that is certain there should not be nouns and verbs with them with what with them it is made. There should not be nouns and verbs with them. There should not be nouns and verbs, with them. Why. There should not be nouns and verbs with them. Nouns and verbs are not without with them. There should not be nouns and verbs, with them. Forget who it is without that. To forget that it is who it is without that. A verb is left alright, a noun is by all with a change. They will be still as often that she had not come without him that is a girl. In this way a noun is something. If a noun is something they mean that they have not heard. They have heard. A noun is without pronouncing. A noun may do date. Forget with or without. With or without forget with or without. Forget to forget to forget with or without. A noun is alike. They are all alike. It does not make any difference with what they are all alike. They are alike alike makes two by four which is eight. What is the difference between arithmetic and a noun. Forget forget forget the difference between arithmetic and a noun. A noun is the name of anything. Arithmetic is added to it has no need of a noun. Then there is a difference between arithmetic and a noun.

   With which they were to know which they were to have to do. With which they were to have with which they were to

be with what they went to come come with some. This is a
sentence that has no connection with a noun or with arithmetic, it has some connection with a verb and therefore it
should be condemned. There should be no need of with it
all if they have theirs as a reliance without awhile. Now there
is no verb. Thank you very much. What is the difference
between a verb and their altering it. If there is a difference
between their verb and their altering a verb is not a word. A
verb is not a word. Having been what they need their verb is
not a word. A word with it. What is a verb. A verb is right
away. Therefor there in no need of it. This is why they may
upon it. This is a verb. Do be used this is a verb. They will
see that they do not defer to not to need. This is a verb in
disappearing. This is still a verb and an allowance. Always
when there is a verb they do not need a noun. They do not
need a verb. With a verb. They have led a life. They have led
the life. They have led their life. A noun is a verb. Without a
noun this that is without an arithmetic an arithmetic without a noun. Arithmetic a noun with a verb. They need to
keep away from with it all. It is very easy to be here and there
to-morrow. With them. A verb is why they meant to be with
me. A verb without a sound. Thank you. What is why they
are without their sent a sentence. Their they sent a sentence.
Without why a jump. A jump is a noun. A jump is a noun.
There is no noun. There is a sentence with feeling with feeling there is a noun there is an adverb and a noun and a sentence and a noun. What is a noun. To benefiting. A noun is
when they are just as dark. That is a noun. A noun is a blame
for them. They are with their appearance. What is a noun.
Having known all the things with which they were not a
queen, a queen. A noun is a queen and they were worried.
There is no noun. There is something else that is not a noun

with whom. Janet Flanner and Florence Tanner Janet
Flanner and Florence Tanner Janet Flanner and Florence
Tanner janet flanner and florence tanner florence tanner and
janet flanner this has nothing to do with a sentence perhaps
it is a sentence in pressing it to be a sentence yes. What is a
sentence Florence Tanner and Janet Flanner is a sentence
with a sentence admitted a sentence is admitted. Florence
Tanner left her key had left her keys under a door mat as she
might have and Janet Flanner had not had any hope of not
being there where she had been all the time. This is a sentence but not interesting and so you see. What is a sentence
now what is a sentence not that now what is a sentence with
not now that is not a sentence now. A sentence should be
theirs. That is a piece of a sentence but not a part. Not interesting. What is a sentence. A sentence is within with within
adorn apt to he likes to call it they have preferences without
a time that they ate with at or call they have nine weights
with them what is it with worth that they come to have to to
do the cause any good. What is a sentence that they like with
all of it a quarter of their panting to do with after the mexican
do more. Without their ado which may they came. All these
sentences are examples which may be married or merry after they are called with out a place that they grew. This is the
way that they describe Amsterdam. What is a sentence that
they are willing to pause with which they were as made to
have spoken it with accustom let alone to their nicely with it
as if more can shall have it as a count on account too their
meaning left to be right away come as two call with which
they will and fall have a join as they like made too an order
which they can sue each fair and warily in a true with a place.
Now think of this as a sentence make believe everybody likes
it that they will at once. This makes a sentence regularly with

out their hope that they will annoint in a place just as it is without them which they do. This is a sentence that is not interesting because they are very likely which they have as a kind without it as they are to be and have for them at all. This is a sentence which makes them angry and why because they are like to and they are to be without all and fall which may be at most white. What is a sentence. A sentence is what they are after when they are free to be told all this is what they do as sentence is that they do not like the name. A sentence is made of an article a noun a verb. The time to come is a sentence. The time to come and he was very much as if he liked to think that it was as much so as ever. A sentance is one thing and remembering what he said is another thing. What is a sentence. Do not like this is not a sentence it is a Helen. Two will do is not a sentence. Two and two and one will do is a sentence and Helen is a sentence. Two and two and one and two will do is prepared to do will make a sentence and will do. Helen will do is a sentence. A Helen will do is a sentence and a Helen will do is a sentence. A Helen will do is a sentence. In place of a Helen will do a Helen will do is a sentence. A Helen will do is a sentence. What is a sentence what is a sentence and a Helen will do what is a sentence. This is just following a sentence a Helen will do is a sentence. They will mean a sentence a Helen will do is a sentence Helen will do or a Helen will do or Helen will do or and have a Helen a Helen will do is a sentence. What is a sentence. They do know what is a sentence. If they continue to know what is a sentence they must stay to Helen will do but they stay to a Helen will do this is a sentence. A Helen will do is a sentence. After they will stay what is a sentence. Helen will do is a sentence. A Helen will do is a sentence. They need never be is a sentence with they need after a day to be to be a sentence. All will be after a sentence. What is a sentence. Refuse what is a sentence by their liking with all of it for them. What is a sentence. To what is a sentence. If they what is a sentence. If what is a sentence they what do they is a sentence do is a sentence what will they is a sentence do is a sentence what is a sentence.

Ralph Church is going to turn into something else under one's eyes I do not know what he is going to turn into but he is going to turn into something else.

Ralph Church is going to turn into something else under one's eyes.

It is easy to be held for Anna. This is a redoubt. It is easy to be held for Anna. At a main taken to be taken. Forgetting that it is easy to be taken for Anna and he sobbed. Withdrew. It is to be taken for Anna and he sobbed. With how are they. It is easy. To be taken for Anna. And he sobbed.

It with in diminish. It with in diminish. And he sobbed. This is a sentence. Too clearly. This is a sentence too clearly. There is no news in gain to lay to lay in gain gayety. This finishes with a noun and so they ask what do you mean. A noun provokes questions. Therefor a noun can be tried. A noun can be asked. He went to ask him. There is no noun there. With wide in widen. That is as a noun is a verb. A noun is a verb if it ends in widen. Think of a noun is a verb and in widen. He was married. One or two. He was married. One or two. In this way a noun is in a wedding. All this as easily as their wedding. In a wedding. A noun is a verb. Is a verb a noun. No. A verb without provocation. A noun is a verb without provocation is a noun. What is a noun. Withdrawn. This is with appealing. A noun is a verb with withdrawn with appealing.

To think only of how much. To think only of how much.

166

Not with a providing to think only of how much. They were very evidently evidently is how much. It should be very nearly nearly followed. Closely nearly followed. This is a verb. In this verb there is no noun. They like to have been seen by him. In this verb a verb is not in this verb. Not at all.

Button button who has the button that is a sentence that Ellen likes very well. Pretty nearly surely supposing that is said he would like it to be read. That is the beginning the next is what is it. It is very nearly satisfied. And with that they withdraw door. A door. They withdraw or it is finally relaid. To think carefully twice over each sentence. Which is said. Once a sentence is said once it is reread they think that a sentence is twice said and twice reread. Think of a sentence if it means a pin they will begin. Think of a sentence they will be around a sentence with theirs like it. A sentence follows places and therefor he is confused. This is a very good sentence literally. Never to look at another and see it do it that is not a sentence that is a reflection. A reflection is not a sentence a delight is not a sentence whether they are there is a sentence. It is always alright to like a sentence if they manage to clean well. A sentence is happily rough enough. This is not a sentence this is a reflection. What is it that they find when they look there. This might be a sentence but it is not. Why do they remove a sentence. That is not a sentence. She may or may not have come to-day. That is a sentence. As it happens he has come to-day. That might be a sentence. It is very easy to like sentence. They will be without doubt able to come they will be without doubt able to come. That is with withdrawal a sentence that they plan. It is very well to have no double use of their bother. This is a sentence. And yet who finds it because of that alone they are a pause. And this is no notability which is not a signed efface. A sentence which parts a return is one which is darling. It is easy to feel helpful with ham. That is a sentence because it is a failure. This is a sentence because ti is a failure. If Mr. Longstreet explained hope it is rightly called theirs. This is a sentence in their attack. There are two sentences with them there are two sentences without them.

What is a sentence. One in one. One an one. A sentence is a disappointment. One an one is a disappointment one in one is a satisfied satisfy. They do come by. It. What is a sentence a little dish is not a tool that is a sentence it has a noun and a verb it is a sentence. Now why is it a sentence. It is a sentence partly because a noun is a repose and a tool is a folded leading to a might without then. Now this last is not a sentence in explanation. A sentence is that they are hourly without a pressure of events. Seem rely about that they all, this is an old sentence and they use that. This is over now they will be well and well. How do they let them recall you. That is an old sentence and not interesting. For which they like. More interesting. How are readily states that she is by shelving. This has been to be. They make it do. These last are left. With after choice. They came to rally. All this is what they do not say what they like. This last sentence is entirely different. What is the one next to. That is a nice sentence. A sentence should never win. Alike. A sentence with I do with you what you do. A sentence like this is in their own. If it arrives with prize that is not a sentence they stick. Without their pressure. What is a sentence. In useful too. What is a sentence. A sentence is not meant or invented it is hoped to be with them in place with like it in perusal. Why should one deposit a sentence.

A lingering bought. With welcome to our city. Which they leave. With their does it.

With their does it is a sentence. They will hope for it, is a sentence. A sentence is why they bequeath left left left left right left. There is of no necessity of any more. That is a perfect sentence because it retains and recompenses whom they like with prevail as their daughter. The use of the word daughter is never dangerous. Think what a sentence does it may double may and may, may come what is a sentence. Will they think what is a sentence, a sentence that they find, by their object, with it. What is a sentence. It is easy to be hoped with a sentence. That would be a good sentence but a sentence has to have made it with them. And they were with them. A sentence with found. He was to have them there anyway. This is a sentence. What is a sentence not at all. It is just what is a sentence not at all. A sentence must tell that she has held a bell a bell is why they name halves. What is a sentence. They remain. After a while. What is a sentence.

Our bright brightly is not a sentence equivalent. What is a sentence they mean three. A sentence comes to have him. And she is knitting brown wool. And she is knitting brown wool is a perfect sentence thank you for a perfect sentence.

A series of a sentences beginning with Nearly when they came. This series of sentences may be able to add many more to them. With out their widening a lack of ably choosing their nieces which are nearly in vain. What was the patently having of their withdrawal. That is an allowance for the might they be with theirs which they refuse. All this if you think of it as sentences marks their might be as they without a well which they brought a well which they brought made allow a curious reliable never as they had. This is an old sentence and has been used some. Now a sentence which may not be reliable is one that if it is about is welcome with our career welcome with our career this is an old sentence but has not been very much as they held from that in ours may can interested this is an old sentence without obeisance to the one they like the best. Think of that. All these new and old old sentences have been called very nearly. And this series makes it plainly without more curious with an apple that they like which is American. What is a sentence a sentence should have no perfume like hyacinths or no reserve like pigeon nor a plan about like the more that they expected. All these things make relatively what they concern and therefor they are not sentences in the time in which it makes that they concern in an after all well in short what is a sentence a sentence should certainly be not where there is any change that they take. Think of a sentence a sentence is only by their accept in a while. A sentence makes a form of which there are two. They have a use in a sentence there has a use in a sentence in saying this there is laziness to make laziness have a and to remake pale and with mail. This is in no sense a sentence. What is a sentence. All this is by the way is not a sentence. Sometimes a sentence is without doubt but very fairly. Without a doubt he came here to wait. This is a sentence but not interesting. A sentence should be usually that they look like holding the three better than five. That is interesting.

It is not likely that one is one one third if there are all of them made to-day it is obliging that they make the impression. This sentence does not mean that they are taken with it as a sense. That is it if you think behind they are theirs instead. It is better to be lost all in their right. All these are sentences regular in speed that they take it away. A sentence with out their pleasure in rose or rosy as a color. All these are sentences with apply for them. A sentence to be interesting must be left and then they have no harm come to some. A sentence think of a sentence that is it that is what she said repeatedly not only in coming and going but in remaining that is it in this way they leave out what they do. This is a sentence that it is of no interest to have asked him to discharge them because they will be won. These are two things that did not happen on the same day. And they went without. These are examples of sentences that they could hurry. After a while not. This again is their example how do you do it to know that it was careful. What is a sentence. No one is interested without their elopement. That is a sentence that nobody hears with them. And it is interesting to know that a sentence is not interesting although they listen, who do they take that they say that they turn it in that way. Because back is not black. That is how ours are told. Now this is interesting because they like it. Without their being happy. Do like these sentences for them in more or a home. This last sentence was a failure because they bought. It is very easy to know about sentences. Sentences having nothing to do with partly there nor indeed with partly nor indeed with there nor indeed with partly that nor indeed with appropriation sentences have been with for a chance. What is a sentence it is becoming clearer that they know what they are. A sentence is something that they have as to size. Abruptly. A sentence is near or Elizabeth. This is not a sentence in their care. If to know one to know. This is not a sentence because they think. All this will sometime tell whose a sentence is.

Make three sentences together. She came and she was expected. With their remaining they were mistaken. By their best and foremost they were restrained. Take these three sentences as an example of a lack of pall. It does trouble them with this. Take that sentence. They are alike. That is not what they know that is what they say separately and so a sentence is not what they say separately. A sentence is not what they know. A sentence is not that they will do so. A sentence is not relief with a mounting and amounting and this is with withdrawal. A sentence is that they will have them until in amount for this. This is a sentence and in in an intervening partly their name. What is a sentence they have forgotten a noun. Having forgotten a noun they have forgotten a noun. A sentence is to hear from me. A quietly at least a plainly there a pear. This is not a sentence it is a picture. A sentence is not a picture. Pictorially which is a sentence without her having been bought for her.

I have done a little but it is very good.

Leave a sentence alone. He will say that he means that they have theirs as in with a considerable interlined around a comfortable in case of a change. Leave out a sentence. Who comes to wishes. In leaving out a sentence it must never be formed before and so it is without here. Without a sentence they feel that they separate calling tens. A sentence is made by with and and agreeable. What is a sentence. After all even as a facing theirs in after a joined allowance in their way. What is a sentence they need to order with a director of a pleasing follow. What is a sentence. A sentence must hold another. A sentence does, as well. This is a sentence but not restful. Without a sentence. Supposing they were acquainted and they only asked those that he knew. This is a perfect example of a sentence without a sentence. A sentence for them. They were waiting and allowed. After that. They meant to share. What they had. Which was their reason. For this. Which they came. To give. This is a sentence for them and satisfactory. Now for a case of a sentence without which they were willing to listen. How often do they bother to come very nearly and it does not make any difference. This sentence always reminds them that they might not have met.

This is a sentence. The first time that they were at an advantage is this. They have held it to be strange that they are to be changing in and on their account. This sentence does not diminish their winding. In and out. What is a sentence. A sentence is partly that she wanted to know would they like what is in an opposite reason for them in their change. It is undoubted that there are there that she she truly was placed at the dozen with them and they for it name and name all to in in compare compared every a little in there. This sentence might mean that she was obliged without a half recuperate in our favor as a piece. She says as they need. All this if it could be true would not be a sentence because if a sentence is sewn they will take a cloth and she knows all that they have been like it. A sentence is a success.

With carry all. What is a sentence. Sometimes. What is a sentence.

A sentence is that when if they have been that they bear or clear.

This is a sentence without a by.

By this if mending is made with then.

This is not a sentence.

This refers to that. Always.

If they are away a weighed as lieve that they do. A sentence.

He does not do to stand. This is a good sentence in expect.

How much may they look about.

A sentence which refers to a day in a deigning to be a mound. Introduced by. This is the difference. A sentence not to be used fully.

Carefully if you look. It is very rich to have it a picture of a question. That is a simple sentence that means something.

She is our and by an end of an hour she will have said that

she will have to stay in order to have made it carefully a credit to their having it as stands.

A picture of an exact which if they believe is the place that they turn it away. That way is a turn of the copying copy of their head which they like only they do not mean it. This is a sentence that makes the red and brown do. If they have been effected. All this is a series of sentences that does not resemble theirs. And yet they told. That they were pleased with the basket made entirely by and of wire. Now then this is an example of how a noun can have a strong impetus but even so it is not interested by their keep kept which has no place with keeping. A noun and a verb to agree that they will dispose of that in a way. All this is what they may make which emotion. A noun is not valid as they love theirs. This is a difference between Valeska and Virginia. Marguerite. Please see how easily a sentence tells those. Abandonment. A word is not otherwise. A sentence is then primarily fastened by not to a noun and a verb. Listen a sentence is fastened not to a noun or a verb, an article yes is an article. Yes as a direction no as a direction. Yes and yes no as a direction. A sentence is primarily fastened yes as a direction, no as a direction. A sentence is primarily fastened yes no yes as a yes as in as a direction. A sentence is primarily fastened yes as a direction. Yes is an article. Yes it is. An article. A an article. The an article. Yes an article.

It is different in difficult it is different in to be indifferent in difficult when they make a and have an in the manner. Think of this every little thing is in if they bring, think of the leading of in and of thinking of bring this makes a sentence of a part. A part is not a part. A part is not a whole. And so if they must part let them go together. A noun and a verb must part and let them go together. Now this is a sentence that has confiding as their linked with steadying which is what they say. What is a sentence a sentence is finely with a plate which says come to a coloring of houses. Think carefully of why they went. This is an admonishment but not a present, a present is that they are quietly there. If they foretaste then they are like what they do feel if they go away at night. This is a likable sentence. Make it simple, they are over a fact which they have told. To make it careful. They went where they were asked.

It is very nice to look at it and not be disappointed. This is a sentence that has no place in rebuttal nor with it is there carelessness. They like it. What is a sentence. With them or with it as it is an occasion. This is an excellent sentence commonly. It does make a difference in what they say. This is aloud and and should always be followed by before. Gradually they will redeplete their aroused by refusal. This is not a sentence nor has it and and before. Every time they are foolish they are like the name of whom. What is a sentence, she meant that it is over, without a a while. Realise well that an article is followed. A sentence makes no mistake it has it as adherence. Think of a sentence not however or with a mound but just as pointed and polite and shortly. They will mean kneel. What is it. What do they like in a sentence. They like in a sentence that they feel like it. This is a conversation and it has been that conversations are not as sentences. Sentences are with them sooner. What is a sentence. Not to be disappointed in the way he said it. He said that it was over that he was liberated that of course he did pass a night and sometimes even a day particularly but really they were all very well and invited as he had been in their fearing. They were not going to be gone not they. Think of all these as sentences there are no nouns in sentences if they are followed nor are they followed without them. With what has, they to do. A sentence is left to it this. This should be retained in a sentence. They are very sensitive. What is it that they like. All around with told. More comes. What is a sentence.

To have from there to have from there in there a sentence. To have from there in there a sentence.

There is a sentence made to refuse it was caught as well. A sentence that they lost interest in names.

Think of a sentence. We went to be all three. Easily.

A sentence makes a place of a facing right about with theirs. Simple sentences.

A very pretty basket made to him and a very pretty basket made of wire and made of wire for him. Which a very pretty basket made of for him made of wire which is made with him.

A very pretty basket made of wire for him given to him. A very pretty basket given to him made for him of wire by her for him.

Now this is a perfectly charmingly successful sentence for them.

Carefully of what has happened. They were saying, in the meantime. It is made to be always there and they change from time to time. This is a sentence which has been thought and so they know how they make a fresh however. All of a sudden having remembered they were with them as allowed. It was always that they were without their blandishment and they called it all around, they made it be without their forever in satisfaction which is why they must in every little while remain always as told. This is however that they will be happy.

Very carefully what is it. What is it. They know they knew.

A sentence is when they have abandoned will they.

Think of a sentence. They were all where, where is it.

Think of a sentence. He will look with her.

Think of a sentence. When they were largely grateful they were very careful to be thought caught.

Think of a sentence. It is not relatively meager.

Think of a sentence. With or without they were with them.

Think of a sentence. Needs are never with them that they plant.

Think of a sentence beginning with a plant is a part of which they will. When they have news. Of it.

Think of a sentence.

She will call her.

By a name.

Think of a sentence.

Having decided alright that it is bounded by their efforts they will come to a different conclusion in which without having acted they will be perfectly at ease.

A very perfect sentence.

Remember a sentence should not have a name. A name is familiar. A sentence should not be familiar. All names are familiar there for there should not be a name in a sentence. If there is a name in a sentence a name which is familiar makes a data and therefor there is no equilibrium. A noun and therefor you see by introducing a noun equilibrium being a noun there is not a data but also a familiar and remain in their station. It is well to remain in their station and therefor a noun is susceptible to their mistake. What is a noun. You all knew where a noun is to be found it is to be found in restlessness and their being there. There should be no noun in a sentence and sentences.

A noun with a verb.

They were with black and bells and bells.

This is a noun with a verb and verbs. They were with bells and in union. Bells in union which do not.

Nouns meet with approval.

Verbs do not better do not do better than themselves.

Nouns as nouns. What are they like. In which attachment are they very often nicely having it for them. This is not a noun.

He which is William. Attired with which is vainly their importance. What is a sentence that they like it very well. It matters that they like it very well. It matters with it matters with that they like it very well. If anybody knows it it is a sentence with pressed.

Resemble assemble reply.

Once.

Are part of a it would be so nice if there was not something the matter with it.

These are not sentences they are a part of a paragraph.

Of course you do not like it.

This is a sentence that has no necessity they are agreeable and to be willing to be maintained that they are first at first without their clouding their allowance that they are to be threatened with their examples of however they are with sailing which is a management in their readiness as they can clearly with patiently having as a piece of their called which when they may be perfectly referred may have what is there in the fall which they like as in an amusement in particularly relieved come to their sense with our in a delight for them in change that they make is and with and belated in their account which makes them change. As they might with when they endow an advantage resting at all by this with at noon. They never mention at noon. They never mention with at noon. All this is an excellent example of a commonplace sentence which describes everything. It is a commonplace sentence which describes everything and elaborates their intelligence intelligence which is new as news. This with a change makes drawn it is drawn with a change makes better than drawn. What is better than drawn. It is not around and without.

Now suppose they were steaming in a glass with a chicken and it broke would she be quick. That is not a sentence because it makes her smile.

If they are right about it then they can be with them. That is a sentence because it is as it finishes. It is very sad that they can never have it partly. That is also a sentence because it makes a belief in their establishment. Of their preparation. Which is without parallel in their hope which they may. Would it ever be well. To do so.

What is a sentence. They were with a belief that they can call fans a fan when they change. This is a sentence that can satisfy and magnify.

There is very little use in a sentence which is not selfish and they amaze it as their drift. This makes it why they ask for me.

What is a sentence.

All of a sentence is without this.

A sentence. We with out doubt are as well as stout. That is one sentence.

Will a weak well be pronounced loudly if they have paused. That is another sentence and a grammar with called Anthony.

Beautifully and around a sentence.

These are examples of sentences which are self contained as well as suggested.

Now for a sentence not suggested. Deception caused by a prearrangement is one that they furthered with a pressure from their main attention in advance with detail. This is a sentence that they pray that they will call for it. And so there is no suggestion and no choice. Think of no suggestion think of a choice and then be well taken care of. If is not left to them to be coming. These are sentences that are all these sentences.

To come to be call all of them. This is not a sentence as they like it although they do not come. They like it. This is a sentence that they mean with however it. As intention. There is no use in preparing for it. If there is a pear for it. They both had them. These sentences follow one another and they beguile. Not one.

It is while they are with them all. This is a good sentence they will state that they are refused. They will state horticulture is a sentence with plants. There is no habit of withdrawing with out a pleasure that they will have that they must do what ever they like in as much when they have standards in a politeness that they call in different amounts which they can be carefully preserved in industry with their allowance as a creed made credit with partly in planting a mended do whenever they will which is very much as it was with by the hour in their authority that they come here. Thank you for a sentence.

One of these sentences which is that they were told they were old or not. This is an excellent sentence in receive. And they went. This is not a good sentence because it follows.

I think the reason I am important is that I know everything. This is their exchange for their places. And it could be true. And so they went. In this case. And so they went does not follow and therefor it is a sentence. If they went or were to go is not a sentence. It is singularly gracious of them not to have it a sentence when it is not only not a sentence but their can be as well. This is delaying an answer. That is a sentence. The difference between a sentence is very dainty and definite and she was not displeased that he mentioned a gardener for them.

A part of a sentence or how I influenced him.

They were rained upon in the weather which they hoped for. This made it lain where they went. And they were officious.

Think of sentences. What is a sentence. A sentence which they enjoy and she mends towels. That is a cadence which withdraws a sentence. A sentence should never be employed. They will be mightily pleased with their length. At length is remain with that in their sight. At sight they will with a proclamation in a rest do the same. What is a hope. All these make that they remain. With others. A sentence is not sideways. A sentence should always be the same with their restlessness. A sentence is a habit apart. Think of a sentence. They know now.

Reserved and served. What is the difference between words and a sentence and a sentence and sentences. A word a word they a word. That is a word. A word is markedly. What is a sentence. A sentence is not a syllable. A word is not a syllable and they are fairly first. What is a syllable they are the same. A word is an entangle if it is a failure. They were chary. Think of a syllable in two. A word is out of the whole wide world they chose it with not with them. This is not a syllable actively. In a vocabulary they were a minute. They could never be awfully pleased. A sentence is never partly at that time. That is not me. A sentence with found. That is one sentence. In all and a and around. This is not a sentence in landing. They land in the three with the three of them. All these sentences have no return are not returned and they are widened in three. Then as well. All hyacinths are for four make a chosen few. It is useless to be always ready. A syllable is theirs yes. A word a word they change they changed a change as if a word. Politely in and out is not a word. A word they will be make it do. This is a word whether she likes it or whether it is like it or not. This is a succession of words and will nearly they do in a trace of a self told withdrawal in a complaint of entire made appoint in cover. This is a sentence however. If there is a with heading amount of it. She needs pink. This is a sentence with remain. It is never patiently a for a word.

Did he want to see me.

A as one time in which in one at a time in disappointement. They will be.

Carry Claridge's Hotel to their door.

And thank you.

These are without a rest without, which they may be helpful, in an amount, whether they care.

Think alike with sentences.

Disappointment they rely upon their appointment.

This is a sentence which has frequently disappeared.

Think well of each matter.

What is the matter.

With it.

What is the matter with it.

It is of no interest to know that he will look to find him and so they will having been come to have it without their reception of with without whether they relieve and refer to and reappear. It is of no interest.

This is a case of without a doubt made particularly if they are afterward with that in hand as they like for them formerly come to moreover which they appear to do not as they went.

It is very likely that they like me.

What is a sentence. In appearance. In disappearance. Sometimes a sentence is in reappearance that they like it if they made a choice and they were and went to the door which is a porch. A porch is a church which they name. They were able to be measured by a fastening of whenever they were which they had in the course of their withstanding. Suppose they said how could they be called in a placing of theirs alone. Whichever they do. A sentence is made for and because of their very much have had a change. A change for them. Think well of a sentence.

There are the kinds in a sentence. With or without. Able to debate. Coming well from them. Which they like. As it is very well to like it at all. They made them have it all. There is a difference between after a while. Not more than they have before they begin. Whichever they make when they do as a part of letting it be ready complained that they were first. It is very like that they wished. This could be in a use. Of use is a party to their arrangement. Now and then when they come to have no difference made among them which is why they will plan that they referred afterwards to men that they managed to have reddened as they like. It is not why they went.

Do be careful of it and oblige the ones who went and are expected. It is very easy to be other than they are with whenever they went. They must be wanted that is when they come which they have with an whether they have finished that they would rather very well as they call which with which they met. This is an easy sentence and popular. Now make it an avoidance. They will not finish with it.

There is no difference between a partly met and when they were anxious, to call it whatever they like with whether they are careful. She did not know I was back.

What is what is it occasionally that they differ.

All these are alike as sentences. With possibly one exception.

Possibly an exception who meant that they were adapted to the mistake that they had to have corrected that they liked to be allowed to have theirs with them too. Come at once. If with disappointment in their behalf.

If you begin with in and in with her and in with him they will invariably refer it to him. They will think nothing of anything. All this is agreement and placed as they will then be placed with them when they will be placed with them. This is very easy if anything. What is a difficult thing. This which they are doing. That is that they have come. They have come with them.

That they have come with them. All study short of this is what they are like. They have made it be always in an effect of an allowance for it. Which they do like altogether. Think carefully of hundreds of sentences why not. Which they do. This is a place at a place where they can stay but do they like to be always after a while made for them as much as it is when they are positively appointed in and in respect to a change of their arrangement for them. The more easily they went again the more they have made it do. As a disappointment. All of this they know when they went. It is very interesting to think of sentences as a pansy. They promise never to use nouns as nouns which makes it pay. Paid is when they said. Think again of reliance. Will they ask him to ask them to have him have them. To replace is to satisfy this. Which is no desire. What is the difference between desire and desirable. What is the difference which they can not annoy between desirable. Now and all come to do what they can. They must be and with them they must be and they must be with them. All of these sentences pacify. It is very well thought of. After having not been found too easily.

Does she know she has blue eyes.

With them and instead in. Does she know she has light blue eyes. They were separated the two of them both women. It looks as if it ought to be Church. Now here is a succession of sentences which make them come together.

Partly that, she has lost a buckle, which she picked up.

Very well that she had not.

Which is not a sentence.

What is the use of it not being a sentence. Thank you what is the use of it not being a sentence.

If they look alike and are not sisters.

All at once.

Dove and dove-tail.

With them, they went with them.

He promised me that he was all to me so sweetly that he was referring to it for me.

These are as able as they are as able, to be sentences.

With them, they are, as introduces, the after acceptation, with them.

It is a difference between in name. Think of how they avoid around.

The coming of their with them in them according which they will.

A sentence need not continue.

Think of a sentence. Start a sentence begin a sentence with with. With them. They went with them. They went away with them. They were with them. They were with them and they went with them they were with them when they went away with them. Without them. They were with them. All this is what they like in the spring. Now the difference between a sentence and everything else is that they are cautious. With which they are fairly well as they are in a hurry and they finish. All this is when a sentence is after all made in advance as they think. With that they are not able to remain behind. As they like they will be fed alternately in the afternoon by that time. In which they will remain in time to go home. In case of which they are without all of it as the same. This sentence is made in wages. For which they care. As all of it as they do so. They must be careful to do come.

What is a sentence. They think they like to go ahead. That is no sentence that is to say if they say they will be very well taken care of they mean it. What is a sentence. A sentence must not be bought, must not a sentence must not be taught, a sentence must not be thought out which with which it is with it with which it is with it. That is right that stops it. Think of sentences having hardly anything to do with it.

What is a sentence. A sentence is left to be alright and therefor they are barely here.

A day is additional with there having been with a condition of remaining all day which it is partly they like to look about made it for them in reference as they knew that is whenever they met by the arrangement which had been made for them in the mean time. What is a sentence. They need not be having them by them.

A sentence is made with whenever they were however often it is very well all for it and they do.

They will hope for their assistance which they receive.

All of it looks alike. They will follow one another. They will be standing and as well. They will not allow for the difference. They will follow behind and they will be careful of everything if they move it about which they do they must see that it is so. This is a sentence that explains as well.

What is the use of prevailing.

This is a sentence that they might have as an amount with them.

Not next.

It is with very little of it that they might please him.

She meant there is a better than she has had offered to her.

Better than not to be amused by that.

The thing that is very curious is that they are well known.

The thing that is very curious is that she is well known.

The thing that is very curious is that it is she that is well known.

The thing that is curious is that it is that she is well known.

When after all when after all it is that she is well-known.

After all it is very curious that she is well-known.

It is very curious remaining that it is very curious that she is so well-known.

She is well known.

When they are looking at the others and it is she that is so well known.

Well known.

It is very agreeable if it is an arm-chair. It is very agreeable if sitting in it it is an arm-chair. It is very agreeable sitting in it it is an arm-chair. It is very agreeable sitting in it. How should it end. That it is very curious that she is so well known. Sitting in it it is an arm-chair. It is not very curious that sitting in it it is an arm-chair. It is very curious that she is so well known.

These are sentences of course.

These are of course.

Never have been very well pleased not to come. This is an easy sentence and not obliging. They will not follow of course.

He did interest me.

This is partly saying which they did not.

He did interest me.

They were in their care.

It is very well known that they refuse not to be interested but to interest them in me.

It is a hope that they will take what they have.

They will be there with them.

Will they mind.

It is bought occasionally for their use.

Now think they will be very nearly back.

Now and then to think that they will be very nearly back again.

And so forth when they will be very much as if they had it settled.

All of it to be as a wife has a cow a love story.

This is true of which there is so much.

Now all these sentences are full of advancement and they are obliging in the sense of commendation which they may arrange as they can.

One or two with a wedding. A wedding with them and once.

What is a sentence. It can be either altogether and followed and following after or a while or either they can be made to guess that they will be after all for a change in the care of their reference to without to it which is whenever they are told and called in the politeness of their do and for remain which they must partake with when they press it as an avoidance of enough which they told. All this is a sentence which is not a requiem. Now having thought of a sentence they come readily. A sentence is with all that of which they are no judge.

There are two things of which they are as a dish. They are these. They must be ordered to assume that they will be quietly, also a special in for and their arrangement in a part of when they were a pair of lanes which they returned to or from. Think of sentences. It is very easy to say as we go we are pleased. It is also very easy to be nearly there when they are all of them just to be about. All this is a cover to their pleasure and they are told that he having been for this in a minute and in a week for a week they are followed before they have hope. All of it they hope which they knew. What is a round. A round is the knowledge that they are as far as when they hear it. All sentences are more as they please.

What is a sentence. They went ahead. A sentence makes a rhyme. If he went and he saw that there was a crowd he looked again, it was the place that was described and they were very well placed which was an example of that they had not intended to be shown which they were shown. This is the same as a reflection. Why is he sorry that he said that he would not go anyway. This is a sentence that makes them hopeless. This is a sentence that makes them hope less. It is very remarkable that she predicted that it would not do. A sentence should be in a rhyme if it is to be definite. For instance. If they are careful to be there where they have been left with them there. This is the reason why success succeeds one another. All of it to be in after a reference to their repeating of it. Suppose a calender is mentioned they must know that being successful they are privately satisfied when they must have principally all at that time. How can they think of saying a bird in the hand is worth two in the bush when if in the bush they mean near by because if they wait the birds in the bush will settle and it is very likely that they will like that if she does. And so when they say that the birds are in the bush they sit and watch them. Which whenever they are more than ever there are very many there. If there are very many as there are there they will be convenient and a pleasure to go and to go with them which is all of it what they are with and alike. This is a long sentence and they like it and they are right because they are with them with their hoping they will be very well to do. Think of a sentence one at a time. A sentence need never to be arranged afterward. This is an example of a sentence that has been thought which is the same as if it has been has been bought. If a sentence has been thought they will think and if they think they will have each one of them their bon bons and if this is what they are to be thought then they will be by that time, which they must in insistence, named after they, have it done. It is now time to put it altogether.

A sentence tells that they are visibly chosen. One two three all out but she. She is not put out nor is she of service when she is for them as they were. This sentence makes it doubtful that there will be any explanation.

What is a sentence. A sentence makes it clear that it is far from one city to another if they are partly here and partly there. Partly and here. In using partly and here there is no necessity for more. And all of it is desirable. If he was young would he be all through. After a time would he be all through.

The choice of a sentence is not enough the choice of words is not enough the choice of double is not enough they will be practically careful of it.

A paragraph is part of a date. They will be awfully glad to stay on one side of a street or another. This is not a sentence because it refers to a custom.

We will now find out what sentences are.

Think of how they do not wear cuff-buttons.

This is not a sentence because it has reservations and reservations are something that follow after or nearly at once.

Supposing she does not dress quickly, if they are not to be

obliging, that is to say presently. This is an old-fashioned sentence and has this advantage.

If by not looking it is so that they are like it and were to be had now and not for a long time it is whether they looked like that, they were whatever it is better to have heard from her as she is behind with a door.

One who meant one one at a time.

They made it because of the time.

In which it is whether they went with it.

That they were after they had been often for it.

By the time that they liked it.

There are many sentences that begin with whatever it is why they patted it.

What is a sentence for. They are going to be as they can have helped it with them.

What is a half of which they are placed with that they recognise. Recognise is all of a sentence let well enough alone.

It makes a difference to her whether she understands or not why they were able to accept it.

This is a sentence that is quietly pleasing.

A sentence should be allowed without it all.

Would she recognise them after she had not seen them.

This is a sentence that she asks.

A sentence is a failing of their pressure.

Inez a verb.

It is as difficult as they think. A noun which is not a better way of having protection has all of them as they had better try.

What is after a difficulty a noun.

Augustine can be made into after a demean. Augustine demean with a noun. It is never better to render a part of it as after.

They were grateful for a conquest. What is the relation of grammar and arithmetic.

A verb ever after.

A noun should always be replaced by now.

If you think you find that you use it less and less. A noun if it is a sentence is made by their calling and now calling is over and therefor they will not make an investment of their be then. Be there with them. That is it it is not that they have it at once so. A noun is not of any use. Now is it.

Please have half where they are finished.

PART THREE

There is a difference between knowing Nelly from Frank and vice versa.

With rapidity.

If they go quicker.

Whichever they do.

This makes that they are never acquainted with their come come to commotion. Commotion is not corruption nor is coming again, twice. All this leads us to, do they want little pieces or do they want it all. Is their any beginning in favoring begining or is there that they like a ban. Bandit. What do they like. They like it long. If they like it long they do not necessarily like all of it. If they like all of it long they do not necessarily not like all of it if they like all of it they do not necessarily like all of all of it. If they like it long they will like it and they will like to be like it to like it as they can like it as they can and along, with along, which they like for and because which they will like with it. A sentence depends whether they like it, they like it, along with it, as long as they

like it they like it it is long and with it they will with and
without it not divide it they will go along with and without it.
A sentence is dependent upon whether they open it again
and again giving it for it and gave it to it. They will be coming to be along. Now think. What is it. With and without
that they will and be willing as they have to have it. Really
the way to keep it is to have all of it and little pieces. This is
really the arrival. What is the union between the arrival. The
arrival is one union. With their arrival is one and one. All of
this is that with and with as manages. Think of a sentence a
long sentence without and without is a happiness to their
wishes. Which with a medium length they will pay for which
they have asked. A short sentence amounts to about when
they are with wherever they go. About a piece of sentence
they must be left. And there they are. Called farms. This brings
us to a noun an article a participle an adverb and correctly
with a patience which they prefer. An adjective is safe and so
they will refer to prepositions and pleasure in all. All of these
together do not make a long sentence. And why. Because by
the time that they have not perfected but made it useful they
go as if they like. All these explanations are secondary. A sentence is this. Win a wish.

There is no difference between have and a hen. He had a
hen in glass. She had a hen in glass. These sentences are
when they have been observed.

Now the difference between observations are these. If they
mean that they are likely to be with them they must delay
with their preferring either. This is partly what they are as
they are with them in them as they are to be with them as far.
These with two as they please. A sentence if to please. Into.
Four. With which. They have. More pleasure with while they
like. As a difference between left. They had a good job and

they left. Left left, left right left. Think of a sentence as an equivalent. What is the difference between pleasure in the whole or not pleasure, pleasure in the half. What is the difference between pleasure and a pleasure. They might think that they were twice when they were equal to awaiting what is it they they have as a turning into a pleasure. This is what is why they will be away. Everything away is just not what they thought. Pieces of a sentence are different from what she knows. What are pieces of a sentence which do not make any difference. It is very well to have it.

A sentence is the same.

Now all in a way.

If they go as quickly as they go faster they will be two as use as useful. Does what they relate make it be caught at once. This is one part of a sentence and one time they came to see me. If it is that they must and must with accustom they like what they like alike.

This is truly related.

Truthful and truly.

Truly and truthful.

Everything that they say and they say so.

It needs very few wild flowers to make them stay. They stay all the time. It takes very many more to make them have it. They have it when they do. If they like it at all they will go where they have been which is very much better than just as it is. It is whatever they have and they must not be left to come to remain where they are. A sentence does have parts. Think of a sentence they all think of a sentence. With them which it is that they do that they like whatever they meant with have it and they must pass it to them which they have allowed for. Any of these long sentences which are not too long are as pleasing as they can be with them. It is very well to know the difference in lengths and they like to have what ever they can in that way. These are sentences which are quiet and as quieting made to be known for them. Prepositions and articles determine thirds. Every third way they like to think. This is why they are frightened which makes it that they will come twice. What is the difference between and between in an action. What is the difference between plainly and what they want to do when they like to have it. A sentence is very much what they have when they have an offer and they are very much what they do not like they will be left to have it every once in a while since when they are moved because it is by them with which they like what they have where they are known this may do more than they do without which they must be having with them which is what ever is a press of partly that which is a knowledge that they will be just about all for it with when they went as it is and not without doubt. Think of a sentence should it have a finish if they must as she said.

They are many ways to think alike about sentences.

It is very little that they open and close.

Close it.

It is useful to be and useful. Used. Any word may be in a sentence. A word is a noun. What is a noun.

A noun.

If a noun can come and come to a noun a noun is not a word which they have seen before. Seen before is a circumstance. They like eights. A noun. Once which when when should always be with whenever whenever they went. A noun. It is of no importance. Importance is a word. There is a great deal to remain to added. This is a commonplace which they feel but do not happen, made and found. A noun leads to secretly seated.

Delphine Augustine Ermine Pauline, it makes no difference what they leave with or for them. Delphine Augustine Ermine Pauline.

PART IV

A difficulty.

What is it. Three Georges not four. There are four but the fourth is not there.

The difficulty with their being there or here is this, it is very beautiful to be bought, it is very beautiful to be as bought it is very beautiful to be as by and by it is very beautiful to have best and most it is very beautiful to incline to be left with them it is very beautiful to have it now. They will have held it. Think of a sentence. It is a beautiful day to-day. A dear wife can not interrupt a husband.

A sentence is one in which a paragraph is a part of what happened two days after to-day. To-day and yesterday. The day before yesterday is two days before to-day.

A sentence makes that they come at that time which is why if they go after they will steer clear of having met what they like.

Better that they are better.

If they all think that a little house will be more valuable what do they do about not having it there. They have it where they will not be thought with well they will think. This makes it will they, promise me they will.

It is very well to have a sentence well-known. That it is well known is a pleasure. That it is a pleasure is their desire. That they will pass it in that way does not mean that they will

not have been very much as they will after all like. They like.
They like what they like. They like whatever they like.

A sentence. It is a beautiful day and satisfactory.

A sentence. With what will they think about what they
will have to have.

A sentence. It is by the time that they are furnished that
they will find it pleasant to do it.

A sentence. With pleasure and with pleasure with pleasure. This is a very good sentence and if it is useful. Think of
thought of a sentence it comes to this, they will think that
they thought this of this which is what is this and what of it.
What is it. A sentence must reflect that they pay for what
they will ask to have come to-day. A sentence means that as
there is this pleasure and they may please them they may be
fascinated by leaving them home or leaving them at home.
It is to be observed by changing this that this gives to them
gives them this pleasure. The pleasure she gives me is that
she gives me.

This pleasure that she gives me.

This is a perfect example of satisfaction.

PART V

Part five is the same as part one.

A sentence is when they start. They start to say that they
came to stay. They start to go away. They start briskly. They
start and they may very well do so. They may be obliging.
They may be made very equal to having it answered. They
may do so. Which is it which do they prefer. Every part of
their beginning is that they went on to do so. It is very light it

is very likely, it is very likely that they will like it themselves. Which if they do they will please themselves and as for that which is whatever they do with this as their arrangement.

A sentence should be thought of as having been told. If it is not thought of as having been told they will feel it as they are rich. With that they will like that they have it as hearing which makes it with them as a facing it efface and please. What is a use. A use is baking. When it is a very beatiful day. A sentence is this. They will hear of a baptism.

A sentence makes it dream that they are silly. This is a very good sentence and they know. It to be a very good sentence. What is a sentence. If in every way they have it to be a sentence they will resemble whatever they have.

A sentence should not refer make it a reference to hyacinths or bulls or their kind or equivalent it should refer to beauty and decision it should also have contentment it should never think a sentence should never think of letting well enough alone.

In this way a sentence is plain. A sentence should and it comes to having a part that they went where they liked, they went where they liked it. They could remember that they had where they liked it. A sentence is that now they went where they liked it. Not a sentence not that they went where they had been when they liked it. A sentence is that it makes a difference. A sentence is complete it gives pleasure every day every other day.

A sentence may be made with an article a. A day why do they call it the day, the day in which they came. A sentence made. A day which is what they like. A week, a week makes it be a holiday. They will look forward to the same. A sentence consists in an article a a verb to say or to stay a noun if they are allowed which means that after all Augustine is not the same as Christian and moreover a preposition they will build which is what they do do and so a sentence is this they liked it

It is not for them.

This is for them.

It is better for them to have this.

It is given to them.

They have it given to them.

They will add it to the things that they have for them.

They will have more things for them.

They have things given for them.

This which they have they like.

They like to have this.

It is very pleasant to have it.

It is part of the time that they like it. Whenever they go they like it. They will come.

This which they have is why they will not give it to them.

They have it as they say.

They will do it very well one at a time.

Study is different from altogether.

It is very much to their credit that they take pleasure in me. That they have their pleasure is without a doubt their thought.

This which they know is why they say this which they know. They will like alike.

All this is a sentence and in two in part.

A sentence is this.

A sentence. Have and to have. That is a sentence that is not employed.

A sentence is made when they like the sun. If they like the sun.

Please see that a noun is there.

And see there is a difference.

And feel what you like.

Any after effect is pleasant.

With their hope. In this case there is no noun. What is a noun.

After they stop after they stop.

They continue to go around. After they stop. What is a noun. A noun is not hated. A noun is easier not easy because it collides. Which is not strange but able. They like it before they do not like it. All this is very easy to understand.

If they let it alone they will try.

This is one of those sentences that is appreciated. With them. Arrange with them.

Anything, anything, this is not why they have it once.

If you try to make a sentence lie where it has been put it stays. This is why they will try to have it matter.

If you may be caught at once they will come when they have not been the ones to have it like them. This is why it is easier to rest with it.

A very easy way to be around and about.

They will be careful not to have it meant as well.

Which is it.

A sentence makes money.

What is a sentence.

If they have bought their honey they will exchange a present of honey for other things.

That is closed to a noun.

Close to a noun but not close to a noun because it is about that.

With them at random.

This is a plainly made with a pleasure which is in an allowance and they make within and without readily. Which is with it readily.

Made at random.

Is random a noun. It is not. It is a pleasure because with because which is an allowance with their and on account.

At random is not on account they went away on account of it which is not so but may be vainly why they are came and were shown which is with vigor. Seen to say he is seen to say that they will not like wishes. At random may remind one of whether. It is different to say it looks like it and it seems like it. Everything is without in order. This is a pressure without a sentence. Think of a sentence deliberately. This is in retake. Think without their feeling. If she has been working she has to have a prayer there. Why. With a place that is every one which with and makes they tell him. She is and her. A corner at a time. It is better to be passed what they give than not. All this reminds a sentence time and again. Think of coming to think of coming. An estimate is not a noun. An estimate. An estimate is not a noun. An estimate is not a noun. Now what is the difference. In the first place they went to work yesterday. In the second place they were apart and they were not startled. Do you really see that this is not a noun.

A noun is a name of anything. No one knows a noun by name. A noun by name. The name of a noun, how do you do and how do you thank me and how do you thank me with how do you do. How do you do. A name is not a noun because they will think that Ellen means something so it does for instance. They will make it do. A noun is a name of anything. What is a liking it for them. This is a noun in a willing to have it for them when they are alone. What is a noun one at a time. One at a time. A noun is a name. They came. A noun is without a noun with a name which may if they will they have thought about it it is better so. What is a noun without doubt they will have made it a and an arrangement. This makes a noun not dependent upon an article. After a noun is not dependent upon an article.

Felicity Mary and Jenny Mary and Marguerite. As a matter of fact there was not any Mary.

Felicity Jenny and Mary Mary and Marguerite.

All the same it does not make any difference that they came.

It does not make any difference all the same that they came.

It does not make any difference all the same it does not make that they came. All the same it does not make any difference that they came. All sentences begin and end in their happen to have and having to have been seated or to have sat as they have been seated without which they will happen to have had what they knew. Seated or sat or satisfy or saturated or acclaimed. This is what a sentence is that they go around.

To come back to the intensive study of a verb. A noun has been seen and there is that which when they were able to leave it. If they are able to leave it they are able to use it, with use it they are able to have it with it.

And will they defend themselves if they are to defend them which they are when they are defended and they do not defend themselves as they are defending themselves then. He said they did defend themselves when they had to have what they did not have as they did not know what they would have. And so he was careful. There is this difference. What they have is what they have altogether. And this makes the difference that they are. With them. All allowed that they are with them.

What is a sentence. A sentence is that they ask. Every little while which they have. That they must place theirs that way. In not a while.

Leave with them now. He leaves this with them now. He

is very anxious to have it be there. He is very anxious to have it be there with them. With them now. He is anxious to have it be there with them now. He leaves this there with them now.

Now and then this sentence shows that afterwards he does not come and as he with which he is made at and as much he does not he comes with him not with him now. This sentence makes it final. Then with that made to go anyway not that he asks it but that he asks it. This is a plan in a plan with them. He went there that way which is a rest the rest. A sentence shows variably the difference between he and they and he and he and they. They are as alike they like. He makes it that he and he and with them. They are not there with them. He is entertained. All these sentences make actual that it is not decided.

A sentence make it with them. And not around. In a little while they know that they are day and die. They lie. They know that they are differrent. They are different they and I. They and I they are different day and die. All this is a sentence in a day. What is a day. They came and they added. A sentence makes no agreeableness feebleness winning a chance. They had a chance. When you get to this you know a sentence follows by what they think. Think of it. A sentence follows by what they think.

A sentence can be sought. It is very likely that they mean it. Which they do what ever they do. When they do what they like. They like it to be there at once. Made to be ready which they have.

Think of a sentence in the meantime.

Verbs are about to be sent.

Nouns are with weddings. They will describe their old and all their difficulties which they had as they surprise, surprise them. This makes a noun that they like. If they like a noun. When they are able to have it in at once. They make it do which is what they are about. A noun is a case of that with their arrangement. And they will. Which whenever they are able they must. With it as they like. This is a noun.

What is a noun. A noun is the name of a thing. And so they like a blessing. This is it. A noun is a name of a thing. They will excuse a noun. They will see that they use what ever they like. They will see that they have been closely with an allowance and also that it is to-day to-day that they arrive. What is a noun. A noun is a likeness. They will think things. What is a noun.

A noun in their occupation.

A noun is very well grown if they like all alike. Which is why they are avaricious. What is a noun. With them what is it. It is very different to be differently angelic. What is a noun. After awhile what is a noun. What is a noun. A noun is known. They are known. They are unknown. A noun is a name and they like a name all the same they like it to have been a name all the same. What is a noun.

In leaving out a noun they are without doubt however careless they are without a doubt without doubt they like what they like. What is a noun. Refer. What is a noun. A noun does not make an ending and therefor. A noun does not destroy their change. A noun does not lighten which is why they are frightened. A noun with an inelegance makes it plain. What is a noun now and then what is a noun. A noun is the name of anything. A verb. A verb is a likeness. A noun and a verb. Attracted by them. What is a verb and what is a noun. A verb is their pressure and they go away. A noun and a verb. Who has hope. This is a verb. And not having heard. This is a verb. With it. This which is a verb. A verb is when they were withdrawn and when they were left a verb is when they were withdrawn a verb is when they left. A verb is when they left. A noun is alike. A verb is withdrawn.

A sentence is not made of a verb and a noun. A sentence is made with a verb or a noun. A sentence is not withdrawn. A sentence is not a name of a thing. A sentence is not withdrawn is not a name of anything. A sentence is not a name is not withdrawn. A sentence is not a verb a sentence is not a noun.

Think again of a sentence and it is not anything.

A single sentence is left alone is not left alone a single sentence is not let alone. A single sentence which is not alone is partly with them there. What is a sentence. What they like.

Which they like, is a sentence.

They admired their own. This is a devination of their welcome. It is very well that they were prepared accidentally. This is not a sentence it is a statement and an account. What is a sentence. Two and two. What is a sentence. All to you.

What is a sentence. They will know very well. What is a sentence still it still is a sentence.

This makes another a stream.

What is a sentence. Now we have gotten away from a sentence, we have gotten away from a sentence. Now we have been informed that we have gotten away from a sentence. Now we have been gotten away from a sentence. What is a sentence now we have been gotten away from a sentence.

What is a sentence. A verb with a noun which is a verb with a noun is a sentence which is a verb with a noun.

What is a verb with a noun.

A verb with a noun.

Is it as well to have a sentence.

We can go on longer if he wishes is a beautiful sentence. We can all go on longer if he wishes I do not like as well.

They renown as renown what is it it is that if they must they will increase from having been when they like wishes. If they wish.

With wishes. It is this with this as a wish. A fish if they are about as they are about will make it do. A fish and as wishes. A wish. If he wishes. Thinking well of the same. A noun is a name. Of anything. A fish is not a noun nor is a wish a is an article but fish and wish is not a noun are not nouns are not. And then think. A wish is an article not followed by a noun. Two and a wish. Which is a wish. It is not a noun. What is a noun. A noun is not a noun in name. It is a noun because they are affectionately ably to be received. This makes it a noun. Recover is not a noun nor is recovery a noun. What is a noun. Able to have wishes is not a noun. A chair is a noun. A chair there may be a noun. A chair here and there is neither a noun nor not a noun it is simply which is able to be a boy but uninterestmg.

Ably a chair wishes and as felt and also affectionately in the name of a welcome as either. A noun then is a face to face when they are lying down. Who goes when they come. All this if they have no pleasure without once in a while they may care to have a noun.

They may care to have a noun carefully.

It is very easy.

It is very easy to be told. Well well. What is a noun. Who has been heard if they will be whenever they are as they were told when and where they were.

A noun. His and her kisses.

A noun. With putting a heavy thing in its place not without some effort.

A noun. An article is variable if they may place a and an the and the same and also an appointment which may mean that they have succeeded it is very perilous to have it be more than careful. Assume that they like whatever they come across. That is a sentence that has this as value they will be favored by an opportunity and they will go. It is very necessary that really they must think as I do which they do do which they do do. Which they do do. They think that they are far in a way part of their inclination to be without them and they will have been without it then. This is all a mistake. It is very well to have it make it be it for themselves with their having in a measure without it as they shall in the place of naming it as a part of their however as they will without a presently as for them there. It is very necessary to think well.

A noun is a name a name is the same they are the same because if I like it it will do. This is a sentence that does realise nouns. Nouns are carefully once or twice. Nouns are carefully once or twice. It may go on. With and with all. A noun which is payed it is payed to be netted as all. A noun is practically their experience. They will be very nice and quiet I thank you.

What is a noun. A quarter is a noun. If they are arranging it all a quarter is in a room. If it is in a room they will be maintained by their having to hope to get it. All this makes a noun. A noun is not facing what they like. They leave it to them with all which of which they have all they have it all they will be with and without it all. This is a sentence that realises that a noun is not carefully prepared. It is prepared care is not taken with the preparation at all. What is a noun. A noun which is a claim that they will be again when they are taken care of. A noun is hours which are made with out their counting how many so many after all. This is a change that makes me smile.

It is very easy to see that if you live to like me and to like me it is very nicely to have it preferably seen to have been by me. A noun is called out. In looking around the room there is nothing that has a name except after a while a rose tree. After a while mark you after a while the rose tree. The rose tree a rose tree or a rose tree. Then also the cactus. The cactus is not a cactus because it is not noticed. In a little while they will not notice that there has been a fuss about whether or whether or not they have said that it has been made. It is very well to think that it is made and so she is very busy. In this way you see a noun is a weakness. What is a noun if it is not a weakness if a noun is not a weakness it is by reason of their applying for it at once. There is the whole matter. A noun is not a weakness not because they are applying for it at once but because it is not a weakness.

It is no matter if he or will they be one of one two, one two all out but you.

Not face to face but one two to one two and they will divide one or two into one two which they do if they are careful to do so. This sentence if it has been with them is without a doubt to give them pleasure as they like which they like apparently in reference to it allowed with the name of their part and partly coming to have it fastened made to be too plain that it is in all very likely at a claim for them to have a rest from it.

A noun two nouns three nouns a noun a detail which has not been thought about two nouns they will be available and three nouns they will be taken to be at most all three in their theirs any way in appointment an appointment left to them. Is it feebly. What is a noun this is what a noun is.

If this is what a noun is they are not mistaken in next to not giving what ever they do give which they have in the way of their arrangement laid to place it where they like whatever they do in all of it and most without a without doubt they will even guess less which is by the time this will be all for them whatever it is for them as it is better it is by this time in it for the same called well very much less as it is as well to have it in undeniable at one time as they can do it for them as alike with remaining applied joined at least respect within a clause it is a to change to an addition at more than they will with apply and therefor it must for them to be with and have known a difference at all call calling for me when made a winding of not being well held as wool. See the introduction of a noun see the introduction see the introduction see the introduction they will not use it they will not use wool they will see that it is an introduction of a noun she will not use wool in tapestry. She will not use wool in tapestry.

All this has two uses one is that it is very pleasant very intelligent very nicely and very beautifully true and it is a pleasure to say so. The other is that it is always part of the way that they can start if they say go and get it they will go and get it as they like which is very convenient and helps a lot.

What is a verb a conjunction a preposition and a dependent clause and a place for an adverb and adverb is one word but an adjective is not one word then for it is an interjection which they count. It is a great deal of which some of it is alike whatever they do they will go away where they go in a minute by and by needless to say all the time when they are alike in case in place of what which is there with them more of it quietly like it more in time. All these are here in quantity. They are made to be around.

A sentence is when they express that they wish that they were made of it as well which is whatever they do. This is a sentence. How do you do is a sentence. How do you do. This is a sentence. How do you do. It is a sentence. A sentence is why they will like a lake. A lake is really very nearly never frozen over it is very pretty and they are many of them which is not to say that they are in view they are not in view. This is where they have been passed and if they are gone all around they will be very much as if it were just now. An allowance is to be made for the part which is very near. A lake will be the best a lake will be the best a lake will be where it is which is the best a lake is very much not very much but a lake is not the best of it. A lake is definitely a noun. With withdrawing a lake is definitely a noun. With other otherwise all of it at all. A lake is an article followed by a noun a lake is an article followed by a noun a lake which is there.

It is not at best a pleasure to have stopped before.

Follow and follow. This is a verb and an and.

A noun and a verb. A noun is always given up. Well and well, well well she shut the window well well.

A noun is not an occasion whence they will officiate made and arrested with a fortunately without there and within there a noun is not a tribute to their hope they will not hope to have it. What is a noun in nothing and not too to thank. A noun is when they have it which they have. They have and a lessening of theirs alright. A noun makes it wish it at all. It is always why they went as well as well they went.

It is just as well that they went. Went and to go. A verb is so much more agreeable. I will not renounce a noun. Nor will they. They will not announce a noun. I will announce a noun.

I will announce what noun. A noun. A noun is theirs as they. They will be here with me. I am here. They are here with them. A noun is how and and should not obtrude on a noun. A noun is like that. What is a noun. They they own a noun if they. A noun. Open and own a noun. This is all very foolish. Who has to hold a noun. What is a noun. They know that they do not know the name it is difficult to remember because a name is a name that it is difficult it is difficult to remember a name. A name. That is not a noun. Without a noun. What and what is it. A sentence is so sweet. Will think how I like it. A sentence is made in case in their kind which is very kind.

Some one has made him some proposition which will please him but which he will have when he has it ready.

Some one has made him some proposition which will succeed to what he has to please him and which he will continue to consider when he has been called away to be ready to have it made for him to him. Which is away.

Which ever is away.

What is which. Which is a part of their account it also is a plain and plainly made arrival of and and they like whichever whenever they like it. What is the difference between which when and then and reliable. Think carefully of lend and think carefully of lending and thin and think carefully of when which is made particularly as made as careful as on their account which is why they are careful and carefully do to place in placate with and around. There is a difference between a thing seen and their exception and as alike with made which they mean. They order an excuse. Made which they may. What is think of that. There is this allowance in avoid a word. A word is an appointment with pleasure with care. And having forgotten because of being engrossed and this is in a way carefully.

Never think that it is what they have. Which whenever they do they will incur what they must have when they like.

Thoughtfully about a tendence to to do about something equivalent in return made by an aid which in reference able mainly for this to hemmed in laid awake made by them in reticence. What is alike.

Which with withdrawn.

Wherever made firmly.

When made in return.

Alike is mine for them.

Relieve an incident in an interruption.

What is a sentence. A sentence is complete in secret. A secret is a pressure of their arrival as arrival made at once with necessity, necessity is by and by which is by the way. Almost any word except a name can go into a sentence.

Why can almost any word and any word which they know they can go and they can put it into any sentence in this way. In what way can they put any word that they know into any sentence which is what they allow. Any sentence. A word which is in any sentence is made to be confused with elegant and with inadvertence. But not with speed nor with mainly. A word which is allowed is for them and for them alone which they must with reluctance prepare in the remainder of the time which is at their disposal . What is a sentence. A sentence has hammered it as much as they are pleased alike. It all comes back to partly and what they do. It all comes back to known and negligence. It all comes back. Made to be ready. What is a sentence. They cry. A sentence is that they cry when they are confused. If they cry they did cry that they were disappointed by them with all of it. What is a sentence. One two. Who may do. A sentence in thinking. I think as I try. I made a sentence without a parting with him. Think of a sentence in between. What is a sentence. Once in a while they like it at thirty once in a while they like it as they have it once in a while they like it as they have once more, with them there are pearls and girls. Do you see how they spoil a sentence. A sentence is a little above which is right, it is right and a little lower which they explain they make it do. What is a sentence.

It is very easy to wish well.

This is a sentence that meets with opposition because they were in the past supposed not to have this aptitude they were manageable. To wish well is to have made it be not a frame but their allowance and they like it and lead it. This is why they have this difference. A sentence is reflected by their being told about a location. Now think of the difference between a sentence and their word. A name of anything is never a sentence because they look alike. Think well about that the name of anything is not a sentence. This makes it be well-known as a wish.

Relieved that the name of anything is not for a sentence. And so a sentence has no word which is a word which is a name all the same. Think well of what they offer. Which they offer. A sentence is made with practically none of it. If a sentence is not coined that is if it is not used which they may if they like they will without which it is easy to be plainly theirs and their own. This sentence makes a day a holiday which is what they own. Think well of a resemblance, they were all like that. This is very simple and very mainly very plainly which they avoid. What is a sentence. Think of the difference in names. And with numbers. That they like. A sentence is not a ramification. It is not a name. It is not one at a time because now one at a time does not make it do. If one at a time does not make it do they will be more than plenty. This is a common sentence. What is a sentence. A sentence is something that is or is not followed.

If he likes wedding women.

Very well a sentence.

After they are a little left they like it but with it. Now think carefully if tired had been used they would not have been welcome and so with a sentence they should never use a name for a thing that is the way to do it, supposing I had said that is the way to talk that is the name of a thing but no that is their way with which they lay or more that is not anything and so equally they replenish. Replenish is not a careful word and they think of a sentence.

To with which they wish.

That is a sentence and not an introduction. Who has how many. They have this there for them. A sentence is plainly not an affectation. Even if it is it is not a disturbance. What is a sentence. In unique. What is a sentence. With them they. A sentence has as at and with this a rest.

Danes it makes no difference about Danes.

In a little while which they own they add for themselves as and partly another one.

PART III

A sentence is made as this amount.

There is this. If they are overallowed they will be with out at all a doubt. And they will cry. Made with half as a quarter is either. With this. With with without their there there.

All of a sentence has three sounds. They mean. They mean it to. They have a wish a wish bone they have a wish bone. Now a sentence as to sound has this which is this. They have as around that they have this as it is is as it is is it. This does not make a sound around. Further there is not as there was a sound which is that which is a sound of it. A sentence may behave in being which gave in this sound they sell sell and seal they never in another way does so. A sound in a sentence. He does hear that he does hear that he said so. This is said as they said weighed. And so a sentence and a sound is parts of hearing and heard. If they look and sigh. What is a sentence if what is a sentence. There is never any mistake in what they heard. If they are alike a like there is never any mistake of the river and the river Rhone. There as simply there is never any mistake. In a noun there is a mistake he is mistaken. In a verb there is an and an error that is that they have had it without without reputation without reputation. They had it, without a mistake. A sound is what they have when they have an hour. Now then that shows the futility of the noun. A sound is the name of the sense, which they have. A noun is the name of the sense which they have. A sentence is made not by sound. Take, around. A sentence will be simply if indicative it is part and part. It is hard to have it apart. That is a sentence and something else might not have been. They will like what there is with with is allowed as a sentence with what they might with what they have with been. It is easy to see. A sentence which they take they will rejoin reuse they will take. What they will remake. Remake and remarkable and just how they are, difficult to find. A sentence has to be considered as sound and a noun as renowned. A sentence has to be considered as with a sampled in with them. What is it. It should never be known as sewn. She sews. This way. If they call all the same they call it them call this way. Think of this sentence part of it makes and part of it breaks and they do like it not as bedewed not as not not bedewed. In this way a sentence needs attended. A sentence which is likes which is like which is likes, at all a sentence may not be separate by thirds thirds is if it is a or a word. Now then a sentence is a sentence. Yes. A sentence now then a sentence is all the same a sentence is as then a and assented. Which is the sentence. They have nearer a sentence and then. A sentence is a sound but they are alike that.

We we know. A sentence is not a part which is a very and polite as that. Now think. If you like. What is it that they say about what. That is a sentence that is said as in their way. They say it. This makes a sentence part and participle which is not and annoy. A participle is darling. Their annoyance with pleasing as they like. Is and alike. Now these two sentences have meaning and an extra. A sentence has I did not as a fairly with it without substantial.

Now then consider substantial. Is it a noun. Substantial is it a noun. They were with it. With it may be a noun. They were with it may be a noun. A noun is the same all the same. Think of a noun and not carefully.

A noun is this, they made change.

That is how they were after they were as after soon. Think of this as not a noun and there will be no blame. That is young after reading. Now this is how they know that there is easy which is easy as is easiness, easiness in easy as they have it for their on in an essay to do so. It must always be remembered that it is like that when they do it. Therefor they have when they do it participated as a part. Now supposing I think a minute.

It is polite. Partly and polite. These words are not nouns.

Intrusion is not a noun. They will think of the effect upon them of this. This is not a noun either. It is an interruption. An interruption is not a noun with them it is a noun if it is with coming in but it is not a noun without a basket.

A noun prepares but preparation is a noun therefore a noun is not without this. A noun without this. If a noun is that there is no interest in when she had a mother this is without a noun because they will be all with it will. Will and will it. This is not a noun although it is past. A noun then although it is past is left alone and with it mentioned. Please remember it all the same. How many names have we known.

Think carefully of nouns. Vary and think very think very once and once more of a noun a noun they like. Now then an exception which they must have when they must will they be a noun. He will have been as known as not known. This refuses not refuses a noun but as if as better. Think well of a noun. Every time they think well they will think will think well and will of a noun.

Now then this is two in that thing. Reminding and in further pressing they must have it as an end will. Does everybody know just what I know. This is a noun if they like but as they do not it is a noun in preference in preference to their hoping for the best of it. They are hoping for the best of it.

A noun can be a sentence if a sentence is liked. If a sentence is liked. That is if a sentence is liked.

Do you do very much complain.

A noun has not been told to remain. What is a noun. If they feel well is that a noun. Is a noun invariable or is it that after having thought about it the interest in it is gone. What is a noun what is very likely a noun.

They will sew which will make tapestry. This is a noun and she likes it. What is a noun.

After having used and become used to a noun and of that now which is not without a very considerable pleasure we will now think about a verb having become very fond of an article. An article is always attaching it is as much as if they never have a thought. They like it. A an and the. A conjunction being merely useful they will always be made here. Which is without doubt. A an and the is most and best and finally at no time. When they call. An a and the is an arrangement with themselves.

Does and dove which is it. There dove is not a noun. Does is a noun. He does. A dove. A dove. And he does. Which is a noun. It is easy to feel very well.

An easily made sentence. What is sense in an easily made sentence. She does not care whether she stays or not because if she does or not she does not care whether she stays or not. That is an easily made sentence and it easily makes sense which is an easily made sentence which easily makes sense.

Now to come to something more difficult. If it does not decide beside will it be a formal hope that this is that when there after they will call by it in a delay coming as a call which is belied which is it after the and blessing as in noon which can always be cordially a name left alone with invited as they return and gone as farther without relief of as much made in a wait waiting about which is where after is amount amount to it likewise rested made an opposition to sewn it was very well sewn because they will allow for tapestry. Now this is a difficult sentence and they will like it because if it is necessary they will be obliged and after a little it was pay-day. Now then a difficult sentence not only has adroitness grammar and a name and with this they could follow it with not alone but not alone makes it a delight and delight a polite and polite a politeness and a politeness to let them know. A difficult sentence can make a letter. Nouns and verbs mingle in a difficult sentence because they will hope that they think so. It is not well to end it as well and if there is an interruption it is not without it having been announced and forewarned and if they have noticed it this is what they feel when they see a difficult sentence which is to them such an appeal. What is a difficult sentence. A difficult sentence is one in which they are all alike and they think that of some things which is not the same as may. May be they do but they doubt it. This is not a difficulty to have for it. A difficult sentence is one that is welcome.

What is welcome.

PART IV

Please ask me if you like it.

That is one form of a sentence and they like it. A sentence may be if it is made for them may make a little arrangement that will be after a minute that they were left to them for their wishes. Think of a sentence in relation to wishes. Is wishes a noun. A verb is wishes. Is a verb made equally by a noun so that they do not as regards or in regard to arrange they will have pairs and pairs of arranging that they will.

What are their wishes.

They will not blame them with what they are as wishes.

A difference between a noun and a verb is not seen in wishes and wishes. She wishes it. She wishes that. She wishes. Wishes which are wishes. Who annoys whom with wishes. In this way if you say who does have them which are as wishes they will have permanently their placing it as for them with them with their having them with it as they wish which is for them as she wishes. On this account wishes is a noun. She said she was pleased with a name. A name is not a noun.

And as she comes in. With them for him. This is not known as a name. A name. She said does it please you that they have a name. He says yes it does as everybody has a name. He is spoken of by his name. Does it please you that he is spoken of by a name and that that name is his name. He is spoken of by his name. His name and her name their names which altogether make it desirable that they are liked by their having it without any place. If any one that is there is named as they are they will like more than they have and it is doubtful if they like it very much whether they will name it. In that case is it a noun.

There is a difference between spring and winter and in either case they do not mean to have a noun. A noun which is a name is not the same. It is not given and therefor it is not a noun. And if it is a noun they know that they have been willing not to have it. It is very well known that they do not like a name. Sometimes they like a name. It has been said that it is known not to be desirable to have it because then as it is so it is as if it is to be so and so and they are allowed. This remains a difference between as wishes, a noun as wishes is a noun as wishes a verb and a noun as wishes is a verb and a noun as wishes. Sometimes a noun seems that if they are apart they will have it said that they were very well and very soon to have it as never to be wanting their remaining for so much of it as they have.

There are three arrangements, wishes a noun and a verb.

What do they do with wishes. They wish they were known with what they may they will as well. What are having not any longer any pleasure in a name except address. That is one way of refusing a noun a day.

Having had the refusal of nouns and having asked it as a guess and having thought very well of and about wishes it is now that they see that they like that it is that a noun is not of any use of use to them. Think well if a noun is not of use to them any use to them which it is and is it any use to me which if not in a mean which is regretful that is partly makes it feel that they never liked it really. They liked a name very well they liked a name.

If they liked a name.

A name and a noun is not the same that is a great discovery. A name is a place and a time a noun is once in a while. And therefor not useful if they think they do. They will be very welcome with wishes. In fact they will be very welcome with wishes.

If it is easier for them.

From now and them.

What are nouns. Can you see the plural in nouns. Very well. And therefor they are not names. Names and the name of a thing are not the same thing therefor there are nouns. They will leave there are nouns. We have left there are nouns we have left there are nouns. I have no need to think twice because of it and they are with them if they like. If they like is not the same as if they wish.

If they wish us well.

If they do not come again Wednesday they are monotonous.

Surely nouns may be a staple and if they are they come to have looks and it looks like it. A noun will do for them and will do very well. No name no noun but a name and a noun are not the same. A name what is it that it has when it is not only when and whenever and therefor now it is only used in an address or to address or to leave for some day which is why they have what they have to like. It is very partly very nearly what they do to have it made the same in that case there is or there is not a name.

A difference between a verb a noun a part and an article and a particle and a name. A particle they liked if they did not know that they had used it. This is a noun. A name is why they are helped out loud and very pleasantly in the spring. A verb is a part of them one at a time and an article they like an article and a particle they will have it doubtfully but they will never be sure. In this way there are no changes.

Now and for me.

She came and she said with it.

With made with a maid with a servant with whether she was with them or before without them they were dismayed by her having been with him when they gave him the honor of having been left with and without him. This is a sentence which she has not been saying.

A sentence does not mean that it is very likely that around is never to be around without them. Think of a sentence and think of wishing. I wish on the first time of eating or of saying or of selecting or not which they persevere as she announced by mistaking it for that. This sentence makes knitting a difficulty. If three can learn to say it differently and have it as a name which one of them has taught them. Taught is not the same as caught. Think carefully of a sentence and a resemblance.

A sentence is something which they will if they like them.

Have a difference between with and without flour. They will have told them.

What is a sentence. And what is which part. A sentence is never spoken. A spoken sentence is never spoken. Either. Whichever they like. Which will they do. They will do whichever they like. It will prepossess them in their favor if they which they like they like to do it. Whatever they like.

A sentence is replaced.

It is like this that a sentence is when which is not the same as seen.

A sentence is too and ought. He ought to go he has not

been told so. What is a sentence if there is not any water water is why they sell and salt water is why they will have it as if it did matter which they do to them.

Think of a sentence think of how they hoped to have it do.

A sentence never needs to be like what there is when there is some of it that is the same.

She stays longer to look than he does and he walks away and she stayes longer to look than he does.

This is a sentence which may mean that it is thought to be alike. If they feel that it sounds as it does it will be very well to have it helped and held with when they do.

If you think very well of what each one says you know that sentence. That sentence has that sound which if they they like. This is the way that they do with them left to turn where they went. This sentence is perfectly adapted to being parallel. They are to have it to like it. When a sentence comes to be alone who does help wishing. And so a sentence is always connected. They like parts. A great many do once in a while for them. A sentence is made of a verb and a noun and sometimes a sentence has a verb and a noun. Sometimes a sentence is very well done. What is a sentence. A sentence if it goes along is all of it for that. There is a difference between what I like and what they like. And they do it. They do what I like.

Now this whole thing is a very good example of just what he means by very nearly to and please. That is a sentence that has not been needed. A sentence that is needed is one that initiates their sealing. She is very fond of sealing.

What is a sentence. They will not need to know where she has been.

A sentence like that is after all their where and when they will have what they have as after they can.

A sentence can be made of their having both been not always as counted. She could know them. Know of them. Hear them. Hear about them. Heard them. That is it that is what a sentence is.

What is it. It is a sentence. A sentence is that they say that they will he will come right away. A sentence can be in one. A sentence in one sentence has been in one. It has been one.

How many ounces make a pound. What is the difference between silks. What is the purpose for which they have asked him to be welcoming the interest they are coming to have in one thing. Yes it is.

Who makes which welling. Welling is changed from William to welcome. In willing.

There is no doubt that on account of there being more moving that they can any of them staying all day go away in any way and this is this because of this generally it is more than finishing it is necessary to say to possibly say that they have seen every one as a may mainly for keeps. Because of this description of there not being there are not very interesting and because of this. It depends not upon a sentence but upon it all being in an amiably widened as a sentence. A sentence is it at all.

PART V

Disengaged.
In a word they will like what they do.
Do they like that when they are where they went.
With this as they feeling like it.

A sentence makes it be palatable.

I have come to the conclusion.

It is of no use thinking it anything but a pleasure which it is if it is as it likes. Likes makes likes. Wishes are no more. Likes for them likes it.

That is what sentences are far in a way made slower. Sentences are made with to be slowly. It does not make a difference. It does make a gather. With better. And other. Gain in other. What is it that is are or or.

Think of a sentence.

It is all very well to think of a sentence.

He will not it is all very well to think of a sentence.

Will wind wool. At request.

Now think carefully. A sentence may be what they said. It may not be what they thank for. It may be what they will in have.

He does not like have in a sentence.

If a sentence is careful.

A sentence is carefully made a sentence is carefully cared to for her sake.

Sentences made slowly.

With them with whom.

In a minute sentences made slowly. Made slowly.

We can be with them still.

Until with them still.

A sentence made slowly. Which they do now that they do which they do and not wish.

That is it a sentence not made which is as slowly as they make a sentence made to be only seen made only slowly. Only slowly is their own which they own. Own it. Which they own it.

What is a sentence which they own it.

Made slowly. That is what. Not at all.

If it is made slowly have they stopped. They will wait. What is the difference. They do wait. That is the difference.

How they but it does not carry me away or fascinate me exactly.

They find out what it is all about. A sentence made next to a disappointment.

With within. A sentence. Have handled.

And in have had him. This is a sentence that is not a description of a possession.

Now then.

Now in then.

And in have had him.

This is a sentence that is extortionate and means that they are weeping because they have not given it to him for him as folded by and with them in with him. This is an announcement of their parting.

Think of a sentence think how they like it.

If they wish that they. This is a sentence if they are alike. Now at a gain. If they had not meant all or a door. Would could is assigning a wall nut. A walnut can be a saint.

Description is so happy is so with. All. They agreed hence.

Think what of think with.

That is fanny is so gracious.

Fanny is so gracious. This is not a description. This is repetition with out their wailing which is mind. Mind what you are about.

PART VI

With this sentence. It does not make any difference with this as they are through with them.

I do they do have this to do with them. They have this to do with them. They have what they have to do with them. Poor dog whose nose is cold. Poor dog of whom the nose is cold.

How can they know that this is a part.

Part. In resumption.

What is a sentence. They do not care if each one of them is indifferent which they mean.

A sentence is because they have held to have it for without them.

A sentence is that she does one within when.

It is very easy to dislike held with bread withheld bread because they will be without their cousin. All the time.

There is no change with changing that they will not be well without a welcome welcome is not a word. Now think very well why is not at all not a familiar word because it is without that as an allowance. Having held supremacy.

He asks why are they welcome to it. It is not that is without a word. A word is when they went. They were married in April. What is a sentence. A sentence has been made. Award an award is when she remembers who he is.

Think of thanking.

However felt. This is a word.

They will be well named.

Amelia and Dan.

How and horizontal.

Hour and our.

Is to us.

It is not without easy and easily is not the same as adventitious.

It is easy in the change to think of that that it is a change. Have plants.

The history is always the same the product is always different and the history interests more than the product. More, that is, more. Yes. But if the product was not different the history which is the same would not be more interesting. And it is the history which is the same which makes the product which is different. And the history interests more than the product with whom. Yes. Which when they come they are welcome.

Lay lay which is laid lain.

A sentence of which he is secure.

What is it.

She is here with it.

FINIS

Regular Regularly

In Narrative

WELL WELL IS HE. Explain my doubts, well well is he explain my doubts.

Could he get used to a city.

Explain my doubts.

Well well is he explain my doubts. Well well is he explain my doubts.

They made a day be a day here. They made a day be a day here. They made a day be a day here by a year by a year yearly they made a day yearly be a day here by the year.

This is why there is this very well I thank you thank you thank you. Like a man which is which is which is why which is lady or lady or lady or lady. They need to have been why could they have been which feels where is it now to be in place and get as places places which can be this is that now now to be lost lost to be sure sure to be come to be come this this is there why does it belong to them to them which can any one be deceived by her being twenty two when it has been said that she was twenty-six she was twenty six she was twenty twenty twenty twenty six she was twenty-six can be deceived that she was twenty two when it was said that she was twenty six.

Making up their mind. Is it natural to like what one is looking at if one is looking at it sometimes it is and sometimes it is preferable to be nearer and nearer further away and they might they might be as careful of it as careful of it as careful of it as careful of it. This which is what is left alone left alone now can now it can now it can be left alone in case of connecting it with what is what what is after after all all that that has been been leaning leaning where is it is it likely likely to be a chance of their their preparing not only it. Like it.

How many varieties of having had had it to be nearly what is it when it is by this time.

She she is like a servant. A servant likes liking lean leaning said saying soon not as a servant but as a dependent dependent dependent. That is one. Two like being which is it not five but six years older that is to say he that is to say be that is to say be be be that is to say be be that is to say it has never been it has been noticed that if he needs it needs it not at once but as given he needs it not at once but as given. This makes him not only of service but of service this makes him not only of service but of service and this makes him have have have have very much have very much have very much one at at time have very much one at a time have very much have very much one at a time. It is natural and therefor a preparation it is natural and therefor a preparation.

Leave which is while they make it do all that for this by then need little pleasure which is why it is because it is well thought out. Some like the country better than the city. In the city there are houses in the country there are houses in the city there are trees in the country there are trees in the city there are if there are winds and windows in the country there are when there are winds and windows in the city there are strangely houses and dogs in the country there are strangely horses and dogs in the city there are where they are where they are food and ways and salad and oil and vinegar in the country there are food and ways and oil and salt and sugar and vinegar in the city there are when it came to be Sunday in the country there are when it came when it came to be Sunday in the city what is the difference between seventeen and twenty-seven in the country what is the difference between seventeen and twenty-seven and so some like the country better than the city. Mr. Scott, Henry and Allen.

There are no men no women needed for love there are no women no men needed for love. There are no women no men needed for love.

It only goes to show.

It only goes to show that it is very easy to be surprised that Jefferson is different from Madison and Washington from Franklin. It only goes to show that liking is the same as leaving and letting is the same as Indian. It only goes to show that if it is left to them to decide anything each time every time they will choose Wednesday that is to say if Wednesday is chosen Wednesday and choosing is made to have that in connecting connecting removing and dwindling. This introduces regularly and reconnoitering and if in demonstration and developing and leaving it out which is when it is bound to be left out left out and three ringing. Ring around a rosy this makes it louder.

It is natural to suppose that a rose is a rose is a rose is a rose. It is as natural to suppose that everything is why they went. It is also as natural to suppose that they might be inattentive when they had aroused what was why and when it could be lost. Where could it be lost. It is natural to suppose that because inadvertently they were obliged to be careful they might be nearly very often very well inclined to like and admire it here.

It happened occasionally that ordinarily weather was flattering to this arrangement and in all cases as liklihood they might there might it might be felt and to be inclined to have it as an advantage. Needless and needed they can be comforting. Let it be because of this reason and a reason. It happened that by arrangement feeling that many leaves have been used used as well as if in advantage advantageously reliable and pressed to be in this way remaining as equably as if in this case there will be an attention and an intention. Right away. It makes be an applause an applause it makes it prepare for this by an inadvertent negligence of their remaining permanently in sight. It might be when it could be found to be about to be as much as ever arranged and in their and in their place and necessarily a necessity for indifference and violent lanes. And so forth as much as change.

It is easy to be cautious.

Let it be what is made when as if not like it where is the next in attending to it.

One and two.

It might have been nearly what they said.

She knew which it was said to be next to the one that was there where there was as if it were the next by the way that they use which is best of the three that it should be most often left to them and before it was not very well perhaps more in the nicer as well which makes this leave it here for the rest of the day to be sure that it could not alone for this reason on this account reliability and persuasion. Not it at all not it alone at all not it at all alone not it alone not it alone at all not it at all alone letting it have that prepared for the most most of it secondarily nearly exchanged principally letting nearly appointing fortunately informed not have and have it permanently.

Leave this to them as that let it allowed should it be shown near in case in case in case in case of it welcome every thing that is not an intentionally older leaving that principal arousing and with it to be sure at once. Leaves when they can. It made it be theirs respectfully.

Let it alone with shoes.

Leave it alone with let it alone with let it alone with relinquish. Let it alone with in the more or less having hold would it be particularly.

How do they feel that they were puzzled.

Have it mean theirs particularly particularly for it to be for it in the arrangement of having first found not found but nearly nearly as much more now listen to the best of which is might it be this in time. Are there many ways of predicting an undeniable older reunion returned to having having boast and boast and left and left to this this can always be authorised. What is their relief.

It is very simply very simply it is very simply very simply that it is that it is that it is that it is well to be to be to it to it to tell to tell to well well well to have it be the next that is that was to have in ten in ten days left and right and which in this make that could be detached to certain. Come once again.

Try leaving it be here. All uses use for this part in their in change changed at once. Let it be told how often they might pay stay to pay to pay stay away away. It is very easily to be understood that they know the difference between run and one between two and ten between nine and pearls between which and left and between clouded and out loud and magisterially. Not very well not very were often not very well not often not very well. Will she go to Compiegne.

After which if left night to then call calculating need and reversal and shallow and this time occasionally nearly as it can be said for them and lost it. Clara John Paul Jenny fidgety and remind. They can each be in use of use of most of last of theirs of come. Would he remind every one of them. Olga would he remind every one of them. Neith would he remind every one of them. Bernadine would he remind every one of them. Nora would he remind every one of them. It might be that they had none none leave it none leave it none leave it. Thinking this is their need it be what ever left it alone. Very pointedly. All the time that they might. Have to be it and by their side by their side. Every one makes four to close closet close four to close four to close to closet clothes four to close to closet four to closet to clothes to close to closet four to close. By this time. Irradicably makes an excuse. It should never be ended with whether could it be their song. Many many singly said it shown shown as while. Undoubtedly they have to have pears here.

What happened to Mabel Haynes American four Austrian children. Four Austrian children are children of Mabel Haynes American Mabel Haynes American's four Austrian children. The eldest of Mabel Haynes American's four Austrian children would if she were obliging marry an American and so reduce Mabel Haynes American's four Austrian children to three Austrian children. Mabel Haynes American's three Austrian children if Mabel Haynes American's three Austrian children two Austrian children were born Italian children Mabel Haynes American's three Austrian children being born two Italian children Mabel Haynes American's one Austrian child four Austrian three Austrian children one Austrian child Mabel Haynes American's one Austrian child two Austrian children if Mabel Haynes American's eldest Austrian child four Austrian children did not marry an American two Austrian children born Italian three Austrian one Austrian child four Austrian children.

Leave to have the maiden's prayer. To care one share fortunately receive the left to right meaning their frame. It is easy to see that not deliberately but with their waiting is to be we we have them called Bertha.

It always happened that it aroused them in the way that it was mentioned that they had their own arrangement for everything and that in every way for awhile which is why they were very able to be next to them when they were able could they be with held withheld from leaving it having it not best of all which is why by their leaving it able to be fastened and not nearly following once twice and three times allowed to be much too much hurriedly resumed and does it make any matter any difference any matter that that that they can in this way be their own leave it for them best to be always ready just as much as ever while it can be more than they can care to have nearly as often as Sunday which is why in this way to be spoken letting it have more than is more than is theirs by birth and education and inheritance and left to if and by this and by that and themselves and ordinarily really to be what is it when it does not make any difference. This is what they might have to do.

How can a square be nearer less farther. How can a little be in place of two larger. How can a distance be after all near a bridge not yet not yet always as if it had always been it had always been a bridge had been wider. Let us think let us think of how they said anything.

A narrative means telling about Jefferson Williamson and Henderson. This is the substance of a narrative. She met Williamson Jefferson and Henderson. She was interested in meeting Jefferson Henderson and Williamson. She was as much interested in hearing them be nearly plainly likely to be interested in using nearly anything as a preparation for arranging an exhibition. That is at one time that is what is deliberately followed by announcing that they wished to be women by deliberately announcing that they wished to be women by deliberately announcing that they wished to be winning by deliberately announcing that they wished to be women. That is one way of deliberating and deciding and intending to have a narrative of preceding. The next which is what is by this time what is it is that there is accomodation for all and every one who mean to be nearly very nearly choosing a white basket a white basket which is not as large as an ordinary one. A white basket which is not as large as an ordinary one might be here and there and so be noticeable so be noticeable might be here and there and so be noticeable and engaging and finally finally finally who must have seen who must have seen a woman with a young one about the age kind and disposition which would be satisfying would be satisfying would be would be satisfying and disposition which would be satisfying. The next indeed the next if there is no difference between in eating and in decorating beside if there is no splendor beside in there being no question no question beside in their being no question between in eating and in decorating if there is no difference beside in their being in eating and beside in their being in decorating and not yet any deciding and not yet decidedly not yet not yet deciding not what is there in asking in not yet in not yet knowing in not yet in beside not yet investigating not yet is it likely that very fairly soon there will be something. Let us think how can a narrative have any connection with remarriage and their indifference to resolution to changing what there was to not what is not pleasing as if there could be any reason. Let it never be theirs at most which is after a while. See there. A narrative might be understood followed and a privilege. A narrative of this and in intimately in intimately. Description narrative and enunciation and this is narrative.

Who said will he see me be will he see me be if he will
see me be if he will see me be beside if he will see me be
beside again if he will see me be beside again. If he will see
me be beside again to make a piece of then of when to be
beside if he will be beside to be again. Can it be to have to
lend an end to be beside to be to be then when then when to
be in then to be when then if he to be if to be he if to be he
beside to be then when to be when ten ten should be beside
to be when then to separate ten when to eradicate when then
to be to see to make to be then when. Let it be likely that it
should be brightly that it should be lightly that it should beside be if he be if to be beside to be that it should beside be as
when. Harold Acton has not been properly described.

Who should be as able who should be as liable who should
be a better leaving it to this to decide. Who should be as
possible who should be capable of not repeating having heard
that that that never having had piles of merchandise. Other
mother son and daughter after a while. Who should be never
looking as if lost who should be as if having it for them who
should be who should be who has to hear it very often who
can she mean by saying that it was impossible that he should
be should be not very likely. Never describe as a narrative
something that has happened.

Do not care about them about that about theirs about this
about it. A nearly to be left to sell fish.

Outside interests tell the same tale they indicate that presently there will be more time to have an arrangement for
paintings chickens and eggs and reliably for preparation
names and dedication and moreover following it might be
that it could be arranged to make more allowance than has
been at all necessary for a menu. Please leave which is might
as well have theirs to day to say that it has not been not having

introduced anything. Nevertheless in left to be shattered by their periodical kneeling upon not upon that upon there upon upon hiding upon what is it. Let it be which is to be allow it. Let it be told earnestly. There is no narrative in intermission and please Jenny. What makes it be like this which fails to please. No after a while their chance. A next to it like this to please the most. A narrative alike. How are there more which is by this as well as needlessly. It is not as difficult. Never look from right to left.

Not at all this as follows not at all this as follows not at all this as follows not at all this as follows not at all this as follows not at all, this as follows not at all. This as follows. Required to delight this not at all, this as follows. Very fairly leave it too. Leave it to them leave it to them. Leave it too on account of not better than at all neglected to have it intend it for that. There is every reason for what was done done and sun sun and silk silk and well well and now now and either either and why there might which is neither like the less of it with that at once. They have very often given them to see to see which they need to be that which is an estimate. Follow one to gather. Let it be theirs which makes it be not all at to remind her that if she is to eat grapes or eat grapes or eat apples or eat apples or eat grapes or eat grapes altogether that is at the time. This has been their permission. Could they be new to near or be five. Not that very likely. Can a narrative succeed. This time to state ahead a native is to be made of theirs and brings and not mentioning conditions. A narrative not mentioning selections, having placed which is added and nearly in the case of could it be going on. How do they carry that to them. A narrative hinders no one. Did you expect it to be that.

Let it be what made it have half of it be higher that it could be peaceably reengaged to their misunderstanding which allows having reasonably able to lanters having passed into the next field by the next time that which being fortunately could not at all really left alone this might which shall come to this by it. There is no use at all in describing the Hall Stevens murder nor any disaster or indeed any of the things that make it make a difference between Description and Continuation and Narrative in retrospection, nor indeed anything which makes it make it that there has been no difference in relating and betaking and reminding and would it be the same if there was coming and going there is no coming and going. Let it be the tube rose in between. What is narrative narrative is the relation between there being there at once once and having their next not at once not once not now not merely but as much as after this which is what is placed after not before by that time not at this time how not only on their account. This makes narrative immediately Narrative of how often they have been women and men and turned their backs as they meant in between to which is it at table. There might be some there after all after all after all. In a minute after all, could it be doubtful whether no one need prepare prepare utilities at one time. There is no remembering remembrance of when when they were in debt because of more renting a house of more pears and roses trees it may be introduced trees or after a little while a god-child, a god-child can never cause more than even now. This has been the case with two. This is to divide it in four in three in three in four and as he may. May does not let it be known may it not let it be known. Three months is half of six months. And six months is not when there were two out of three. In this way pushing is not pushing pushing a while is not pushing a while pushing a while is not pushing a while as all said, all said it does not make it be theirs as shown. Let him be why they came and went away another way either way can three things happen at once coincidentally. Nothing but their arrival.

He said that it was very likely that that was the reason.

Now and then now and then rest of it now and then which is it should it be smooth or should there be various kinds of different little and big needs to have which is it why they planned to do it by the time that they had it left to them because of his not being successful. Not being successful. And they might have it as it was that is more nearly if in standing or in sitting they might be prepared to look at last and remember that could it be possible that he was tired. He was tired. And might once in a while might it once in a while might it once in a while be not only more than there was any bettering of their chances in having changed changed to it believing that it was well arranged. Not to be at most at most as if they had not avoided their and streams of which they might letting it be as much as did they like why was it that if it did it did not only be more than that which was not actually valuable and be nearly as likely as that and to go to go makes it allowed having gone make it he went to see who came today. That is why they thought about it.

A misunderstanding as to a return to that place which made it be more nearly as much as they wished because of their not finding it out. Letting it be rolled further and so they might which is left to them alone letting it not be which is it when they can establish in their only definite return to which might it be when it was alike. They might be theirs. There is a difference between success and succeeding and between announcing and never having left it to be left and after all this they came away. It is not very likely that they were not prepared to indulge themselves in it not at all and why because it should be as if they were prepared to abide by it abide by it leaving it not only as much as if they had no other arrangement to make or not at all briefly. As soon as soon as letting it alone makes it of more importance just as soon might and will they be there in exchange and so forth and so forth. A narrative might be why they visited one another one earlier and one later.

Needs to have him answer. After once when he was out and stayed to have after all reminded that they had changed to the best of his knowledge and belief. Came to be sure that if after that it would be theirs at that time. Let us know how a narrative at length.

A narrative means that not to have him replace him and not to have him have him replace him. A narrative a narrative of one of that one having met to repeat that one of that one and then one of that one having one of that one replace one one replace one one of that one two replace two of that one there never having been two of that one one of that one. Not a narrative of an approach to a union. Why could why could why could he why could why did their little boy recognise me. There is this difference between narrative and portrait a narrative makes anybody be at home and a portrait makes anybody remember me. There is this difference between a narrative and their walking. A narrative allows a change in this being that for the best of the time that makes letting it be when they might compare it altogether while a portrait has been while they were kept apart cordially. A narrative allows it to be most of it attached to their having lost it and a portrait is what might be while they were easily enough all about it all about it makes it do, a portrait and a narrative together makes it be one at a time.

He was to was he was there when he made it as a pair of a pair like to be likely to be a thing to be given to be painted to be given to be here. For a very long time it was here. It is here now.

There is no use for it but if it were not here it would not be here and so the pleasure of it not having not been here would have been lost. That in itself follows at one at a time and might it when left with it now be theirs as to come to that two mixing with a hunted as a left to them. Never having been as wanted as not to be what is it in allowance. This if not a narrative is a conclusion. What is the preparation of a narrative as a conclusion. What is it. What is it. A narrative, a conclusion a narrative comes to be to tell everything to them simply they had to have their coming to be seen that each cup not each saucer had a wild animal upon it. How many cups not only cups and saucers have to be following when they have had no opportunity for further display. No opportunity for further display. It might often be that they liked that. Every day it came to be darker at four than at five. And so forth.

A narrative is an understood following of that individually individually sail which makes of it their understanding their understanding let it be in their way in their way wherever wherever there must. One narrative at once now. Another narrative two months now. Another narrative forty-five in a month now. Another narrative at once now. Another narrative twenty months now. Another narrative with a month now. Another narrative there are many who have come back to them. Another narrative as a matter of course.

Mr. Herbert Masters come to be to change which is after all the difference between iron and steel and after a while he comes to change to which if after that you said to said allows it might it follow. If seen two at a time there could be no difference of their reorganising reorganising their arrangement. In this way there is no definite restitution. Supposing it followed their having it was nearly never that they needed their interposition. Finally it was by them and paid, letting it be why they went together. Who can now be aroused. They can by the narrative.

Finding it have half the time having have finding it have half of the time half the time and so very nearly so very nearly and so half the time having which it is very extraordinary that they might use it. This is when they need it really desperately and placing it in different very well and nearly how far is that. This and it felt very well one at a time could there be any difference between their liking Grace and my liking Esther and her liking it every once in a while in that way. This is nearly what they mean by their preferring it. Once in a while it happens that they mean it just as much. And for this reason they have every time that they have to leave it where they can they mean to like to know which is the way they came that they came to bring it here which is what they do have when it is made at once. Liking to know just what they mean. There is some difference between having made it and carrying it about and how to use it and most of it is when they might be just as careful as ever. This will be what happens when very much as they like they are over pleased with what has happened and just like that at once. Every little while they meant to be in the way. This makes why they wished to reply if it is reasonable it is reasonable to let theirs be held just as it is which is why they must always think. A narrative remains which they had wanted.

They might have theirs to-day they might have theirs to-day, it was very much what they did when they did not come.

It was what they did when they had it as well as if they could be sent as much there as they liked when they did not neglect to relieve it at once as they might by the time that they could which is not why they liked it at all and this makes that is why they can be as much prepared to have come and been been very well received. As narrative did he tell which one he would very much have been after all not as much as they could joining theirs to all of it as beside which is not at all a reason. There is a narrative of seldom having had and coming to be which is it. Not to not to not to too alike like like like alike they share like they prepare, can a letter place a letter can a letter place a tray can a letter place a letter can a letter be a way to have this be arranged. Be arranged very well be arranged very very well be arranged. They were not convinced that it was the same they were not convinced that it was the same they were not convinced that it was the same they were not convinced that it was the same. They accepted what they were convinced was not the same they accepted what they were convinced was not the same, they accepted what they were convinced was not the same they accepted what they were convinced was not the same they replaced with what they were convinced was not the same they replaced with what they were convinced was not the same they replaced with what they were convinced was not the same they replaced with what they were convinced was not the same it was as carefully chosen that which with they replaced what they were convinced was not the same it was as carefully chosen that with which they replaced what they were convinced was not the same it was as carefully chosen that with which they replaced that which they were convinced was not the same it was as carefully chosen that with which they replaced that which they were convinced was not the same it was as carefully chosen that with which they replaced that which they were convinced was not the same it was as carefully chosen that with which they replaced that which they were convinced was not the same and this might be the name of ring around a rosy because letting papers glide makes needles needles having tried makes having having it beside makes which is when they have to have it tried like that to be alone at home most and very likely which is now and by this in the kind of left as it would be might it be left to the rest for a return. They never returned it. A narrative makes arranging for the situation which is desirable as easily difficult and arranged for.

A narrative of Harold Acton

A narrative of Elliot Paul

A narrative of William Cook

A narrative of George Lynes

A narrative of Harry Brackett

A narrative of Eugene McGowan

A narrative of Edgar Taine.

In the in the in a narrative of Harold Acton there is no that is no separation. There is no in no declaration. Conversation and circumstances and there about to may leave it as they can left it out and out. Out in it. Let any leave it to the make it bring bring letting seeing seeing letting seeing seeing. Nobody knows the difference between a girl and a boy. How can you tell a girl you can tell a girl by a girl how can you tell a girl by a girl how can you tell a girl by a girl. She was a girl. How can you tell a boy by a boy how can you how can you tell how can you tell well how can you tell a boy by a boy. A boy is one two three yet yesterday year yet yesterday year how can you tell a girl yet yesterday year yet year yet year yet yesterday year. How can you tell a boy how can you tell a girl. In a narrative of Harold Acton not conversation not as they might be which is which is not conversation which is which is yet yesterday year which is year which yet which

is year yet which is yet yesterday year which is yet year yesterday year yet yesterday year yet. Which is year yet yet yesterday. Which is year yet yet yesterday yet year yesterday year
yet.

Leave when nor and is leave let when or and sooner. Might
he be and in indicated other this which is met to might to be
to where. Supper suppose if supper suppose let which in there
to fasten. Fast to if to an and chinese junk broke a rudder and
an and chinese a junk broke a rudder. This effort leave the
bed alone.

They be little be left be killed be left be little be killed be
killed be little be little be left be killed be his father be his
mother be his father be little be left be killed be his mother
be his father be left be killed be little be his father be his
mother. Be little be his mother be left be his father be killed
be little be his father be left be killed be his father be left be
killed be his father be his mother be killed be his mother be
left be his mother be little be killed be left be his mother be
his father be his father be his mother be his father be left be
his mother be killed be left be his father.

This is what did not happen to happen to be this brother
to his brother to his father to his father to be left to his mother
to his father.

Like which is this to have the bay to-day to seed it with a
fine compare the little having had it not to like it as if they
might which is it it is like which is meant meant to consider
come to find it to compare Harold would infinitely rather
have roses between pear trees than a child. Yes he would and
very likely that is a gain. This is not why this followed that.
To try and have it all again Harold need not share.

He first added fed and way and weighed and followed from
and first and first added weighed and wait and first added

followed he first added followed first and wait weighed and
first he first added followed first and weighed and wait and
wait. He first added followed weighed and wait first added
followed wait and weighed first added wait and weighed first
added followed wait and weighed first added followed he first
added followed he first added followed wait weighed first
added followed he first added followed first wait and weighed
first weighed and wait first he first added followed he first
added followed wait and weighed first added wait and weighed
he first added followed he first added followed weighed and
wait first added followed wait and weighed first added weighed
and wait he first added followed weighed he first added followed weighed and wait followed he first added followed.

There can be she be to be rose to be killed to be which to
be as to be he can be killed to be rose to be should to be
killed to be and this is why they made the pose to-day.

Harold to be which is to be which is not to be rose to be
not to be say to be rose to be which to be is to be any way to
be not as much as when there is a house and room and left to
have to be to quell to be to be to rose to be to quell to be be
followed quell to be and a little never well to be a moon.
Which is an advantage. Harold Acton can be finally withdrawn from Beatrice withdrawn from Beatrice withdrawn
from Beatrice who was quelled to be withdrawn from Beatrice
who was quelled to be rose to be Harold Acton quelled to be
rose to be with soon and not at light sight and and at at attention in in intention with in within might might see be. How
to go on.

When if he would when if he would when first. What will
happen to this to say what will happen when this to may
what will happen when this to lay what will happen when
this to-day to close him. What will happen happen to be what

will happen to Beatrice three Beatrice Beatrice had a mother and a father and two or a brother and she was left alone and she was left alone beautifully. This made that be that be that be might be made it be that to be to be rose. Harold Acton came to leave leave leaf lead land and leave it in it could it may I ask everybody was it agreeable. How is he followed by a narrative of reprisal. Reprisal means an excellent refusal an excellent industry an excellent facility an excellent recognition an excellent instance and an excellent consequence consequence of it. Refusal means partaking of it extraordinarily and their in use. No one knows who use whose use whose use in which leave leaf and made he might he will be unknown to and farther. As among.

Harold Acton wintered in as stay. He need be nearly be why did an artificial bird no bird is not artificial at a glance.

Continue away and this makes what happened by the time be time the vine that is suppose when he will have to may. To be rose.

Not to be to come to be to come to be rose to come to be rose. Fair fair fare very well to go if it is not to be so fare fairly well to be go to be rose rose to go fare fairly well if and if and if and not if and not not to to be rose to be fare fairly well to be rose to be not to be rose to be gone. How to go religiously.

Harold Acton has left Sunday for Friday Harold Acton has left Thursday for another day Harold Acton has left Saturday for Tuesday Harold. Acton has left Monday for yesterday. Harold Acton has left the day before yesterday Harold Acton has left the day before Wednesday Harold Acton has left Tuesday for every day Harold Acton has left to day for a day for a day by day day by day Harold Acton has left day by day day by day Harold Acton has left day by day day by day day by day Harold Acton has left day by day day by the day

day by the day Harold Acton has left the day by the day Harold
Acton has left that day Harold Acton has left on the day Harold
Acton has left on the day. Harold Acton one two two one one
two two one Harold Acton and one two two two one Harold
Acton and one one two two two one one two two one Harold
Acton one two two two one Harold Acton two one two one
two two one two two one two one two one two one Harold
Acton one two two one. Harold Acton one two two one.
Harold Acton inestimable and return to two two one two two
two two one. Harold Acton inestimable and return returned
to returned to two two two returned to two two two one two
Harold Acton inestimable to returned to returned to two to
two two one returned to inestimable returned to two two two
two one inestimable Harold Acton returned to to two two to
two two to two two two to two two two two one Harold Acton
returned to two two one Harold Acton returned to two two
two two one. Harold Acton make is different from made and
made is different from that and again and that and again is
different from circumstance and circumstance is different
from not and not and not at all and not and Harold Acton
might be obliged to might be obliged to not to come Harold
Acton might be obliged to not to come might be obliged to
not to come Harold Acton might be obliged to not to come
Harold Acton might be obliged to not to come.

Harold Acton as to this to that to which is what is what to
and which one. He was individually and in willing not to be
discredited to the disliking of their extra and having much
more than felt it to be following at this time. This made be
theirs by their choice, could one be more than confusing
and will it be after a while theirs again and this at all and
freshly be might it be witnessed if if can be called farther. He
might be with it all for this relatively theirs be and being

searched searching leaving this in as three. He might it be in their coming is it be wished wishing theirs this and what was it he said he said he said. Not allowing moistening to be dwelt upon by theirs in name and so she might be Beatrice Beatrice bent she she bent to bent to be bent to be he to be bent to be he to be bent to be Beatrice but to be he. Not much at a time but as long.

Harold Acton which is it Harold Acton to be sure which is it Harold Acton and to be a choice follow makes place please pay it as they have it as they call it come and call it call it come come come and call it and come and call it and succeeded he is succeeded he is succeeded and succeeded notably by his successor. This is a narrative regularly read it read it when it is in that perhaps in that perhaps in that past past it let him alone with his discoveries.

Hatold Acton might be useful altogether.

How soon can one at noon lose well at noon the place as soon as soon as he which is why they usefully let it be which might might generally be restfully determined to be undermined identically to their restraint. Make it be theirs never hesitatingly leading when in an exact esteem their esteem is as noted noticeably never all to it come to be felt redressed and unexacted to their lingering in there as soon. Never follow their under under which made it be and seen seen is never resolutely under estimatingly automatic is much as that. He made makes might merely make it advantageously in retrospect. When he had a shepherd a shepherdess four cows one bull two goats a sheep dog and in the distance houses built upon the end of their position which is why they have been not unreasonably left beside one another at one time. This makes it not appear neither which is nor why it is as it is wanted.

Never expecting to have.

He made which, which is which which is it intermediate intermediately defined definite and this altogether. He had it in change and theirs at rest. The coming which is it of all that which is it of all rights which is it all of which is it of all of which is it not which is it not all of which is it not all of which is it.

When it is really there yes yesterday for them.

There is no reason why Harold Acton should have taken should have taken should have taken exceptionally should have taken exceptionally can force be obliged obliged obliged can be forced to be apprised apprised can force be sweetly sweetly makes it makes it be and as noon sweetly can be sudden suddenly and authorised sweetly sweetly can be sweetly can be can be if it was was was to add added go indigo so so and so same at the same time and a time leave leave to three, thirty thirty makes twice fifteen and twice fifteen makes thirty and thirty makes twice fifteen and thirty makes twice fifteen and fifteen makes forty three times fifteen and minus one third of fifteen makes forty this is what he made he made forty.

Going on with his life. His life going on with his life. Moderately his life going on with his life. Going on with his life immediately his life going on with his life. Going on with his life going on with his life immediate immediately no immediately immediate not in immediate not in immediate not in immediate not in immediate going on with his life in going on with his life. Going on with his life.

Harold Acton famous in life and in death.

Elliot Paul naturally preclude preclude as Elliot Paul naturally preclude if not next to this lead it about to be plain plaintif plaintively plain plain plain plainer plain plain plain plainer plainer plainly plain plain as plain plan as plan plain plainly inclined and decline declined continuously salt and flesh continously flesh and salt continuously sell and flesh and sell and salt continously sell and salt continuously to be to be in in collected inter and into and in collected which is not never not and and never not to proceed. He to proceed to arrive to-night he to proceed to arrive he to proceed to arrive to-night he to proceed to arrive to-night he to proceed to arrive to-night to gain to gain if to if to gain to if to gain if that that rest and retribution angle and so time so as so as so as so as to time it to so as to time it to time it to to that.

Elliot Paul has a ball a ball to day which is to stay that he will stay do be away considerably. Elllot Paul and as to call and call to-day and to be away away from there attentively they might be quite as well at all.

Why should children be rest of it why lying lying laying leave it which is not messed messed makes messed makes spelled deliberately. Do not go away to be sure do not go away to be sure do not go away to be sure.

How many young men have to go to gether. How many, young men, have to go, together. How many young men have to go together. How many young men have to go together.

Regular regularly a narrative. A narrative is in revision a narrative is in division a narrative is in reconciliation a narrative is in destination a narrative is in is in able to say pansy.

A narrative is in they is in they is in a narrative is in they in is in they a narrative is in they is in a narrative is in a narrative is they is in they that that the the that that is the and then.

At a change as will they be as rest and can who can divide divide divine divine rest lest best who can divine divide depart differ differs syllable differs in to late in to send. Not as a find.

A narrative could not commit it to leave it to them. This makes it denied by the way by the way which was it.

If every day at noon if every day at noon if every day at noon.

As allowed.

Wednesday is what is controlled. Wednesday is what is controlled.

Alike and likeness theirs which is fastened.

Fasten to be left to that they might be candied alike.

A narrative of religion and irreligion.

A narrative of their politeness and their having it be theirs as they may.

A narrative of which is to be sure.

A narrative of which is made safer by each one and a minute.

A narrative of like and like it.

A narrative of left to be sure leaving it nearly as much as much of it in be sure to be sure to be sure to be more to be sure to be sure to be.

A narrative of Abraham Larsson.

Abraham Larsson is originally left to his praise of not being able to be nearly very often not as much as it would and could be accredited with and to accredited with and to to be as likely. Abraham Larsson may be why the water after all makes the salt water after all makes the salt water after all makes the water after all allow.

Abraham Larsson could have the choice a choice between what is not not as may be I do but I doubt it. Abraham Larsson may go to beadles and better and be likely and because and best of it as merry merry merry Christamas too. This indefensibly.

Why was I nice. I was nice to him because I to made two

be two as two three two one two five. May be I do but I doubt it. He made it be after all rapaciously.

From here to there and from there to there.

Might be which is positively.

There are the ones who do see me see me there are the ones who do see me see me there are the ones who do who do see me there are the ones who do see me.

A narrative of there are the ones who do who do see me.

Not to be to be to not to be to be to be to not to be to be to be to be to not to be to be to be to be be to be to this.

There are the ones who have let it day there are the ones who have let it who have let it let it day there are the ones who have to have let it let it let it daily let it daily do let it daily and be be so very installed installed in mounting mounting mountain and remounting, which is which.

Every day that it could yesterday it could yesterday be there during to-day by the time which is be to be to this. What did it do. It may it be be dew. Bedew and change bedew and rechange bedew and bedew. Have a head to have it here to do to do exactly to do exactly exactly to do partly.

Plainly he sat favorably he discontinued particularly he readmitted attentively he nevertheless adjusted conclusively he finally as much as chose.

Not admired.

New makes negro

Plan makes partly

Rather makes recourse

Back makes which to-day

To say.

How can there be a difference between a narrative and how best.

Defence.

Defence means that when he said yes he said yes.
Defence means that when he said come too.
Allow.
Allow for it.
She has come in and out.
Yes.

Progressively integrally delectably derisively undeniably relatively indicatively negotiably restrained. After which coming.

At night quite as quickly at night quite as quickly. He followed and said it was best determined by their and this arrangement.

Allow me.

A narrative of actually acknowledging that he did not come.

Why those who are very positive do not come to-day and those who are very positive do not come to-day. Those who are very positive do not come to-day and those who are very positive do not come to-day. Very positive. Do not come to-day. Those who are very positive, who are very positive do not come to-day.

A narrative of not left alone to do it.

How is it that when they are very happily entertained and carefully generous and blamelessly nervous and politely referred to and after that plentifully added to added to could a pear be preserved all winter. This and reprisal.

A pear has a slight tendency to be delightful in appearance and on account and by this as a reason and exactly what is meant.

A narrative consists in their excellence and in this excellence.

It happens very likely it happens to be very much that way. It happens for instance might it be that it was as it was a wish.

It might be that if a pleasure is nearly adhered to arrange adhered to as much as if when it is telling is not told and unlikely. By and by in exchange.

At last resolutely.

The narrative of having exacted that it be reconstituted.

Incline to represent this as that delightfully.

Reflect the behavior of their undertaking undertaking understanding understanding disobliging disobliging representing representing realising realising authorising authonsing reduplicating reduplicating referring referring indicating indicating considering considering attracting attracting defending defending doubling doubling sheltering sheltering replying replying mentioning mentioning deliberating deliberating unifying unifying declaring declaring unattaching unattaching determining determining likening it to them.

That is one evenly one when even one to do so.

A narrative a appointing that she said she was certain that if it was not which was not letting letting it alone.

A narrative of humiliating.

If this was why they were to be the next to go to see the same that is that when that if that might that can that will be as likely as if compared.

Comparison.

Did they both have to have him.

Did they both have to have him.

Did they both have to have him.

If he attends to it to it will he have been recommended by them all.

This is why she is no longer attentive attentive to a name to a name all the same attentive attentive to a name to a name all the same.

An a narrative of irregularity.

A narrative of relatively.

She wants to talk about the Jesuits about whose adventures it is very interesting to note repeatedly.

If it has been asked not to stay to leave not to stay to leave not to stay if it has been asked not to stay relatively to leave not to stay if it has been asked to leave relatively not to stay to leave not to stay.

Once in a while.

Relatively.

Relatively once in a while.

A narrative of relatively.

They have thought out about they have beckoned them to go in one at a time.

They have thought out about encouraging. They have thought out about encouraging they have thought out about encouraging. They have thought out about encouraging them encouraging them out about encouraging them to begin to begin to anticipate why they went and why they came to anticipate why they came came to surprise apprise one day to retaliate one day or on a day a day or two.

By majestically. If a suspicion to a suspicion three a suspicion four a suspicion four a suspicion five a suspicion five a suspicion five a suspicion five a suspicion to be too around. This makes it pitiable not pitiable but palatable not palatable but inordinate inordinate not habitually in their excess. This can do cautiously content content to content to be to be to be told. To be told.

A narrative of undermine.

Undermine in their interest.

Rescue planned planned. Rescue planned planned. Rescue planned planned. Rescue planned planned. Rescue planned planned. Rescue planned rescue planned planned.

If if the chateau d'If. The son of Juan Gris If if the chateau d'If. Faded. The flowers of friendship if if the chateau d'If. The flowers faded. The son of Juan Gris the flowers faded if if the chateau d'If the son of Juan Gris the flowers faded.

If if the chateau d'If the son of Juan Gris.

The son of Juan Gris if. The son of Juan Gris, if, the chateau d'If. The son of Juan Gris the flowers faded.

PART II

The place for Grant.

I often wondered whether I would have liked it better if he had not taken the name Ulysses Simpson which made U. S. Grant United States Grant Unconditional Surrender Grant but had kept the name Hiram Ulysses which could not have been used in that way.

He knew he couldn't that is he knew he couldn't.

He knew he couldn't.

To be went to be added to be went to be.

Grant Ulysses Grant, Simpson U.S. Grant made at one time very differently made at one time made at one time.

Very well.

Made at one time.

General Grant the general in general General Grant.

Very nearly knew that Sherwood Anderson would know would know General Grant knew General Grant. Very general now in general.

One time when at one time having heard read and read having read heard read read and read the history of the Civil war General Grant General Grant was the most important general General Grant.

General Grant was the most important general. General Grant was the most important general.

General Grant was the most important general General Grant General Grant was the most important general.

Why was General Grant the most important general because he was the most important general.

Collaborators collaborators tell how in union there is strength.

Collaborators collaborators tell how in union there is strength.

Collaborators tell how in union there is strength.

Next.

Collaborators are which when they when they to be theirs to be theirs to be theirs. Little and restraint and by the way and trade and trade and by the way and restraint and little and authentic and identify and surround and left at that and by this and on account and by the time that this as if indifferently and recapitulated and not more than if they please and repeatedly unfasten and find it to be not as much as if they liked and likely and likely to be and likely to be mine. Mine mine mine mine mine mind to mind to mind it.

How different when it is as they said.

How different when it is as they said.

How different when it is as they said.

How different when it is as they said.

One three four two to be sure.

Two there two there to be sure.

Harold manifestly does wish not to relate but to be sure that changed is not changed and changed is not changed. He went to meet him meet him as he went. He went to meet them meet them to be sent. He went to meet them meet them and he meant he went to meet them meet them as he would he be not to-day. There is a very pretty piece of left to it. Left to it. How very nicely.

A narrative of individual frightening. If she were frightened would she be nearly have to be to have to be have to be what is it when there is silver silver in a photograph. Once. The second left to it makes it not be not only a wish left to their being not while one begins to end end to end.

Let alone a narrative.

Regular regularly let alone a narrative.

A narrative aimlessly.

Let alone a narrative aimlessly.

Let alone a narrative aimlessly regular regularly let alone a narrative.

Let alone a narrative aimlessly.

Let alone a narrative aimlessly.

Not nearly young when not nearly young when not nearly young when when let alone when let alone when regular regularly let alone when not nearly young when let alone when when let alone aimlessly let alone nearly young when aimlessly let alone nearly let alone when nearly young when nearly when regular regularly nearly young when let alone nearly let alone when aimlessly nearly young when let alone regular regularly nearly young when. Let alone aimlessly. This is how they had the president presently regular regularly president presently.

They have rearrange tries by by and cries rearrange nearly when aimlessly let alone nearly when nearly when let alone nearly when rearrange cries cries tries nearly when rearrange let alone aimlessly let alone nearly when nearly when rearrange tries nearly when nearly when tries nearly when nearly when rearrange nearly when regular regularly nearly when president presently nearly when tries let alone aimlessly nearly when regular regularly nearly when tries.

That makes narration recede from all around narration recede from all around narration receded recedes recedes receded regular regularly as nearly left and left he had a good job and he left left left left right left.

Change to a pay to a pay change to a pay to a pay to a pay. Change to a pay.

He is to right to a right to he is to a right to in betterment is to a betterment follow follow practically renouncing practically renouncing practically renouncing practically renouncing practically.

Follow to be sure.

To follow to be sure.

To follow to be sure to follow to be sure to be sure to follow. To follow to be sure.

What to follow to be sure to be sure what to follow. What to follow what to follow what to follow to be sure. To be sure.

By leave and leaves.

It makes shells be placed differently.

A long as odd.

Odd add added oddly old oldened and and and iron iron wood wood circumstance circumstances in included plain plainly in indicated mean meant and obliged. Obliged to go to go to go.

Obliged to go.

With held withheld will will withheld with withheld withheld out and out.

Never not to be too noon too noon to be too too noon. To see to too too noon to see to to see to to see to noon.

This is what happened ever to be see to see to be to see what happened.

Having held her having held her having held her to it.

To see to see to it to see to it to see to it what happened what happened to see to it to see to it. To see to it what happened.

By this and on their account.

By this and by this and by their and on their and on their account.

Anyhing to be.

It is in tenderly time and time.

Never come to be come to be come to be their stay never come to never come to be their stay.

Not making it do be do be do be at all do be.

What is that that difference.

Not to describe why I did not go.

A story of remain reman remain tell well tell. This is what is to be what Max Ewing Max Ewing said.

After every time might which let me.

After every time might which let me might which let me.

George Lynes is appreciated.

Everything they do.

Regular regularly a narrative.

Expect to be to be fought expect to be to be fought expect to be to be fought expect to be to be fought expected expected expected in that relief relief to be fought expected in that relief expect in that relief expect in that in that relief expect in that relief expect in that relief to be fought expected in that expect in that relief expect in that relief to be fought.

Parts and parted.

Regular irregular regularly.

Parts parted be stop be stop be stop be stop be stop be stop to be be stopped to be stop to be a part. That intuitively.

How can it be not which is in which as which having having having once two two to be having having having having once once two to be once once once two to be that which means make means make make make it do.

This is entirely so.

Sherwood Anderson came to see me not with a letter from any one but with the consent of being related to it. That was what was understood as very nice. Several years later he came to be one another and one another too more too more one another to more to more to more one another to more. He came to to size to size makes it be happy. Anyone came. That is one narrative. A narrative has to be equally redelivered.

A narrative has to be equally redelivered.

One, two three one, two three a narrative has actually to be redelivered.

Writing letters a narrative not separated a narrative not detained a narrative not an advantage a narrative not silk or water a narrative not as not alike a narrative not in the left it to them a narrative not easily a narrative not nearly aloud a narrative not never to be when it was which one a narrative not planned to replace it a narrative not once when it was useful a narrative not exactly a narrative.

To expect reverence a narrative.

The manner of treating very nearly when it came a narrative in place of not chinese scissors a narrative this makes it a reassembly of which it was a narrative.

How like a narrative.

Easily, a narrative.

Seven maltese crosses under a sheep a narrative.

They made be perfectly around a narrative.

At a time a narrative.

Why not which they sent and now very very soon there will be plenty of opportunity plenty of opportunity plenty plenty of opportunity plenty plenty plenty plenty of opportunity plenty plenty of opportunity very likely a narrative.

A narrative makes individual separations between what to please when it pleases them. A narrative.

In add advancing the this the best in add in adding in advancing which is way to be capable able added to be added adding adding to be wide widening widening a boulevard a street a village or an avenue an avenue of eucalyptus trees eucalyptus trees admirably in an arbor in an arbor gently Max Ewing gently Max when this is very nearly as admirably in keeping. This is what it sounds like when it is not by him not by him not by him not not not by him this is what it sounds like when it is not by him.

A narrative is why equally why not equally is why not only not only not why not equally a narrative is an arrangement of settlement settlements once in addition once in addition.

He said individually five out of how many are five out of five. Leaving it all to him to them. If there is no change why go if there is no change why not go if there is no change why not go if there is no change why not go.

Just alike prefer to be preferred to be. He always heard it between between between which is which is which is built be with. There is not any use in remembering five fifty in lends bewilderment there aroused.

Might be just as once as once request requested certainly not to see so.

If there is no change who has whose whose hear whom whom hear hear hear hear to me to me me differs too to for me for me form me for me.

Interruptedly might just be more theirs as connectedly. Connectedly can always be river boats and not a city see to see to be to connected. Even connected.

Their might just as just as just as much as with it all all to altogether all too shown. Shown especially specially by choice bewilder choice bewilder be and wilder wilder come to gain come to gain in their remarkably establishing. A narrative

makes does make does does it make does it make enchain.
Does it make enchain.

Never stop to be between and to say so to say so to say so
never stop to be between. Remember chosen and choosing.
Remember chosen and choosing. Remember chosen and
choosing.

Remember chosen and choosing.

Might it not be theirs.

Just how did she meet Helen.

Why makes what they did why makes what what they did
why why makes what what they did as much.

Let it be plain just how many days Miriam waited.

Supposing everything is open and they have no reason to
have confidence in hours and hours.

At once at once to be left at once.

Action and reaction action and reaction out and aloud
allowed makes makes find find allow allow why why will they
cloak cloak shoes why will they cloak shoes ordinarily why
will they cloak shoes ordinarily why why will will they cloak
shoes ordinarily in our way our way our way in will they will
they cloak cloak shoes will they they cloak shoes in our way
our way ordinarily our way cloak shoes. Why will they cloak
shoes. Ordinarily. In our way.

Preparing for opera.

If she passes at that time what does it depend upon. It
depends upon them.

She has never been able to eat fish. It depends upon them.

If she is not only not obliged to recall that there is no
return to be to come to it. Come to it is not as it was.

Then this is that to them to like it to have this to it to call
to do to do could it do it for them.

Could it do it for them.

Not find not to find forget forgotten not to find not to find not to find it here.

After a while they were pleased to be asked would they like what they had not only but also as it is very likely to be adaptable.

Even when sitting and not sighing even when sitting and not protecting even when sitting and it is not a temptation who is whose.

This is why they rush along.

Eludes me it eludes me it does elude me. Narrative regular regularly eludes me it eludes me.

If she came in and not having seen her brings it might she be might it be useful. She had had an and rest.

Not that that they had had for them. For them.

Having forgotten all of them as they were not as they were. As they were were they.

Worthy of idolatry.

Follow foot steps.

Worthy of idolatry follow foot-steps.

In addition.

Finances. Peter.

Peter. Certainly.

Certainly did.

Did. Not.

Not. Tell.

Tell. Her.

Her. Finances.

Intermediately.

May be yes may.

Very well my new when be no way be not satisfies me.

At all but she.

There when when it is by the way to be as bequeath she need to have called it called it as a way.

What does he know.

About it.

A great many do a great many do as rung.

What does he know a great many do as rung.

Every three times to go further a great many three times to go further.

White and blue.

And for you.

A great many to be three times and to be to go whether. Whether it is whether it is as to redoubt it.

Three times to go whether whether to go three times to go whether to go whether whether to go three times to go whether. Forty three times. Forgiving identity cards.

Indifferent to narrative regular regularly.

There is no narrative in expedition expeditions.

Finally regularly narrative.

A narrative indicative.

A narrative Cook Houser Blanche and orange.

A narrative of how Cook was met when he was going to a house which had been built very lately.

A narrative of at that time.

A narrative seated by the time.

A narrative to be allowed to have it arranged very well.

One thing at a time.

A narrative back to it back to back.

One two one two one two one two not what is it to be to see to see to be not what which in why does why does why does it why is why is it entertaining.

Way a way away.

A narrative I know a narrative a narrative to be sure.

A narrative of next to next to next to an addressing.

Once once at all very here let it mean that it came to be all of it shown at all like that now as much as much so.

Piece of place of best as it is.

When does come again say or say or say say said sailed.

Finally from it back at once.

A narrative disliked.

Prepare a narrative of all which has held it.

Prepare a narrative of all which has held it.

Prepare a narrative of prepare a narrative of all which has held it.

Out of the whole.

Out of the whole wide world I chose it.

Out of the whole wide world I chose it.

Not in as a candied and by and by.

Candied and by and by.

Narrate how they asked why why it was.

In time.

At least as less as why as will they too.

More orderly.

By itself.

What happened when everything is in there.

Just as likely.

And pleasantly.

With them themselves.

To come as they finish.

And clouded the sky was clouded and there was some wind.

Right away everybody knew that this was what was the matter with it.

No once can return purses altogether.

And allow it.

To be sure they can call it that.

Find it at first as they came here with this as it was in that near at hand made by them to be can leave it with that not

with it and now they must come to be with what it was as
nearly as they can which is when allowed might with it be
that named as much as theirs can be as it might with it to be
known come to be at that said by the time of which it was
meant let it be the most that it had and leant mean which is
for them as it was by that for them to be with it was now to be
come in this at all that it should be shown with with with the
kind of them that is now now plainly as it is to be theirs all
day to be which is it letting them to be known around down
and multiplication which is it as is most in demand for this
as finality to be and proclaimed once in this as interval when
reinstated much has in it well this is with it as they can near
nearly lending mine mine at a time if in particularly which
is united letting in be reclaimed as one if it is not by their
change changing with it too interval with it.

Petted add is fell to be said and selling settled as shall see
shall see shall see to in that this is the sacrilege there this that
the same to to intend to to to intend to color cloud and cloudy
as a house house to house held here and in it this that being
be to be to be tall to be which is mention the rest of it to seize
leave add in on as in actively redenominated in that way and
a mistake to mistake mistaken un under underlying underlying in that time time to to be sure to be to be left to be to be
and to be in to be to be not this is that neither here nor there
merchantly which is reactively leaving left alone not as it
might be to imagine let and letting it in now. They do not
recognise him. By which in mean mean leave it there there
with the nicely to be netted with it now. Not in this to this
extent. Shown as why why did he why did he do that.

This is in the way of their not being left to have it had to
be in time in time to to be a little as it should it be their say.
Difference between say and say so.

She cannot see when it is thrown as it is given to very soon to be there.

Leave it to them a narrative of leave it to them.

A narrative of leave it to them right away.

They both came at one time.

Pretty well to be the most and left for them to send it with it there in that case which is why it is not all that in the way that that is there which is why will it be if it it is in not to be with it as it is in it left to the rest of it in find and leave as will in share and best there will it with it when with with it when with it as it as it in it is is it is it at least at least as left as left to lean to lean around around it colored call and can and carry choose and dot and dot and do declare and unaccustomed change and very nearly as aroused and by the time with this with their in change and as it is by this by this fancy fancy theirs in ribbon in which is it when is it is it a back or is it back to back or is it why they went away every little while and just as sound as sound to sound to be sent to be sent to sound to be sent to sound why they went.

Once or twice.

Why they went.

Once or twice why they went.

Once or twice why they went this is to be here rashly for and by changes with with it might might be become freshly in that case be very much what they asked for as it is very much whether it could be or might it be blindly blindly means furnishes and furnishes as they were as they were let which is might it be not only a declaration of part and parts and leave it leave it alone alone there as is what they might relay they might relay that that kindly that kindly too two in once or twice connectedly as nimble and presently once or twice preferred preferred can be around and left to them left to them into into reinstated cautiously in a place. After this by that time in plenty of leaving it be with that which was best where they must if indifferently rest more than they do.

Very well then.

And climbing.

An authority for that.

By the time that they went.

By the time that they went.

By the time.

That they went.

Alright by the time that they went alright by the time that they went.

In which is it.

Left and might might and will will and come come and now now and sit sit and leave leave and as to have it have it have it all the same. Very many might be once in a while. Once in a while might be many might be once in a while might be once in a while many might be once in a while. Every little while they are to to be what is more after all than Elizabeth. What is more after all than Elizabeth what is more after all than Elizabeth what is more after all than Elizabeth what is more after all than Elizabeth.

There there where where every where where every where where where there.

Follow to two.

This is how they understood one two three all out but she.

That is how they understood one and two all out but you.

This is how they understood one two three four this is how they understood less than twenty.

In letting it follow what is the best thing to do.

What is the best thing to do.

Virgil Thompson comes to-day he will very certainly stay Virgil Thompson comes to-day naturally.

Virgil Thompson comes to stay Virgil Thompson comes to-day he comes to-day naturally.

Once or twice means more than either or before before what.

Very simply if he ate he ate this.

If he ate he ate this.

To-day she said that Josephine was looking very well.

She said that intentionally she was with them now.

She said by that time she said by that time.

She said that she was not while it was there.

She said do that too.

She said leave it to be that she lived to leave it to be that she said leave it to be that the sound of apples.

The sound of apples.

She said leave it to be that.

By calling for it.

Neither have to have it with with with wedding wedding wedding it for them for them as startling as startling ready ready more more to to be be to to be be to to be too.

In inclined.

Cut it as they might to might to might it do to might to do to them.

If Bravig Virgil Elliot Wilfred and Glenway start and pause where where do they carry to and particularly separately in that regard advantages.

Act as if at once at an instant and infringe and matter.

Follow in you in you in you unison too wise.

Where can poetry lead.

Poetry can lead to altogether to lead to poetry can lead to.

Where can poetry lead to.

Regular regularly a narrative.

In there to stay to stay in there.

Have it to show to show it to to them as they as they wish to wish to with it with it by and by having heard with at last that mistletoe is mine.

How do you like what you have.

Once said twice wed once made twice paid once one at a time twice two at a time gradually.

This is theirs too.

Said it did not need one.

In admittance.

Never without one.

With one.

Without one.

Admittance.

Without one

Never without one

With one

Without one

Never without one

With one

Never without one.

In admittance admittance in admittance never without one with one never without one.

One at a time.

Never without one.

Admittance

Never without one

In admittance

Never without one.

Plain and plainly never without one plainly in admittance plainly never without one.

One all.
Never without one.
With one.
Never without one.
This might be sometime.
Just as if they knew
This might be sometime.
Sometime.
Is extra.
Sometime is extra.

It is not necessary to have to go it is not necessary to have to go. It is not necessary to have to go. It is not necessary to have to go generally.

Never mention honorable mention never mention honorable mention.

Never mention.

Honorable mention.

A narrative regularly.

To praise a narrative regularly.

Who could remember that they were Elizabeth.

Elizabeth was will and will also be what is it, to do what has it to do with the future. Elizabeth will be as if when very angry as in shall it be not only some but summoned irregularly irregularly feeling not felt so and as the difference and differences between as as well.

This makes having never and now never known very well that married married well well as much as ever if easily upset if easily upset. Follow what is said what is it and when if angry and when if angry never to fear if when if angry never to fear if when never to fear if angry never to fear never to fear never to fear if angry if when if angry.

The next which is why in mother mother to be said.

Sarah was a mother Estelle was a mother Harriet was a mother Adele was a mother Isabelle was a mother Gabrielle was a mother Emily was not a mother neither was Janet or Katherine or Helen. This makes them a mother.

Boys and girls tease the seas and this makes them either a mother or it makes them either a mother. After they left. Then theirs it was theirs which was theirs by this time which was which was it whose is followed by whose and at least at least makes it at least a leash makes it at least and having to wait two weeks having to wait two weeks makes it at least.

They need not be as hard-working as colonists.

Once every once or twice obliging and obliged and obliged to go and obliged to go there for them.

Obliged to go there for them ineradicably.

The thing to remember is that if it is not if it is not what having left it to them makes it be very likely as likely as they would be after all after all choosing choosing to be here on time.

What happened when this is true. All this has been in introduction. Now there will be a narrative of undertaking to weigh them every day every day after a while.

An undertaking to weigh them every day after a while and a narrative of their using it now.

Believing that it is studied they are believing it as it is studied.

Studied does make a difference between Versailles and Vincennes. At Versailles they have a palace at Vincennes they have races. So much for fountains and after a while.

A narrative of undertaking to be only very well attended is what they used they are used they used it for it. A narrative of undertaking to be chosen not solely because of probably remaining.

A narrative to go on.

There is no difference between ten twenty eighty and five hundred. Thank you very much.

Narratives indeed.

A narrative of found in time also a narrative of sequences.

How many loaned it to them at once loaned it to them at once.

Go on.

Come along.

Come on.

A narrative of what wishes what it wishes it to be.

It wishes it to be not by the time that they were there. Ten years as little twenty years to be twenty years very well read twenty years having them come ten years remaining to come remaining to come to come. Come along.

Come on.

That is at once.

Twenty years in their day their day twenty years after this twenty years which is when it was by that time twenty years leaving it be nearly fifteen fifteen has to be has to be five five could be said five and twenty to have the habit of twenty-five.

A narrative in union in union there is strength.

A narrative not only allowed.

It sounds very like a narrative not only it sounds very like a narrative not only allowed allowed for it it sounds very like a narrative to me. To me.

Wider than in and out as wide as they wished they wished to talk.

If they wished to talk why did they delight delight makes it one at at time. This makes it a narrative of obligation. He was very much obliged for it. He was as very much obliged as he could be. He was very much obliged particularly as they went everywhere together. When they did they were particularly nicely finally they did it too and very likely. Which was it that they decided after all was the best. Going that way they might see flowers not as early as they would if they were left to do it at once left to do it at once is why they were very affably indeed coming to think of it. Nearly all of it was what they might like for themselves. In this way remarkably in this way very remarkably very remarkably as much as if they were always not believing it just for that. By the time that they were foolish. Who could be liking to do it when this was all that they were able to finish and because they were estranged they were very evenly which was as before when they could and divested of it as an interest.

How could she read.

What is it that they do when they go to the country. What is it that they do when they go to the country.

A narrative of lucidity.

Everybody likes to pay for it.

A narrative of elegance.

They must be left to themselves.

A narrative of irritability.

How old is it when it is very likely.

A narrative of intrusion.

They arrived famished at the best hotel.

A narrative in place of this and blame.

They might be willing.

A narrative mean to I mean to be going to be once said.

Follow is exchanged for follow.

This is one.

One one one.

Parti-color may be united.

United and untied.

Never as obliged.

United and untied.

Thank you for sewing.

This is the way to see identically.

Now a narrative to state that every day and every weight is nine.

A narrative in order.

There is no necessity for resemblance.

Easily reminded of it.

Emptily on purpose.

Used to be confined to it.

A narrative means that larks sky larks come to settle at a distance and likely as much as they arrange not to mind it.

In their intention in place and a place if it is not by the time that it can be having been where if having passed it like that very nearly when it did show itself as very accurate. When to come. Almonds eaten every day all day disastrous. Advising advising advising very very much very much much repeatedly wish which dating it from their having been twice two times leaving this as left in time. When an impression when an impression when an impression aloud to do so when an impression aloud to do so with it all. This must be it. Neglecting bread not to notice butter. This any day any day orderly. Relieve a difference between. Succeeding is one differing is one deferring is one defeating is one one and one one to go there one detaching one one one from one it never can be so to to be so to be so which is to be so. Intermediate commencing. A narrative of in union there is strength.

Wonder wonderfully.

By by the by.

They this their there to there there is there this this to to this is is in in the nearly adding in the next. What is the difference between building rock and fertiliser. This makes additionally.

Any day which say say which is it which is it to be asking

after after it is certainly ensued. By means of originally and master and master pieces of it stupid stooping large enlarging reputably ring ringing as it is.

In sight.

It never came to be there more more which is it.

How can emptying be around. Which follows by the way. Leave housing housing makes it come to be in violetly voicing leaving same same the same the same too. Continues to be sure to be sure to be sure to be sure to be sure.

Evenly as which a house which a house there.

It this in this this is this is this is culminating with in within within which is which is why delicate denuding of depriving this when when is it. To follow another by asking.

Can a narrative be dependable.

A narrative of their having known when they were leaving as they were to go and by the time that they went they were to be certain that it was as much as if they could have done it.

An essay on narrative.

A narrative has been feeling that they might be seated.

Now and at a time they were before it was as before the interpellating of in reunion, a narrative of in union there is strength easily.

Around two houses.

He went having been in.

Around two houses of theirs presently believed.

Accustomed.

Prevented preventing inordinately relieving which in best best of believing this mingled frantically remarkable extravagantly letting it alone.

They might with a win window win window wish able held in preference reference send invitingly so so.

An account on account in in to be dismissed by that time.

It was ready it was ready readily readily refrained from it to within hearing mainly as if in presently if it was left to them usefully usually very easily in referring in fact in fact to it. Any award will do it.

A narrative in union.

Letting it be he came back.

Finally to say so.

She came in.

Sedately to arrange arranging actually there was was having been left leaving announcement of twenty times not twenty times as they would of course they would.

What is the difference between narrative and conversation.

The difference between narrative and conversation in conversation really in narrative rather often.

Very good.

The difference between narrative and description narrative as if it was while they came description leaving it in plenty of time to do it.

Difference between conversation and description all all to go and description all all of it very much what when it might happen happen comes to them now.

Anything described is other other patiently with by leaving it much of it to do so.

Anything else.

A narrative leaning out of it by apples. To like it as they made it out of it by their on their account.

Having never been to be gone once.

Marion Lane Ripley has been met again or so.

Found found fond fondling fond to fond to fond to fasten fastening leave out.

Not at all.

Hannah Seton Richards bend becomes doubtless registered and hurry questioned by that price if it is a name.

Hurried half and rapidly in the in fact she was most admired.

It could kind by greater greatest example of less for it when this among the with this be for now.

Amongst.

Never to deceive by all by all.

Just as balanced.

There is a difference between forty minutes and forty miles.

It is.

They grew.

It is.

Bay grew

It is.

Bay obey tea tasselated as let red send being twice as it was leaving in this are as much extolled. Extolled two range arrange at my time.

Have have ahead ahead of time.

In place of feather.

Whether.

In place of weather.

Leather.

In place of leather.

In place of leather.

Accounting.

It is very well known that they would be sunk.

Much more not be them.

Much more not be them.

Much more not be them.

Fully out and out outer.

Do do which is true true to gracious.

Advancing as much as much so much so much still still as it it is arranged arranged longer.

Could it in return.

Returning.

Light.

Lighter.

There is no one two three there is with the with the wild and layer.

Supposing two were too many.

They do not mind.

To consist in a bench bench of theirs with the chairs with the chairs the chairs stairs stairs come out in come out in come out. There can be no confusion.

There can.

There can not be any confusion.

This is why before before water this is why before before water this is why before water before water before water.

It is not necessary to have that.

A narrative.

Be used.

Relatively refused.

Refuse.

Relatively.

To refuse.

Very nearly right.

Very nearly.

Right.

It will be all of it a day.

They never say.

A

A day.

Having escaped it.

A narrative of audacity.
Did not dislike to have a room.
Alone.
A narrative of their appeal.
Either why or either need it now.
Some say.
It is under but not over.
Once at its best.
Not now.
Stopping makes a narrative not stopping but stopping.
Very likely crossed as high.

PART II

That may help.
More or less that.
Identical.
More or less that.
Which is that.
More or less that.
Identical.
Which is that.
Daffodil he will he will Jonquil he will he will.

In this way remember and tries. In this way not left to in time. In this way it might be clear. In this way it comes in time to do so and at highly left to it.

To let it come next.

A narrative of made a mistake.

A narrative of made a mistake. To know now a narrative to know now now to know a narrative is like explanation it says so. A description is not like narrative it does not say so. A narrative is not like in a minute it does say so a narrative does say so it is not like description it does say so. A narrative is not like description a narrative does say so.

After this a narrative.

A question is not an answer. What is the difference between a narrative is not what is the difference what is the difference. A narrative is different. A narrative regular regularly a narrative.

A narrative.

A narrative tells in tells a daffodil he will he will a jonquil he will he will.

A jonquil he will he will a daffodil he will he will. A daffodil is different from a description a jonquil is different from a description. A narrative is different from a description. A narrative is different from a description.

Will, an undertaking.

Not to come to be to be to be orange.

It is not to be to be to be to be sure that they they all day all day to be sure it is not to be to be to be to be sure that narrative means all the time they walked away.

What is a narrative collaterally.

Inclined.

A narrative has to do without it.

A narrative and in an especial an estimable an indefensible an understood excursion.

A narrative makes how to do how to do how to do aimless. A narrative makes it might it be made minutely in their delay.

A narrative in their detail.

A narrative separates delay and detail letting it be in forget me not plainly. A narrative shall be rejected by their delivery and in employment. A narrative left idly. A narrative in escaped places. Why is lightly in escaped places resumed and unused and violently and denial and deed and in deed indeed crowdedly. A narrative makes bewilderment bewilder in their and high highly has to be heard. A narrative which beneath beneath led to them to them indicative indicatively bright. A narrative to be wounded. Wounded. Wounded. A narrative leave leave precluded with their made to it be well as well.

A narrative will be will be wedded wedded wide widened to them at at to relieve relieve live light butter unusual reluctant time is it time to be here.

Having refused a narrative and with reason.

Having refused to do to do to do to do to do as well as that.

Having refused a narrative.

Having refused narrative and for a reason. A reason for having refused a reason for having refused refused narrative for a reason.

A reason for having refused a narrative for having refused a narrative for reason for reasons for refusing for reasons refusing narratives for reasons refusing narrative refusing for reason refusing reason for refusing narrative for reason refusing narrative a reason for refusing for refusing narratives narratives for a reason.

Easter easter is a time.

In time to regulate ministration and administration and letting it easily reduce their denial as if in lain as it were allowed allowed to be deliberately rejoiced and went again two even as it is so.

Very you likely as very likely will as you will.

In time.

Never a name never a name surname a name a name never a name never a name in time.

Imagine two leave.

Imagine two leave in time two leave a leaf a leaf as leaf as a leaf as a leaf two leave two leave as two leave as two leave at a time.

By their beside beside two beside beside and beside beside which which is when to tremble tremble to to tremble to to side to side to aside aside by by a side by side by side side by side tranquilly.

Makes meadows so and so so and so so and so makes meadows if it should be hereditary and delighted and daily and returned and indubitably and with a grain and left or right and might it be enchained enchained and robust and with come to color.

What is the difference between a follower and follow me not and be so beside. What is the difference between deliberation and their delight. Narrative and surface who says so who says so how many surfaces are there at easter.

Who says so should be once again. If meadows are believed believed believed with one or two.

A narrative of there for instance.

A narrative might be as once in a while they would be having to go to Africa.

What is the difference between travel and to travel and a description of their engaging it to have been what they would wonder if it was not all all of it.

Remember narratives are continuous.

A narrative might be what if older older than they were said said so might be said so might be said so.

A narrative is as they wish.

A great many people to see Africa.

To see Africa.

Glenway Westcott to see Africa. A narrative of to see Africa a narrative of to see to see Africa.

What is their difference.

Arthur E. Donaldson meant to be one of those who had been included in a roll call and he went and there is a title a courtesy title a title to be called Arthur E. Donaldson and often to have been very welcome originally and always. They might willingly know the difference individually and authorise reluctantly that and finally and taking place integrally.

Would it be his to-day.

It is very true that usually they were surrounded.

Who makes which of them do this now.

Prepare there.

It must be as at once.

As at once alight.

It must be as at once neither of which made theirs speak.

A narrative is at present not necessary.

That is theirs.

Theirs is theirs.

They have been what is the difference between skilled and will.

What is the difference between will and very well.

It is disappointing disappointing disappointing what is disappointing.

Appointing disappointing.

What is the difference between will between at will between at and at and at and at additionally additionally which means in and uniting and uniting theirs and they they are related.

Might any one be advantageously as they went away.

As they went away might any one be advantageously and at entirely at a time.

Why which is as wishes.

Not in kind. Kindness.

Allen and a trade.

Edward be saved.
John be in a stand.
Albert as wishes.
Which is wishes.
Which is as wishes as should be renounced.
There is no difference between net and nets.
Why nets.
Allan and in a trade.
Allan be sure.
Allan to be sure.
Allan to be sure and in a trade.
Remind mines.
And alike.
What happened every day.
They were discouraged.
If you are discouraged what do you do.
Able plentifully to have this for them. In reminding.
Every one two any one two candle sticks can make a noise.
Allow it.
Need it and fine find find finding inalterably.
Could any narrative be a a more. In more.

Finally George

A Vocabulary of Thinking

A PLAIN GIRL let it be Susan. Finally George.

George is the name of George Lynes George, George Bracque, George Ullman George Joinville, George Williams and will with it and George Middleton. This makes it recognisable as the name George.

Bay likely.

A bay is a body of water surrounded on all sides by a coast and at one end of it it is by a passage which can be very well arranged open to view. And this if there is a climate which makes it attractive makes it be as much as ever attractive. It replaces a wider named gulf.

They if they see that Burgundy is a prettier country than where they see to it that they are in preparation for life. He loves to be left. And she she loves to be left. He loves to be called Philip and she she loves to be called Camille. She loves to be called Mrs. Helen Landor. He loves to be here with her. He called on her with the two of them and not with him.

It makes no difference if it is colder than she says since she is anxious that they should like it.

It might be that they would die.

If a man has been at all theirs to be known as finally it is more than they like.

Probable probably is the most that they can say.

Find it for them is the most that they can say.

Very easily measured but it would be very much worth it.

How can they too many try.

There is no use in joining purchase to porches

To know what to say.

Anything that means two fishes. Two fishes are enough for three people.

Out and out.

How many are coming in while how many are going out.

She looked like it because it is said to be a resemblance to an exact reduplication of their being captured, as it is announced to be very often for them.

He might leave all of it for them.

Identical twins do not look alike, they have beside that being one more and the other less less likely.

How many houses have changed enough so that some one has been left to see to it.

All for George.

Any George.

It is best of all to be met and meant for it.

George was born and his name call him Edgar. He was twenty two when it was known that it was indefinite. As a little boy very little and playing there surrounded with them made it that it was kept. He knew left to right and trees and shields and a Jesuit Father. They were all taught to be left to them when they were standing. This is what is made of it sufficiently.

Perhaps.

If it rains and they are not heard the rain drops and if it is to be certainly agreeable she will be reflected as very well known to them. Twenty and plenty.

Much alike.

Why do they like it to come to an end so that they can try. Why. The end is that some time when china lilies smell like chinamen.

If they can be angry two days.

Like to try if they can be angry three days.

Like to try if they can be angry three days.

Like to try if they can be angry two days.

Like to try if they can be angry three days.

There is no reason to be alike when mother love is very much more than if they were indifferent. Assistance. Very different but much more by themselves. And very much more with it as they were to be more all of it to be among. A disappointment in being in between.

George Masters.

If two and new makes it smell of prepared leather it is very winning of them to be allowed to smile when they are very much known to them as one who had been found not to have been killed by the men who had killed them because he had been with them and this made it be not more than ten years after and he was very pleased that they gave it to him. He could have been.

George is a very full and resounding name and has been given where it is suitable but it must always be given first it must always be be given first.

Some know how George is gentle and bewildering gentle and bewildering. His name is George. He is meant to be superfluous and he is very much more than in the meantime. And how often is it that they do not cry. In the place. Of many cases. Of what they might. Like just as well.

A makes aimless.

It is very much needed exchange changing this for that.

George shines out one two three four about it.

What difference does it make what they do if they are getting up sitting down and walking around.

George is sadder Monday than Wednesday if they like

Gerald and William Thomson. George is fascinated by liking it fairly well. It is monotonous to be fortunately preferred and to be very well known as much as that. And very likely it is by that time that they are very much as they like. Now then.

When they say two do they write two. Do they.

When they say five do they write five.

This is theirs yesterday.

When they say I will be as much liked as ever are they pronouncing themselves to have been in presence of an arrangement which they have left to them to need it before and after.

They do not say one two two through. They see it after they have no after why and why after by and by after now and now after then.

This is not what they say.

What is the difference between what they say they say how much is there there.

They do not say that.

They do not see that.

Now and then.

Now.

And then.

Neither is divided by the other. And so they do not say so. They say what they think. They see what they saw. They will when they have. And more than often. Back again. What is the difference between repeating and back again.

Think and thought, hear and bought. Shoves rhymes with loves, and shook rhymes with nook.

Conversation. Conversation is not heard they like to leave well enough alone.

It is not necessary to be troubled by their not wanting it

because their not wanting it is not a trouble because later it gives it away to them.

Did he live to believe that it is not well enough done.

But it is when they look that they have one half of it given to them. How many do not deny it when it is best to have it only to this end that it is not an obstacle.

They made twenty times more preparation for it. And how much to they say they are to be opposed to having it be theirs and left where it was when they were able to have it given them to be added in case of its being very useful and a pleasure.

It is mainly for themselves alone that they are employed. And very much of it to be known as very well and very well at all.

Writing may be made between the ear and the eye and the ear and the eye the eye will be well and the ear will be well.

To be faithful to George who has not been very much needed nor very much in the past and the present and the future. Very much to be examined as if in a bank of very fragrant very fragrant and beneficial very beneficial and preparation very much in preparation.

George did see eye to eye and did hear ear to ear.

George Banks George Danbury and Georgie Cheetham who looked like Lord Roberts George Lynes made fairly. What is it. Is it that you have grown tall or that the houses have grown small.

George may he.

It does not look like two and four it does not look like this and therefor it does not look like the rest and remain we know John John made George come George made it be much more in and for a reason.

George is very well known after all is said and done. Will they need to call them to come if they need them to call them to come.

Perfectly true.

She would like it for dinner. It is true that it can be transfigured all the same.

Begin now.

It has to be of no use to remember.

That to remember very well.

It has to be of no use to remember that to remember very well.

Now will weight and well enough alone count.

A narrative is a piece of what is made to be that they do no wish to be let alone to be hurried.

Let it alone to be hurried.

Slowly remembering another George. George Levenenko.

George Washington on horseback is printed.

Averagely book of Georges.

See them ask willing to be of the center or once after the last of the twenty in the beginning of the extent of the ones that furnish the found and facing the interim in interval of in the end and the coincident handling of increment an assistance within therein in a point of recognition made generally by the time they invite rightly within their resigning as much as for their attention to be whether very much again in private and pertaining to which was formerly an interval to be more convincingly an inestimable distracted allowance of relating their rejoining to individual with standing as they wish it to have more relative marking more than is at issue. A plethora of particular without fright merely how do you do that for them.

Come to be a queen for George.

George Banks thanks for having had a division between himself and his two brothers one old Alfred Banks and one younger Edward Banks and their neighbors over which they ride. Do not be mistaken. Remarkable to be clearly intoned. In if it is to be left what did he say. Not remembered. What did he say. He said that they would very manifestly advocate an alignment in favor of their experience. They would partially inaugurate their remaining permitting it to be of use to any one of them as they prevail upon them to be kind. Shown and shone an argument. A phase of elocution and their voice and their restraint and their result and their vertically and unallowed within the placing of irresistible depression which can make meandering a reason for a cold river out loud. Now preventing in the time in which love is sought and so how do you deliberate in place of their allowance for well enough alone. It might be George Bracque.

George was in a minute with the pleasure of their half and half to-day. At present.

It is quite politely a precedent.

That is conversation which means greeting.

Georges Allans Pauls Christians and Virgils.

Coming to be pearls.

He is very well which is an advantage when he is resting. It is very much a disadvantage to them by the time that it is furnished partly to be carefully adjusted within the appearance of their establishing bilaterally an indication that to the most attractive interpretation in an announcement they will be having it bestowed upon them by a particular detailed origin of this and nearby an impediment in their rejoining. Come to call him. It is leading it before and behind. A bed of a river when it is very wide and only shows the evidence of snow in winter not in the spring nor in the summer can be delighted by and by by their being more if it can it which it is. Forward to their distance and for which and for this that it is pointedly known. What can they be when they are carefully shown. To be attracted to the making of irregular exhibition of with standing a distance. Tenderly to own. It is not often that a name is forgotten forgotten but is it theirs to be named with it. George is the name of George Lynes also of George also of George Danbury also it was the name of George Banks. George Banks had had an illness.

Does George wish to be the only one to come if he does wish to be the only one to come it is because they have been finding it very much what is it when there has never been a George who has not a brother.

Georges Allans Pauls Christians and Virgils.

Accompanied by fifteen women.

They meet on the grass which has been newly cut.

Four or five Georges three or four Allans five or six Pauls one or two Christians and two or three Virgils.

Contemporary Georges. Having to be in ice fields to sunsets with pink clouds and a plan. Rice fields te sunsets of pink clouds and a broad sword with ice fields with drawing a plan. Contemporary Georges withdrawing a plan.

It is very well to believe that it all happened at once.

Georges have half the time in which to place it where it will be covered by a rose or roses on the cover. At least just as well as whether withstood. They were as quickly near it as if they had been enthralled and by the time that a space is made with cement and surrounded by their stationing it with their representing one or two or three or four or five or six or seven or eight or nine or ten or eleven or twelve or thirteen or fourteen principal places principally. This made it that they stood in the center. And looked about.

It is very well to have made it be almost when it is that a leaning it behind with whom makes it be inclement and it was a very beautiful day with very little wind and every way ordinarily after day before Wednesday. They came to be left to it as closely. As if in on a ground of making it be a factor in suspense. They liked women wishing. It is not before theirs in which by in relief to the most and when it matters as much as an allowance to determine that hoarsely is not because of told. It was made fortunately as to-day. To-day and a peek into which leaving readily as might it be when very well wished. Very well as an instance of theirs so gloriously. It must be quite a while.

Not half of it have to like it all the same. And so they have a name for it.

Have to be almost lost and known as well as when there is very much to doubt about whether it can be claimed to be and not be known better than by the time that there is very much to be given for it as they please themselves and have to have a name for it. It is wonderfully reasonable of it to be known as an alternative for it by the time that they have been wishing for more of it all the time. And so they might if it is better liked than it has been. Which makes it be that George and Georges who are contemporary just like as when it is bestowed by their folding it one at a time tranquilly with it in place of their changing an effort to be allowed to be told of it. And as much as they can. So Georges feel very much better than if it were only one at a time carefully to be lost to be told. Very many frighten very often as much as it is best to see to it and is more than theirs and just as elaborately. Kindly be very much engaged with all of it that can interest them further which is just what it is.

The best they have when they look like that is that it is

very like the relieving of it by the one who felt that it was very well for it to be like that alone and left to them as fortunately it would be by the having it planted like it and formidably pursued with and for itself as much so as ever.

Who can say that they like it very well when it has been removed particularly in an outstanding habitually left to their consequences of having very likely bought it for them. They were out-lived by being half as well known as ever partly with by the time that it is left to them they have it as their share of more than all of it which is more easily known as wanted. Leave it to them. They can be as much when it is more than a case of their being willing which is why when it is very well known as having been beside that allowed they may be advantageously left to it in irresistible withdrawing of their allowing it to have not possibly seen it yet.

It is more than they had with it as very well known principally to be now after it after the pleasure of whether they would do so which was what they wished in their doubtless leaving it as an impression. Undoubtedly they do.

They made it just as durable and they do not very often and otherwise believe it to be as may be just as well as within when they wished and nutritive is very well established as better than their sight. They might be within reason very well known as may be they can be careless with what is as much theirs as before if they are very well because it is nearly by the time that they can which may be why they like it so much they will be withdrawing what is of no matter to any one if they are without it as more than at once very narrowly left to be coming as much as they were very often better than it is made between leaving it and having it made as a mention of their being honorable. They like why is it that they must see to it that they more away from the next to more of it as it has been after all.

Laying one at a time where they put it might do.

This is in a place of Georges. Georges have many names where they are awfully well prepared to like to do it now and it is not because of that that there is nothing to say about it they were indefatigably pleased to remember which had been partly to blame in leaving it to them to discover the indifference there could be to their annoyance every once in a while considerably nearer than that more with it as in a contribution to their originally failing to be as much as well as that. In consequence.

It is very nearly that they like it so.

Place to return.

To wonder if it can be called remaining it might do for that which is perfectly paralleled and rusted with in union without making it be just alike very much as a merit for it to have remaining almost as much as they stand with and without their not knowing it to be why they have it in as much as when it is only slate and they were very much confused perhaps because with and without clearly not much for them to see.

It is not only close to it. With them they were just as useful. They were prepared to be very nearly gained and it is not only individually but for theirs a use that they can not be what is it when there is preference because it is invoked in the same way with means and it is a blank well without it which is why they are nearly so. It is not only all the time that they are abused and believing with it as an exchange because why varied with it in eternally reminding them of what they did which was just a chance. It was not more than it is like it that it is indelibly left to them to be very much aghast when they were left to it which is not what they are willing to have seen. They were always once allowed quietly and left to have it not more than they can raise it so much as they need to be

thought very well on account of having more with it in the
afternoon of their returning it for them as it is by nearly most
of it. Which makes it do. Mainly for them. With it as a part of
their having it be always in an aspect of changing it around
for them as they like it which is why they use it too. They
might be often there. It was more than they had to give them.
Leave it out. Which is what it made. And it is always very
well known.

They might be indifferent to all of their not indicating
which one they went away from it every once more that they
were changing it as conveniently as it was acting in a way
when they were very much better if it was not to be placed
there very much too much as they knew. It is because of their
wading in and about which makes them certain to an aloof-
ness to their pleasure with it for them principally nicely to be
by the time that it was shaping it into a next to their wonder
which made it obliging. Leave it to be so that it is there when
they come. Idleness and it is not more than they must be for
them to be whether it is more than just very well if it was a
pity that they would not be further occupied as they had refused. It is for or for them.

Made to-day it is as a better than believing in leaving it
inevitably as their change. Surrounding one two or having
blamed George for just as much changing the return for
across. It was what they had beneath in care and in allowance made it be plaintively as change. Hours and hours.
When they were this that allowing more chance predicting
classes of windows that made a place which they made. At a
time as they were with it all in excess mentally in
reincorporation of their having had twenty times in excuse.
Reasonably so.

By the time went away. At the same with clauses. The

clauses were that he would need to come up from the south and they were mainly in question. It would be a plan to be more than drying the thing that is if it could be a likeness. Very well then.

It is a mistake to like George William Paul Christian and Virgil interminably if it was to be that there joining brought it back to Henry. Henry and Henry. It is very much as much.

To find it do may be so if it is this which is it. When it is in the meantime there is with it as a principal with it in in the meantime as it is not to be in the next after it is not to change this soon soon then send it left to this which is in climbing to be soon to be that it is as if it is with it all in time to settle it as well as all that it is in estranging them frequently lying alone in the best of it all to them and as scarce as when it is much as it in the middle of an interval to oblige coming there as nearly by the change of it to them when it is more mellow for that in the likelihood of the most exchange of never the less then in an instance better if when there coming to be the next which is when value and variety to be sent with in the mounting of their insistence to be closed calling for the with it just the same then and so much of it to be with it as left in a distinct refusal to be shown that it is not with it in between left to them very sent to be to known around with it in the same establishing with it frequently in around may be nearly this and so much for this frequently to be made will it.

It is very much as to too and better needed with the best of it coming to be leaving likely as it was to have sharing left more than in in every allowing it without in doubt frequenting needfully to be nearly when it is in shall with it more as it could be left for it to them counting why is it in a place of the nearest to them where in it is more desirable for instance.

Come to Jesus.

It is about this time that there is more beneficence than there will be for a cloth made very well made with blonde fur and a hat in the shape of a helmet made of black felt that is silky and very light in weight.

From there to there.

It is very difficult to know whether that makes it so.

How to account. Refuse for it.

Georges just the same.

It is a remembered fact that they like it just for that as they do.

While they have to be there just for the time that it takes for them to have the time in which if when he is bed ridden bed made plainly by being higher it is better that the one who at a distance by the sea shore does not ignore nor preserve it for this industriously as if when it is yours with held mine withheld plainly to be known by a conversion of believing that animatedly not frightened it is by an infusion of their ostensibly not having rightly recaptured their abandonment of including it as a fancy for having in the past refused their shame to be ashamed to be particularly with it in pursuance of their liking which is fairly when it is believed that not an instance of it being attractive by reason of their using an inclusive title to having fifty to thirty years run around so quickly. That is why they must be nearly as well as when they can be found in addition to their refusal of mending it as formally if it were asked as advice and moreover there are rose bushes that can be sold at five francs a piece in the value of money as it is at this time.

The Georges can be divided to sign themselves Albert Joseph.

It is alright for the most of them who when not entangled may be called and accredited with not knowing whether it is manifestly in exchange because of the tendency to reunite and to insert when well known to be a cause of their rejoining not because of it peculiarly in the arrangement of their denial which if in the behavior of their announcement might be advantageously calming it as well as it could in place of it being an insistence upon the melody of which it is a strangely and passively arranged denial of their preserving it as placed once in a while differently a measure of their relating it to their renewal of finally leaving it as much as if within in certain as especially with drawn and disliked underdeveloping of it in place of it with it in and on account of their estrangement comparing it indefinitely with the urgence of the leaving it to the known neglect of their referring to it particularly which can be nearly what is as much theirs as when they can relatively be called away. It is by no means what it can be left to be known as calling it feverishly the same as well to do and all more by the way of it in the circumstances of it in with and because of the withdrawal of their being more than half of it in the best of their planning in a circumstance which makes it casually theirs in the meantime as they have of course to be lost with them. It is splendidly in behalf of not only not enlightening them to be affronted as well as they may within the particular relation of whether it is the cause of their withdrawal of when in preparation they plan it. It can be learned.

It is partly the same and they need not indicate which may be separated by relieving it for them as they must do when it is not to be called in ostentation withheld and preferred in its advantage when because of an interval where there beside it is in reference to theirs in the plan which they made as it can with all and beside more so. Frank could be called George if one were used to it but one is not.

After all an abandonment. It is very much with when it is in an entanglement of wool and stripped of after all their might be as much in reliving what could be called distance and a colony. Moreover there is in pageantry which can within and imperfectly restrain more nearly when it is an incessant release of their abandoning it partly where in and behind behind and besides should be eradicated as completely as withstanding made it pay literally as perplexing which is their might it be an effort of their arrangement which it is if they are recalled as having noticeably made it be what ever is made with and without them. It is past and best known as their delight and they can encourage it with more than it is within and called for as it has without any reserve been left to them. It has been left to them. Could homes be known as not known.

This is it with it as it is. It is better to have two and seven that is two longer and seven smaller than to be left to be delightful as they please and they do please they like to have it known as very much which within when they made it change from their having been all alike owning for them what is after all to guess well as much as for the change of their adding this to nearly there which is why it is not intangibly left to the meaning of why they ask whose has it been in change and they are inclined to doubt what it is that makes it perfectly clear where it is fastened to their obligation to have all of it told to be no bother as much as ever which is why they like the most that they can do as much as they ever choose which is very well thought out not only as it has to be very much adjoining left to them partly as to know how very much any very likely it is unanimous although left alone very clearly as it is at sight that they have known it as very wounding to be intentionally and very frequently leaving it to hers to be left almost as much as when it could not do that any more than it would to be perfectly happy and not by the time it was very well arranged to be often thought out as much as ever as they wish which is fairly well known and partly all the time very much as it is wise and careful of them to like it or not if they choose as well as ever if it is told that very much as it were to be laid alike and too many have to know do they like it as well as they could be certainly shared with them for this and by all it is very much whatever they can affection-ately leave it like that coming as it is when there is more than there ever has been very nearly likely to be thinking that it is very friendly as much as when it is not with it if it is wished to be alike and they do call it as much as ever they can their time one at a time and once when they were said to be with it all as much as to be careful of seconding them reasonably partly as they are to like it to be more than they had with it and willing which is why they were unable to be always when it was more than they liked which is why they are attractive and remarkably as much as it is very reasonable of them to be calmed as much as they are by being in place when it is mentioned which is very much their delight all the same which after all means something as it does which is why they can be all very selfish and they do know that it is attributable to partly why they went and they came whenever they liked which can make it do as much as ever they must when it is very likely theirs all the time as it must be if there is not more than they can when they might be more and more very nearly always after they can be most unfortunate in having heard bells and be all of it with them and once more they can be said to be nearing it just as they were.

It was too many altogether and it is more than very much in a place and they might with and without it being not at all as it is made to be all with them in particularly arranging for it which is quite harmless and made it most without it in pressing upon them to like it all the time which they do. They do have to have the most that is where they like what is in a difficultly pointed adding of why in a way there is more arrangement than they have with it in immediate leaving it for the most in no order at all which makes it place it finally at once when they were welcome and it is not more than if it is more in with and all they may coming to be though very hardily arranging to be more with it worth it worth while of them all and so very much as it was it can be more to be sure than sufficiently with it in place of theirs in union. It is more than they liked.

Does one have to ask about how it happened that we saw them doing it. And whom should one ask. Would one be satisfied with the answer if there was every certainty that the answer would be given. Certainly yes even if immediately after there would be another occasion of telling about it and having not an answer at that time but an uncertainty and so at no time would there be any doubt that it was very much what they had up there in looking up and observing it as well as the one who had not been any farther away. This always comes to that. And that to them. Is there any difference at all in being certain.

Once very often they might be known to have left it as much as ever it could be come to be as might when and can should and would almost be awfully well pleased to know about it.

A name if she asked why is it not known as something then they do not like to like to have to be meaning to be not more than an excuse.

The Georges whom I have known have been pleasant not uninteresting and finally one and finally more often very well estimated as succeeding intelligibly and not more than is necessary as presidents are useful. They are useful in extremes. So can there be doubt of Pauls Christians Virgils and Williams and even Franks and Michaels and James and pleasures. They can be united in resemblance and acquaintance.

A nightingale makes it be less expensive.

It is not a better thing to provide splendidly for their best way of learning it for them to have in place of often with it at will which is when in estimation and this is called with this at once when in a change they make and might be challenged to show that they have no more use for their entanglement than they had when they were indisputable masters of their amount of mine and with it with an impress of not having particularly a thing which is an advantage in literacy with and between and ardor for because in entitled firmly to be more than in time to be conditionally when left to it as it is when it is why they come to be most indifferent to having tried to cry as they very well could if they heard a sad story suddenly as it were within a part of the time in which it is more than especially allowed to be an absence of their withdrawal of by and by very likely to be more than ever intending to explain in what way they were inviting one at a time to be fortunately left to that alone with them where they were once at hand as with it it was most often plainly as much as by preference in a detail of their intention to be detained as very likely to have happen to have leave it for them in the way that it is best to allow it to change nicely which is why they arrange as for instance in the way of their rejoining partly of in exchange and by the time that it is mostly increased by their attention to undeniable interdiction of their remonstrance for which thanking is not pointedly in place and reddened as if with and because of their return of their very many parts of their understanding finally what any one has seen which makes having it do it very much whenever they like which is why they add it and leave it every bit to them as is very often made to be shared as plainly as ever if they please which they do conditionally in the meantime for their sake which makes it leave it to them at once more than they ever have if they like it in plenty of time to diminish their having it with great difficulty as best known to themselves in more than any case which they would because of it as it is more than they like. It is more than partly that in carefully trying in leaving attachments and more than with that temporarily in case of it having been that it is very much with it might it have been left to them to cry and plainly when it is a betrothal they may be an authority in their arrangement which may make it cautiously be circumscribed by their renewal of their obligation to be called that it is more nearly an effort to be more plainly wishing to have it made therefor that it is in the more than betrayed finally an instance of their fashion of leaving it to them to please it with the only hope that there is there. May be they will but may doubt it and can it be felt as much independently and within use that plainly it is a partly interrupted and firmly intended part of their pressure which is brought to bear to make them leave it as if they were prepared to be useful to them too in the way of adding instances of their arrangement which is methodical.

George and Georgey no name to be used when it is a pleasure to know that there is no difference and to tell them so.

It is partly their way to win.

It is next to leaving it for them that makes it be undeniably partly in plenty of care for them as they were to be stationed one at a time so that it could if it were to be balanced very well that they were indulged particularly as for instance it might be that it could be more in order that it is partly with them in actual reconsideration of when it is to be more than it is plainly as much as by the time it is allowed which is in relation and in connection with it as an enjoyment of their pretention to not normally leaving it as part of the time to them in the place of their surrounding it temporarily to be within sight of why they went. It is very much to be deplored naturally. If they found him in the snow would they be sorry and would they try once he was well to remember that there never is any snow there even if it is said that it is very much like but that it is not merely not only not temporary but admittedly not an advantage and it clearly is as there has been very much sorrow taught by their expecting to be nearly in plenty of time since they did go away. It is more often than not troublesome to be obliged to ask have they thought of it. And so do they like to leave it for the most and very well known additional example of their having it partly at one time and left alone which might be why they continue to measure it as they do with the difference that it can be left to the most and very obliging person who with it could be leaving very many to them. Why do they try if they care to be left to one or two as much as yesterday which is supplied be more than it can place as much as that with it at once. Which they do. They might and it is always what is asked that makes it have it as failing to be satisfied with at the moment of their preceding it as an appointment which is absolutely what is usual. And it is always very well done. Remembering it could be known that they could be visiting every one that had been having it very much as it was when they were there. And how do they like to be left to themselves. It is always what they do when they might be worth having it liberally as much as they could see it in the most and very nicely thought out way of distributing it to them here where they have placed it as they say. It was almost their voice.

Not in the morning because in the morning it can relieve them of the necessity of having to choose not between but because of the most that they can state by the time that it is not thought of as a relief to it if by any chance he and she were to come together and state that the time which was more than enough to have to have as if it could be ascertained that they arrange the rest of it in the meantime as believing left to them with an alteration of their arrangement with soothing and left to it mostly as an elevation of their allowance which must be strange as they are inclined to have it very nearly as much in an allowance of their pressing as if when left to them they try to be not very much with and behind in the part of the arrangement which cannot force them to be patient as long as there is more in the place of their arrangement and closing it to them as much as if it were partly only playfully left to be dangerous to an inundating plan of their having oceans of intervals and mostly as they liked. It is part of it as it is in a blunder. They were called and more than they could they were perfectly plainly understood to allow that it is undoubtedly dear and perfectly with it as an understood trial in intensity which can be compared to invidious and partly theirs which whenever it is bestowed fairly often at the same time as their surrounding might it which can be most authoritative have it as plainly as their being willing to know it of them that it is bewildering to liken them to their not withstanding disappointment in arousing chiefly the most that it is best to be artlessly left to their order to join in ordinary anticipation of plainly adding which when it is a disappointment they can reunite at most actively in the interests of their allowance which is advantageously left to be genuine as they say with no additional interruption in the attraction of their opposite. It might be that he would marry. He could and it would be of no disadvantage that she would be wealthy excepting that it would be of no disadvantage if it placed them here and there in the indifference of their collecting their really pressing necessity of interupting as it were they very much like so to speak generously it has been noticed of three.

Having undertaken never to be renounced never to be diminutive never to be in consequence never to be with and delayed never to be placing it with and because it is an interval it is extremely difficult not to make sense extremely difficult not to make sense extremely difficult not to make sense and excuse.

A very little way so they say go away a very little way go away go away to obey as they say go away any day to obey as they say to go away to say to obey to go away every little while because beguile instinctively necessarily ubiquitously in addition to their surprise that it is by reason of their making it an advantage that they could be more than it is as ludicrous which is why they were faintly pronounced as indicating left to it in the interests of their allowance and it may be why it is deplorable that they do need to be not withstanding as more than it is because of their attaching as plainly as when with and partly it could more than is witnessed as their disadvantage more reliably connected by the best of it all as it could and more frequently an inspiration to their belittling it as it is without any doubt an interesting and disliked ability to be a phase of their best and very agitated relief within and very much as they were without it being more than attributed to withstand their hope of bettering it melodiously and refreshingly as it is within and out of it in plainly to be perfectly resting without any disquiet in connection with an inevitable reliance upon their exacting it to be noted at once which when it is he has not met him which is a pity.

With whether it stands. Allowance of whether they are right. It is a pity that very many who have meant to call them feel that it is right to be overwhelmed by a comparison between whether it is anticipated that they might have been very much as much as at a disadvantage because whenever it is met at once and finally there may be no mistake as to inequality in their obedience to their denial that in exchange they may include their persuasion of restlessly being in an unbelievable likeness to the most that is encouraged as plainly as when in authority they complain that it is very well as happening because in interminably they do not reestablish what is partly as measured which can be in contradiction to their allowance of unpretending resting upon the best of this in it as for and plainly they can join without the renewal of it in a pleasanter relation to the newly accepted relief of their having made in the interval as noiseless as when they establish their decision to be more than it is in preparation for their entirely having the most of it in the effort to prolong their allowance of the more easily advised pleasure of the more than better effort to be thought equally so in the decision of not only fairly but merely as it is as thoughtfully betrayed by variety of their aiming to the more adequately esteemed origin of notably adjusting this frequently in the arrangement of their appointing the denial of the chance to be of use in the practically allowed behavior of the rejoicing obtained by it at once. They might even not be certain that it can be predicted in time to be very much with the movement of their having in the meanwhile left it to replace the joining of their autonomy which is a provision of liking it as a widening of the appearance of their appointment of the remainder of the obstacles which make it like it is which can be inordinately as preferring the indication of the anointment of the vanguard of appealing their might in pretending to refusing the moistened end of the calamity which can replace the outstanding emptying of their persuading the integral in event when it is by the most attenuated belief because of it in addition to the value of their having been inclined to surreptitiously leave it in behalf of the more painstaking liking of the most which is why they are hurried. Anybody can recognise a fancy.

It is a delight to love it and to be the most after all worth while of them all

Having explained pardonably they with what is more than indeed relaxing as elegance in their having it majestically surveyed which is when it is not to have it frighten them to be more than satisfactorily courageous and planting and their with it with it do to more than after all as labor in exchange for their placing it in within to be more noiselessly fancifully if it means that when and for this as persuasion which can invidiously refrain from their suggesting it as more than noisily. After a while they do it first.

George can do if it is to tell them that he is attracted George can do what might be very favorably left to them as their having been with it as a chance to be more restlessly predicted it is not very much as if they like it. Having feared as well as hoped.

It is as they know the regulation made abundantly in relieving the absent thoughtfulness which particularly in the middle which is not toward the end they might favorably if with in the next of having by attacking the genuinely relaxed fermenting of the intermediate explanation of their allowing without which it is integrally their reliance upon the most which is an advantage and now she opens it just as they said she would.

Georges and Georges George and Mary George and James George and Jenny George and George and George without her George is a George advantageously George may be seated in the midst of company which means that every forestalling is done. George and time and may be they have to be very much prepared to be said to be without it any more. Any more candidly. It is very much better not to be fearful in the face of plenty and plenty of time. How do they like it. They do to do it as much as is in advance of having made a mistake. It is back again to one and twenty which is twenty one one and twenty and they are like the very most that they can name. Relieving it as they do and not to be more easily playing with the advantage of their being told that they do not follow a another another day to-day if the rest of it is by the time that it is in division. To explain non continuity by experience makes it be very much because the have it as the rest of the exchange to the pursuit of banality which is a pleasure a pleasure is a treasure trove a treasure trove is when she knocks sooner she does not knock she calls.

In an ineradicable arrangement with them they eschew their delight in rising alone in the afternoon of the middle of the planning for their release by means of it at one time as left to the more nearly having an advantage in politely adhering to their intentional robust devotion to their tidings. It is mainly so.

If fairly well she saw it sell and it was not very good because it wa-s so large that if it were reproduced there would be and is the largeness of the grains that make it inedible and it is particularly there are as many as if there is in estimation of believing that if it is to fall it can come to be all out but not as with it as a purpose just as he is which is manifestly not fairly well established in allowance because and with it in a peculiarity of their containing and whether it is more than delicious it makes it narrowly have it more than if in impenetrable rapidly without and peculiarly in outwardly having chances of their applying for it in the partly chosen expression of their pleasure in it as much as they may care to do which when certainly more having it fairly prepared and on this account they may be theoretically be chosen as more than when it is by word of mouth in copying from this to that in order to have it be no more than it was a pleasure which can be at last more than half and half in the preparation of their intermingling which without and by the mention of their not unreliably attaining to more than forty of all the most which has been as very well seen by reason of the behavior that makes it have within and laterally laid down without their having sent it a little way further which when it can be mostly reliable is with it as an authority in the meantime as an arrangement of their relation to the pleasure of their surrounding and mostly it is a very good thing to like it very much. They might be very much as if they were left to be having more than is usual in no time at all and they may without any question have it in view and perhaps when after it is to be called when they can it may if there is a pleasure in their not letting it be more than a pleasure at that time it is fortunately because of their wishes that they do not betray themselves in the habitual resolve to be cherished with nearly that which is indubitably and made it in renumeration when they have not without release of more than fifty birds made it without and a pleasure to have managed to be artificially related to the next to prepared interference with their leaving it as it may by very much of it in integral independence more than it is without and leaving and it may be more than they have by reason of it elevating their certainty to the exposure of release which when without their amounting to their ocasional resemblance do more than change which is very jointly their deliberation which is in the occupation of their bewailing made plenty of traditional liking for the next and very much appointed union of independence and denial of why they came which they did in time and widely as it is shown that they will place partly more than it is more than notoriously without hindrance in so far as they do search and more pleasantly advise the nearly possible advantage in their deliberation which is when it is more often aware of the renewal of the most willing to be needed as how and why they do not behaving as unitedly as they need within the more than their praise of the aftermath of settled arrangement to prepare to come to have it do. It is very nearly very well liked as it is which is the most available release of their beside this when it is nicely postponed to the artifice which makes it usual in the so to speak liberty to radiate the capacity to withhold which when common to the needle and the pleasantness of possible silk using this as a withdrawal of their appointing it to be what is if when there is no use for it the best of their habit of having in plenty of time nicely rearranged to their advantage which when it is of benefit may accrue to the more advised pleasure of their relieving it at once of the nearly played part of their payed attention in excuse and apology for following one with another. It is partly a trial of the pleasure of their knowing that it is possibly a reminder of which it is that is in the ordinary allowance of more than having half of it in repealing the most that can be said if they were to replace another which can always be an arrival of their precision in being along when they came which they did as they heard that they were to be sure to be able to go where when they did they must at all times be not very much disposed to have an attention to the disappointing leaving of it as it is to be in the future mainly without and a pleasure to their having it more than it is within the way that they say they can account for without it being at all their fault. This is why they do not have it without any pleasure in particular places of which more hereafter when it is more suitable to have it known that they will go away and it is by various practices that they make it of some account which is just why it is when they are very often told to be better known and very likely they are exceedingly reduced to the most entertaining form of deliberation because while within a given space of time they might be disclosing just the thing that they want known which is very presently what they will do and in this way they might without reason have half of it continually which is just what they will do as they said. They were more than very likely pleased to say so as well as to do so which they do and they were very lucidly leaving it to the best known avoiding it more than it could have been done by this when that is where they are to leave it when it is done and so forth.

It is a way of letting it be partly hers and theirs and it is also a way of their leaving it one at a time as often as it is of any use to any one. It is moreover as much as they care to allow them to arrange it and it is by the time that they are ready very much as ever plainly put their for their pleasure and they enjoy it which very likely they do.

Coming with and an arrangement of their being more than half placed in an allowance of the most elaborate and very careful interchange of left to them in case that at a distance he would not undertake to meet him which he did not refuse to do. It might be the most and very much a great difficulty to see that five are more than four when three of them are dead two not responsible for being living and one perhaps refusing in addition. And they were how to be left to them inescapably and with an enduring pleasure in surrounding it as with one. In so much they were of use to them and at the request of one who had refused the matter was arranged so they thought and so they did and as much as it is in hopes of their being more than quite often never mistaken. Never to remember any more of wishes. Just a little of the most that they can do. They need to have had it planned for them. They like to know to what extent it will be done. They must surprise them with what is not by any means rarely attained by their having without any placid fervor seen that it is more than an especially politely and whether or not pointedly praised insistence upon that at that time and if it is with when they come it is more than if without it there is to be left where it is in following blindly very well with eyes shut.

In speeches never to refuse what he has said coming handily from word to mouth in pleasure and excess of the more than ever usual having it plainly returned if it is possible to hear them turn the way they did in precisely a pleasure of having it placed upon the most uninterrupted jeapordising of their return to an advantage in an instance behind the merely added whether it is beside which it can be entangled very much as if in whether never to be said to be clearly an infringement of their patently admired reconsideration of their regular provision of having one taken out of two. One taken out of two two are there and one is taken one taken out of two.

In very much attending to this as the most when there is that it is difficult to know whether they wanted it to be so and

it is a plainly admired presentation of their resemblance to
the renewal of the advantage that they have in their allowing
it not to be pointedly known as once and for all as they could
attribute it to the nicely left admitting it to be more often in
inestimable recurrence of their determining when it comes
to be that there will be changing to the nicely thought out
reversal of their uniting it to the more advantageously placed
betrayal of evenly once to be not obliged to refer to them in
choice which is because of the newly arranged flourishing
bestowal of the might have been handled to be inarticulating
it without more than because of their deciding leaving it more
than it has more often to about arrange the continuance of
their deliberately satisfying the choosing of the elaborate arrival of why it does not come to be furnished which is more
than having it be in a preliminary charge of intentional restlessness as they say because of without the more left of the
interpretation on their account it might easily be that they
were discouraged by not half of it having the same as ending
where they were beginning. It is doubtful if by beginning
they mean in the first place.

Sound sight and sense around sound by sight with sense
around by with sound sight and sense will they apologise
truthfully. Come to allowing.

As often as not as often as not they as often as not were to
be going away.

A plan that is made and causes it to be that if they were
after all not behaving as if they could by an indifference to
an extravagantly prepared advantage which is by nearly their
importance advising them to be more than as well as if by
the time that it is to be comparatively obtained in an intentional adjustment of the renewal and bestowal of whether by
the chance of their adjoining they may be colliding without

an impatience which can be changed to an addition of their bestowal which is in a way might it be shadowed as because of this which is an objection to their having whether it can be an interval of it just the same which is preferably not only a reason because they may be that is if it could be to notice that having looked to see. It should never be an exact copy. What is the difference between starting and starting and when may they like it looking part of the time as is very much their hope that they will be without in the meantime furnishing it as an advantage which it is to the more delighted explanation of their being very ready to send very many apples.

Politically do they have to be known as George Middleton or George Mayhew or George Wilson or George Arthur or George Leroy or George Watson or George Hardien or George Pleace or George Veron or George Arlen. Might they have measure in all things. Might they be politically orthodox and expect to place it where it is which is very well known that if she does not every day hear what she sees she may be mistaken but this is not at all likely because in the very best hope of glass and resistance there should never be any mention of either at once. One at a time makes it be very much as if when a large and larger to be doubtful lest they are wary.

Very much as they do they may be the most that they have as an advantage to delineate the more than hopeful withdrawal of their arrangement and may do more than with and they can have it be as much as in comparison which having it challenged and replaced they will without the most refractory denial be saving it as partly as they would in annoying it which is for them as a better than their usual ingratiating arrival of partly without it as with them that when it is most and preparatory to a renouncement of their indignation they can insultingly agree to be disposed to like to have not known that it is at all as they could which very prettily makes it do it as they have more than on that account beside the arrival of their disappointing wonder as to whenever it is to be thought very well of. It is very difficult to avoid parts of it. Once in a while they may cheaply leave coasts where they were. They must be very often told to look alike and they do not please every one as they should because if after all they are in the more than half of it as ready as they could illustrate their occupation of arising from a meal every three at a time in the interval of occasionally replacing theirs in estimation and coming comfortably to the most as an advantage they will call. It is more than they can as a surface follow fellow and the hope that it is said of them. Begin now. It is more practically as they like that it is as much as they ever have and it is more believed than it could be in the meantime that they are all in derision of never fearing as a word to be chosen because of the unitedness of their having had a home. How much can they be as much liked as ever. Anyway now. It is because of sighing that it is very much that they have of preparation in leaving it to them. Anything as an attachment whom did they used to know. It was as if they could be very likely as in an interminable using of collecting it as more than without an appointment to have it be coming to have with and precisely in comparison to be an arousing of the peculiar and more than effort to be known to be hourly which is in subdivision in lots to suit. It is plainly their desirability which creates what it is in the pointedly ineffaceably refusing of their reiteration of appointment to be nearly left to it alone which is more than has been attended to and may be of importance really. It is very absently altogether which is more than in transfiguration which means this is what they call them when they are very placidly disturbed by the name of a

street. They like to do it. They are very early at it. They do
not deny themselves what is more than having it and they
are very much the better for it and they are using the best
and very nearly their voice to decide it. It is as much as they
care for. They do what ever they like. They never relax and
they are very pleasant when they come to-day. They know
the difference they look about them and they find it where
they wish to put it and after all it is more than that. It is partly
that they could contain what they heard in that way. It is very
well to be open to influences. And it is not at all what they
asked for. To continue to come and go come to them and
they will come to you.

Once in a while as any one can say it is very well to have
it have it better as it is in case they should in place of after all
knowing that it is the same as that. Do they like to have them.

In the morning and at noon and after noon they were
occupied in reading and when not in other things which
occupied them because having made a list it was practically
never a possibility to carry out all the activities indicated because although there were no interruptions nor differences
of direction naturally there would be a completion of each
activity and in so much so there would be more time occupied in the interval of passing from one to the other even
when that was ever so quickly accomplished that inevitably
and also as there were small interpellations which not withstanding an allowance were allowed for might with the very
best management add minutes to partly hours which makes
of it without question a division of partly needing to add coming to relieving and were there as is very often a habitual
accomodation to their reasoning that they were inevitably
what would leave one poor would not make another one rich
which was partly why they had prepared more than it was

ever at all likely that they would partake of as in unavoidably
referring to what may be in a management of indifference to
an estimation of their appointing it as a principal failing of
having it be believed as their own without an interview which
made it be with renouncement and so if when because and
fairly they were without and bestowed as changing they might
which is in origin because of their willingness to be re-
proached which is in all at once without an arrival of their
indulging possibly in the most as if when and believing it
categorically as being without a doubtful pleasure in their
renouncing the most advantageous arrangement of their suc-
cessively desiring to be wondering about it. Coming to have
it better than it was without more attraction than could be
earnestly belonging to the more intricate plainly attributed
the more often represented changing of theirs to them particularly as in an effort to not remember actually the color
actually as they said actually to be sure more than it is by way
of this which when it is aroused very well as they must with
and by the mending of their applauding of it with and without especial leaving it as very well to be added to presently by
that time which without any after laying it to be known peri-
odically without their renewal of it as it can be shown which
differently from when that and altogether it is not beside that
that they are urged they might have it be very much to blame
as they could without it being partly as if they were more
than they could without their having been differently aroused
to unite it in their particular variety of making it do. And
now then allow then and not to be unequal to an apparent
likeness to their approach which they may do and partly holding it as their arrangement which can without a part of their
arrangement makes it have an application of their withhold-
ing because proverbially with it and by their with and all

leaving it which when having rejected their announcement partly and enjoined with and more than which when they can indifferently rally to the most that they can do exclusively. It is more than they had with it they were very much pleased to have it be gaily adjoined to the realising of wherein they were more than acquitting themselves of the advantage of which when they had they were by the change of their being reasonable which is by the most of which they have beautifully released it from them which is why when they have it as a joy they were plainly allowing it to be more than they had without it being merely finally bestowing upon it in the more than ever that it is without their being thought very well of and they may by the time that they do and do have it as an employment they might and it is without their only pretence of having it be left yesterday may be without which and because of their very well choosing what is more than partly every little while they may interruptedly be more than it is to be nearly fairly every once more their own which is in a choice and they can be very well known as having been very much more briefly left to them very readily with it as an interval of their being not only more so but as wholesome which is a change from that it is by the time that they are with and without as they were more than as carefully as ever being when they were to be asking it of them centrally which may be an offence but can never be as much as they would have been known to have as an annoyance which they might very well to be left to it as it can be originally an allowance of with and more than peculiarly without an acceptation of why they were to do it too which they did as indeed is very well known because by the time that they are indifferent they may be more than having it made in methodically refusing to advance every time that it does make a difference which might never be what they wanted altogether if they were very well pleased with it because it is not by any manner of means what they liked they were to like it just as they did and they were to say so just as they said so and they were to go just as they went and they were to have it be partly at their disposition and they were to be disappointed as they were expecting to have more left for the next who were to see to it which is why they were praising it to every one and then after this they were to move it away and they were to allow it to be left where it could do the most good which it did in just that way and they were very well placed to see to it and it is not only because of that but by liking it very well that they were to be always more and more regularly left to go out as often as they came which they did and it was very much as often as they were pleasing it which they can without more ado have it shown and they may be perfectly right and they may not have to have it be left more than every twice in ten times which makes one in five times and they do like it and they were as often mentioned as they could be without any effect upon the ones who were leaving it to them.

It is more than without the more that it can be with a challenge to them to be known which is very well as the murmur of their not being placed in such a way that they can be more than forceful and they may wind it as much as if when it is by any chance theirs to be more than having it made regularly with and by the time it is in memory of their not needing it to be more than devoutly which makes it change and they were very much as much as having it be not only without the annoyance of their doing more than they had done hardly that and without any reaction to their doubt of having been without a placing of it more at once which is why by any chance they may like it and after that very much

as if with the reversal of their leaving they may be in referring to it have it which is why they like it as much as they do
they were to be not very well or very little known to like it
and they must come again to tell of it as they are more than
ever just what they can do without doubt as much as it is
which is really very nearly more not a burden and they may
come to half of the time have it be why they went away and
they came and it is left and because of that they are to have it
themselves very much much can be much mistaken and so
can it without any acquittal of it for and to them which might
be without it being usefully in the more than that having it
as an astonishment which when within and they were as very
often as if counting they can be very cosily and as much as
with it because of this and that amounting to it which it does
when they can be acquainted with their allowing it to be
having more than they had because of it as it is to be thought
out and very well best of it as it is. It is not known that they
are to go there. It is not known that they are to go there which
is when they have not only to be late in going but they are
very pleased to stay and they are very pleased they are also
very pleased to go which they are. They are very pleased with
everything it is not at all an ordinary thing for them to be
delighted to have it be changed as much as it is when they
are to come to do it and they do not allow for it which makes
a difference. They were very well pleased to have it do.

At no time is there very much of the same thing that they
like and they like to ask for it. It is a great pleasure to know
this and to be very much at their service and to be very much
more agreeable than if it were only that they were pleased. It
is also not only partly but altogether true that it is as they
wished. They may be very much obliged as they are when
they accept what they do and they are very often very pleased

to see it. They may be also as much as ever without doubt not at all more than half of the time with it because without it half of it the half of it is more than they care to very readily declare to be what they must know about it and they like to be without wishes which one of them does not because by the time that they are very lively they are beside all that very nearly vivacious and they may be in doubt which is more than they are very careful to have as their having thought that it is not more than without it which it is not as they may very well say and moreover and not any one can follow without it being more than a rejoicing which is an example of their having it as a more than in plenty of time and it is with and for nearly a half of the appointing of their being without it which is in very much of it without it and more than by the chance of their referring to it as it is more than why they ask. Why do they ask. They ask because they answer and they do say how do you do when they are far apart. They allow that for them. This makes them try it for themselves and they are partly wishing to have it alike which makes it very often in between and they with very little of it to be lost to them can be joined. It is very ardently their wish that they might be kept very much as much as if it is what is not without partly their coming to be having it to do which may be an advantage partly within there.

They may be with a better half of which is with the more that they can do when they are without that that is by this time not to have it felt as much as they can to displace the next that they can find without it having been not only not neglected but with it as an instance of the most that they have in joining it relatively to the more that it can be traced without an opportunity to declare that they might be very much as well as they have known that they can be left to which it is in regularly being more than worshipped which makes it an alternative to having theirs meaning it for this at once precisely to determine without and behalf because it is not only theirs to enjoy which can within and by the time it naturally can be aroused which makes it plainly follow in the more that it is known in leaving it like that they were not this is the remainder of which very likely it must be fortunately in the performance of their burning it as a pretext to be submitted to embroidering without it have it to be left as it can mediocre in reestablishment of what they wanted to do well by the way of their impeding it from the next to the best that which may be in a trifle of the welcome that they have with what they come to get by the part of the time in which they partly have it lawfully to do as it is as if it could when to wish partly in halting in one place they may languish as when it is primarily what is used as willing to be seen restlessly enjoined in mainly repairing it being theirs especially as when they wonder as it is more than they have to do securely to arouse the partly without vindication if it is what is meant when they came they were to be much of it to the use of their peril which is as plainly as if when it is more than they have as a likely to being sent as a message that they were pleased which not in argument makes it around but they are barely with them to be spared from the continuation of leaving it out which makes them do it as often as just the moment that they with the middle are able to do not the account of the winding it partly around and it is satisfactory at least he says so to the explanation of their having willing leaving in return with the named pointing to the privilege of which when they sent they occurred to them in boundary of which if it could be with welcome as joining in establishment of their penetrating which is told to be left partly to the exchange of their surveillance and in trying it is not what they could have asked them to do by the time it is furnished to them inadequately employed as a renewal of which they were in interval of minding it as when they are privately having it made joined to the liking it as much which they did they said they were fascinated. It is very easy to stop first. And a disappointment makes it a promise of certainly the next time making it twenty five percent better even in detail because being a finished after the mainly out willing it to have because of their beside which it is in partly they may come to be with the fact that it is not what they sought as it is more than they can allow which they mean to have as strings and they do not wish to have it after the littler one is not more than they can be nearly very well certainly as they do not offer it to them without it has been for them a very interesting time as they can be not only very much in intention but they do more often have it left to the best of it because very finally they must be when they are to be known as much as they have to be all told like it. It is more than ever their own to do with as they choose because it is very heavily lost by their being willing to leave it in the more particularly partly left to them to keep which they have. They might do it even more often because it is by the way of their being thought to be nearer to it very likely that they are with more readiness to be chosen as around in the neighborhood of adding in plenty of time advisedly in restfulness which is why they make a joke and they do not measure it as which it is by the place because it is made primarily as a condition of their having fancied it would change which it might do providing it and they were to leave it to them to more than engage them to verify it as a pretension to the most annihilated part of the beginning of their intention to be wistful in as much as when landing they may be not only sought out and congratulated very much as they would like also they could relieve it from the minute detail of naturally changing the rest of it as it is more than invigorating plainly and as a use which when in plenty of more than when they must be patiently fortunate they do not much like to say it by the fashion in which it is amusing and it is guided to the best place that they can see as a fancy of the opinion that it is whatever they have had enough for it which can make them hold more than ever of the combining of it in plenty of time for them they may can please themselves very much as they do do it is not hurtful that they should change if for once more which they have as they very much like to be outlining it with the middle very much richer than it could be in part of it added prevailing upon it to be with as able as they do not countenance them to like it because it is very much where they have had it be nicely around and thought because it is with pleasure very much with pleasure. They were to know it at once. Once or twice once or twice once or twice once. They were to be very much at a time in the arrangement which can be made as frequently as they have to have a favor and they were in the place of their being more than it is in coming to it which they can do for them it is not left to them to be more than it is not which it is coming to have it be what ever it is of it to be not only nearly with and without holes. Can in place of than. It is thicker than water milk is not thicker than water tea is a different color and can be golden or yellow brown or brown and fresher than ever which is why they are possibly ready to put it in place of black.

If they two they and they away from there that sounds like it. So that they may be favorably asking how do they compare with it if it is very different from left more of it than they expected to which is what they must do if they are passing it along in the most that is why they are asked to have it which is more than they like as they need to be at all very nearly appointed to join without any of it coming to be around when they were more than it is in rejecting their amount of which it is when they are frequently told how much of it they like and they do mean to have it be what they had by the time they were to come all at once which is now. Out and out. Come one come all this rock shall fly from its firm base as soon as I.

It is very much what they had when once in a while in a way they made it be what is not particularly their characteristic. They were to be caught by an outline and also they were to be very much moved by having it be more than related to the appointment of their having it do without they also could without blame be very much in after it was to be thought much when they could in preparation come to be calmer which is what they did do in asking it is about the time that they are to take which when to and for and mostly it is not by the time that they are not any more in preparation which is a pity. Not to mind it. Do as they choose. Follow it or not. Prepare it carefully and let it be whatever whenever and wherever there is more than they can like and they must be after all very nearly perfect. They must be coming. They must be changing it in every way because if it is to be what they can estimate how many houses are there. Houses should never be known at home. This is why they must be very careful to have it do. Our Mr. Goodfellow this is the name of Nellie's lawyer at least she thought he was her lawyer but as it turns out he is Albert and Sidney's lawyer not Ada Ada has no lawyer she is to have a lawyer. They are partly to blame. So deeply does she feel her distress she can not but breathe out her bitterness.

Allowances have been made. They are very pleasing and engender this as reliance upon the recurrence of their departure which makes finally it be not in preparation but by and long and notoriously which is in refutal of the resemblance in recalling it artificially for appreciation. It might be that there is a caligraphy of repudiation which makes it vainly a rectification of the reliance that they have upon the prevalence of appointing it as with them mainly in recalling permanently those who have left which unavoidably is debarring them from the deliberation which has plainly been retained and so fairly left to it in timely assumption of their indifference to maintaining it in costlier appointments of it at one time because without it necessarily entailing more in prosperity they might being very disappointed leave it to them to procede in joining which is always worth smiling by nearly very intently judging the distance. It might whether they were to be bitter or not they would with a fairly added arranging of interruption deny it for them. George's article as to the newness of difference if there had been quarries underneath made it of itself be without highly denying justice in itself which becomes originally their allowance and they may be finely placed where they may care to do it as alone when they must which is why they are coming up and down in response. Pardoning the delay.

Two nuns inside a motor omnibus and a nun driving it that is it. They got out before they came to their destination. No one is anxious about anything within the meantime whether they are likely to prove adequate to the situation.

Not to regret that it was what they wanted and they would rather have to be what they gave when it is as if in the case of some one asking for it at the same time that they had moreover because of an actual refusal of the desirability of leaving

it in a pleasing frame of mind without an arrest of their playful accessibility to the original distraction of relighting the
usefulness of their withstanding by an appointing of it in actually being painstaking which is why there can be no remittance of their alienation from the understood admonishing
betrayal of alacrity without reappointing it for Friday which
alarming them to the meadow which is in undated and afterward frozen does placate the reasonably assuredly boister-
ousness of their inviolability to the nuisance of not winding
it up measuredly with the resistance of their redistribution
and plaintively allowing it to pass muster as without it there
may be plentifully remained as coincidentally attributing to
it the noiselessness of their reunion which is in denial of the
might of weight which vainly could be a research in the
amount when it is continued as only at all comparing the
account by means of an announcement coming actively to
be volatile because addedly they might considerably in profusion come to be variegatedly left to the betrayal of their
instigation which without noiseless as much continues with
an announcement of lending it partly plainly as if merely
connecting more than should be chosen at a very well known
place where they can be seen to have more of the come to
like itas much as they have done in the past which is why
they need not be so carefully placed as it is when they like to
know more of it then without this as a change bewaring of
naturally planning to appoint them more capaciously than
hitherto as can be readily perceived with in no case an instance of noxious poisoning of the sources of their relinquish-
ment of intermediate pressure considered as in an interval of
not only having known it without more ado as it can be in
exchange of the more mystery which is pointless unless needing a pronunciation of with and whether and withstood and

inability and consideration and violently prevailing in order
not to be thoughtless of which it is more than controlled
without connection to be refraining invariably commenced
for this alone more in a place which favorably situated causes
violet to be known totally and they care framing it as moistened essential collaborate in traversing unifiedly please to
be seen in alternate windows which can place them with a
hundred and more twelves which is as sewn barely on account of the annoyance of would it do to ask it of those who
do not remind them more than they care to be sought as
claiming singularly partly with all pressing it for this as a purpose maintained conceding the alleging of conditionally fortunately pointedly with spoons as made in a bill of lading
which makes it regrettable that there are these conditions
which do prevail and yesterday make it not have it gently
pressed as concisely leading mainly with all the remainder
of not as it is politely vindicated as a negative changing of
pointing to it in appointing this which is badly renewed as an
imposition of which in ignorance eliminating more than is
prevailing with an amount of it not adversely countenanced
as promulgated in pacifically which is sweet to be which is as
sweet to be as cane sugar growing not on a tropical island but
a temperate climate which is known best and never has it
been allocated to the primary use of Bertie Applegarth or
Esther Pain or Ida Jaffa or Victor Frisia a train of which meant
to be in an ordinance of furnishing it for them. The amount
of it is as they know very much very useful very needful very
well and very contentedly measured which is why it is most
material to have it very well known very much as they do it
very nearly all of it very happily with it very precisely
antagonised by their remonstrance which may be why they
never know that they can be followed which whenever they

are coming to be sure of why there is the combination of time and again they are always very uneasy and they prepare to fancy that they are coming to be known as farmers which is not only as they wish and could wish but also as they wish and could wish and on this account they are worth needing more than they have in their parallel of nervously lending it ahead and in so far asking of it that it should combine tremendous and invited colored and invited and a calamitous withering of willows which have not been properly planted and will concisely praise the considerable and favorable judgement that is very often passed in commendation merely by a aggregation of vainly disturbing the most that can be heard which is why when they are ready they might say that they will do as they like it makes no difference what has happened nor does it matter by which elimination they are forced to confess that it is dangerous and might they like it if it could be brought about that there is no mention of pleasing them by the same as a token of without which they are harmlessly widening it considerably leaving it for them to decide because it is a matter which is not more than it has been understood will be undertaken mainly as an expression of their willingness to come again because it is by the time that they are all called to come out that they come out which is hardly what they meant by liking it by liking it as they never will admit that more than that they are more than they are appointed to refer to it principally fortunately it is not what they wish that they call they call come one come all fortunately it is what they wish they wish that they were to be left to be added to the part of which they now see that they can without difficulty share partly altogether in an absorbing of without ways and measures of combining in plenty of work which makes it definite that men are more fragile than women that men are more fragile than women and it is not an accident that with or without that the most that can be had in a very faulty appointment of more rather than the ones which have been known recklessly to leave it to them may be it is whenever it is a pleasure to be shown all of it as nearly as they can being convinced that it is practicable because by the time that there is this arrangement there will be about as much as is truly kept in that way more than in investigation it can be shown that afterwards there is petrification which lends in rebound to more than very well as very well known very well known part of it might it be what is desirable when they do care to know that it is very plentiful which is it. It is as much like it which is when they are partly very pleased. They would rather read about the sun.

It is at last made in a way known in case of perplexity assailable prevailing for instance as a cause to be doubtless playfully caressing with a chance providing in a advantageous collection relating to a nondescript weathering of pointedly choosing violently withal namely in place conditionally without in plenty of rallying surely in appointment bestowing combinedly permanently choose with on account of the past point of adhesion to the principle of why and better not notice the announcement of winter coming to be known as the shortest day because it is nonsense as many as are able will sing they will sing water boy which is a negro song but not a psalm it is a song of not asking for the plenty which is abundant nor for the noisiness which makes them say Mary and makes Mary say something but not only without changing little for let and letting it be very much having it join that. Mary could be a color. Stella could be a color. Alexandra could be a color. Katherine could be a color. Pauline could be a color. Nancy could be a color. Susan could be a color.

Hilda could be a color. Four more in plenty of advantage.
Afterwards they were in especial after nearly awhile made
considerably entwined changing precisely indicating eliminating dominate with whimsically joined collaborating even
if unknown pointedly long undoubtedly lining combined in
precaution perplexed more chambers where there around
benighted as a fashion of willing it as a recollecting coming
known allowed with or without made easily a plantation of
winding it with wool made in a place where it is well known
that they can be candidly frightened almost as much at once
which whenever once a week come to be so much with pleasing it for them who when can not go to be an amount where
it is but more than when it can should it reach more than
once when they go in a while candidly leaving it better than
by the most enlightenment of their destination which chiefly
in a harmonious collection of many minutes more allowed
to an elegance of prevailing more left for the moment as is
what they know coming in silently with in need come shall
with but as now for the near latin is a wonder come shall
known to in call vainly they might allow but not for a considerable time an advantage to be only needed to the more insistent variety of which by nearly all of it in appointment
come to be not without the management of periodical vague
without more dear and me come which to send it as vehe-
mently adjoining the carrying on of when inadequately re-
signed to the date of installation made without consultation
and might coming in at once in the chase of panoply which
is not appointed to mention where they were left to themselves as they were left to themselves heroically in the politeness of whether should never be followed by wither and this
again should never be followed by whither and this again
should never be followed by endeavor and this again is an

amount of resignation when will it win came to be next of kin which left to him and they are very much inclined to be puzzled which is what makes the difference between a part and left around as is very well known especially when they care to have them it is more that than anything coming very much to a finish and it is an amount of many cases of once in a while where they are not at all better than the condition of not judging it to be a particular bluster of without it who are they they are like that as is very much why they were sent to be staying another time left to it more than on account of a choice of not only without more than is this as allowance for very pointedly leaving it for them which makes them smile while it is a very much better to know that they like it left to nine out of ten and never now which because nor is it meant known collected with a way of following two by three. It is a great pleasure to have the light change it is one of the things that makes sitting in a room very pleasant. It is also an advisable allowance of memory to wonder did or did he not give it in the moment of division and it is also what ever they may choose a very considerable importantly lost avoidance next to say is it as different as that and was she not mistaken and was he not appointed to do so and could it be preferable to know afterwards correctly that they would like to have it and very soon it could be if all their wishes were gratified a most admirable thing to be flattered.

They may be caught by considerable of what is more than they have to know as one two three and also it is not easily allowed that they should do what they think is the best. It is by appointing them to like it themselves that they wonder if it is always desirable to be very hasty and to be without at all soliciting for it in a wonderfully chosen maintaining mentioning allowance of better known adjudicating without the more robust thoughtfulness of whether it is more than they liked which is only without the nearly advantageous collusion which makes it be a pleasure to have it financially placed upon a sound footing which means that they will not interfere. It may not be worth while. It is very likely that they will be thought to have it feverishly near to the origin of their allowance because absurdly as they may wound they will without doubt shoulder as much of the conclusion as it is to their interest to dominate without a speck of difference of opinion regulating the withdrawal of their authority should consider alternately a pleasure predicting a related inharmonious willow which by the time it is curved may be fairly voiced as a comparative extra enjoyment in the sense of their predicament impersonating fluently the announcement of well being in relatively abundant chicanery amounting in twenty times two and four and they might believing gradually in their allowance be at most which is least ways a plant there without as if conclude never plainly estimating made it call shall an advantage be taken of an interval which makes hesitation famous and they lost it lest they may be all with and without deplorably laming more than a congestion of appointing them partly to have lost it that is what they say. Once in a while it happens that they come to know them apart which they like very much they say how do you do and it is always a pleasure to be partial. How many hours are there in the twenty four and in the forty eight. Merry Christmas and happy New Year when this you hear.

Four books of four Georges who have been said of them that they were in superiority as it is not a one that there is a great deal of wind but also a great deal of rain in between also it is often said that the one who was accidently met by them is the one who has since without it being an extravagance to think made plentifully as a choice of their minding it as much as they do. It is more or less true. Once in a while they think of everything naturally on that account they were very willing to come not alone with them but without them. They were awfully sorry that it is too much trouble and excitement to be partly left alone without as much as it is made carefully in extenuation of their needing even which it is more than an affectation to be deprived of it amounting to that.

Accidentally because of that that is how he likes her.

In need which when never in fear in formally be having elaborating in in change if it could with hold plausibly stated made in chagrin usable forty balancing this slightly made regrettable chosen coming foundationally attributing without displeasure in allowance when in case he with it wishes destroyed astoundingly never the less it is to commence commencing indubitably left to acknowledging as to might considerably choosing come to be amount which when comforting this union made to wait left it this more that they had. There is no reason. Many unite with them. This makes George seem everything neglecting anything that is that he has said to him you had better go with him, go with him, which indelibly unforeseen in indelibly refusing having being an opportunity to be eligibly welcoming playfully weathering made inextricably without which in formation can be identically refusing it without him to be never exactly reproducing and this is in amount which care not to be adding it is mainly Josephine and Joseph and adjoining and without investigating it is plainly not at all what is it when they have to go it is more than they have and very likely it is abominable which is just what there is to say and it is partly why they like to not be very often without more than they do with what they have which is very speedily mainly for this purpose as they can not

344

by any means let it alone just as they did they may do very well with it and they may not. It does not make an atom of difference to them alone if they are ever likely to make it with hesitation because when it is very well partly coming to be sure they know and and should be received for a little while by coming to be through with them for them. They might like to have it. Avoiding it comes to not ever new come to be seen what with able to say join more in it because of shall having not at all very much faster it is an obliging way to not at all have it do which it is very nearly they had to divide it all the time it is coming to not be part of it at all without trouble by the time they have eaten it as well tell him. He is all that they have when they go away coming it is what no one doubted that it would be like that. Which it is. It is very much never to know that angels could not be produced just lax with wood just lax with wood angels could do so more evenly attributed and not connecting how many dates are there in coining it coming to cover it half of the way in ambition to be a prize come to have which is it left to the quantity a quantity out loud it is made fortunately more than ever it is more at a timely she knew come this can be a name to some which is it made in plenty of their suspending water as a plastering of leaving it about which made it an alteration to know how it came there they might unitedly too more than is when they were without this. This is always that nobody knows that cyclamens are rose. George gave them this he knew that if it could be called water boy they would sing slowly if it could be called Jo they would sing slowly if it could be called Katherine they would sing if it could be called Julia Julia would be its name and fastening it was more than which it came about. She was disappointed so was he.

Now do none dare they leave with them this that they

find very difficult of understanding and it is why they leave it they must be counting they must have meant to have a basket and a best at that time with vainly it is more than they meant when it is nearly coming to that if it is difficult which by the time that tell them that they could be only very much about why they combine to admit for it it is not coming as it is with a will which is might be in time to have it thought out loud they like it very much much of it not at all which when ever they show more escaping let it lighten they might anyway have it be at a time it is like it like it might be very much what they and now to make it depend upon whichever with hanging made it come to be more should and when it is around. They like it very much. It is partly why they went. Very much. Once to be getting it made with it it is very well to be not at a coining six which lubricating feels very much like it. It does it feels very much like it. What is it. It feels very much like it.

When the time it takes to leave made it be the most with which they may be having it established as what they knew. It is not only very much as if practically they could be doubting if it was what ever they made it have changed in changing in relief announcing coming they were without willing to have it be known in the bewilderment of why in the chance of not only be very welcome allowing namely the prevailing joint of the jointure which is why be in behalf not only not nominally twice in the way they were inalienably leaving it to them at first which wherever because in time they were carefully purchased in employing what to call them to do it for them they were better than that to promise that they would like it made only believing without which it is if a noise can always mean sleeping not with or without it made to order they must change more than they like because it is not by that that they are known to be not a noise to commence it was lost without it in time. What did he do he changed nothing. It is not without this that they were there they were to go and be not by this which it is in unifying left to it as an establishing of alighting from the once in a while destroyed it as a momento. It is very much as they thought. It is most of it very pretty. It is partly left to go together with what they have. It is not why they went but where they went and when it came they were always appointing it very much as they would know it to be to be sure surely comes to be at all what it is as they can be separated. It is a help to them that one of them can have a difference between white and a ribbon. It is very much better as it is.

Precisely my dear, it will give us a very great deal of pleasure to have you leave it to them. Precisely my dear it will give us a very great deal of pleasure if you are to leave it to them to come. A great deal of pleasure in having it be ready for us when we come. A measure of pleasure in receiving it even if it is not precisely what is desired by us as a gift on this day which is a day of giving and receiving particularly as from those who generally send something which is not in the nature of a surprise and when it is is sometimes acceptable and sometimes not there has been in place of what was promised something in flower which has made for beauty and gaiety and is very probably to last quite as long as it has afterwards been explained that it would. The difference between paid and repayed the difference between payed and unpayed. There is a difference between payed and repayed. She could have said said and unsaid it would not have been different as it is because in adding a prefix it changes its meaning.

She likes it very much she likes it too much to say so. Pages point pilgrims which in retaliation succumb to the maximum intrepidly fan shaped without reason better than

they can which makes it noisily at most morosely be patently
theirs as a pastime which they like very well as it is what they
have when they are around it is not at all pointedly left to
them making it be a middle which they fancy they might
relish because without their having any denial they can be
urgent and most of it caught without nearly enough to be a
change with and without make it do that is what they said it
was occasioned by leaving it for them as they please may be
it is partly whenever they come forward in more than shall it
be partly as if by their way of having it be not at all more than
moistened in a preliminary which is why they are rapacious
making it have it sightly as a well known variation of what is
it without a better half of their thinking it to be a shame that
is what they are inclined to like it for by more than without
pleasure which is just why they make it have it should it
moreover be declared not surely as is vitally named coming
not by reason of its having needed silence to still it they made
it with which they were delighted and coming it was not to
tell if of more than frequently not more it could without having heard mention of the violence of notwithstanding delicacy of changing by the most that they had which is why
they inquired and it was more than ever theirs at one time
which might equal it it is not more than they have if it should
please them to like it it is always made just to have it known
now that without more ado they will have better than if it
was just that which very likely it is just as they think which is
whenever it is part of the time that they have more in an
allowance made to be sure that it is not why they are obliging and a candidate for their not having been obliged to go
which is never what they only mean to like as it is why they
are held half of it more melodiously very likely when they
were it is not only that they are rarely added mind it as they

do which is more than they have felt it coming for the indignation of minding it as they may please to call it when they go they are more than ever quite capable of ministrations and they account for everybody at once to be where when they like they must admitting it to be deplorably furtive which is why they went when they came right away as it were made to order just as it was because after all what made it particularly primitive more than they can share it as part of their winnowing more in exchange of politeness why they like having it told as they were careful to be always needing nodding at one time more than they care without which they are very much simply left to undermine any way in which it is placed and they without that may be confiding having it chosen as a very much better known than there is in any way one day making it feel part of the time that they are there. They are there which is not at all why they were more than ever individually wishing that treasures are agedly fishes because many marry too and it is well known that the church admits that if the child is born in wedlock even although the marriage is not legal by any arrangement nevertheless the child of such a marriage is without doubt legitimate if they like and anybody can like.

It is meritorious to manage adequately that they would give it which is why they might be known as avaricious they may be coming to have it as a fancy and if they like they would admire that they should having been solidly on one side make it to be forlornly leaving it to them to come again and sadden any one not only not knowing but in time without which it is in solitary restlessness that they are adding the more maligned relief of their being obnoxious which can be not lightly but without welcome fairly at once made in charming indifference raise in elegantly shambling without which they would hold as they might be theirs as they will claim what have they in place of theirs as an advantage which makes it readily not mixing in amounting that is what is known as they ran. They may be made more without their knowing that it is deliberation. It is very much all of it an allowance of their kindling it as a praise of what is it in the account of their being more than with all changing joining it indolently without tricks as they might be better known it is because this amount may be what ever is beware of that in spite of in case which when they linger they make it appoint it for this in their disappointment to be truly made as a choice of their in dwelling as in amount that it may be coming to have more in it in insistence that is as the never thought out choice of what was it that they ordered. They ordered it just as they wished.

Forgetting all of that in allowance. Might once might once if it is changed to an indivisible letting it shall join they may seventy four do it may be as they glance that there is more than an interval should it be calling for it as a perplexity that is translated and traduced as a blinding of what they had as a point without which they were surely to know that it is as radically as if without fail they were to be together which may be when hesitating it is predicted voluntarily to gather that they may he outlined vertically smaller by nearly as many as they with cinches include playing more for it with or without this in collusion which is a method that they may be coming finally invidiously more than a change that they gather without count it is more than there is a pleasure to have satisfaction it is arising made nearly with plenty of animadversions in such a definite aggravation not needed in stalling more than likely where with whether it is known as a tolerably allowance of their prevarication made it styling it as a renewal they were there to choose it is more than a blush and a promise of not should it be cared for in violation of plenty of witness of what is in which which they were willing to be privately an adventure of their knowing that it is mine. It is by half of it. Very well when they were in a plain where without doubt they were counted.

It is a judicious interruption of the noise that made it come clearly be with all of it a prevarication in announcing reasons because it is in legality that they are equally choosing it must by very well done to have it plain. They might within and without doubt make a floor have it hold it is not only why they were willing that it is out there out there might be nearer made to be in order very much cheering it as it is not only gainly but just not now now that it is without a particular care making it a reminder of when is it that they liked it. It is more than they must be known to have in a place where they can easily frown as being known should it be by the advise of their needing it for themselves. It is merely a practice that they could be thoughtless and very much if they had what is known temporarily as without doubt they gracefully should be a rather widened river which if going down going down made it be by a day it is not always when they frown and when they drown they must be as it is very well at once to show it as in the more advantage that it is it is by and without it at any rate and they must be all more than they could should it be without being strange they must like it they must shoulder it they must with withdrawal be not what is it when they are without doubt theirs as they have to see and saw as they know it is a deplorable change and they will without willows come to be not often made ready to come stealing and they are fastidious principally because it is that kind and it is made without their being noteworthy and left to the change which it makes if they are to have it which they do they do do the same and it is very often lawful they like it they do not despair they must be selfish they must come one at a time they must take it together they will be with them they can have it in effect and they are to be known without wishing it is not what they like but what they linger linger longer Lucy made it stand it does have this effect they will be staring they will be principally they must shut it as they go they know it as that they will be first and last they without doubt as more than ever ready to have it they can be more than ever ready without it they are in the midst of whatever is by the time that they shall chant coming through the rye because of course they do it is very well known through them that is what is always meant by readily in kind of wanting it be chosen as an interval in which they are very likely to be tired if it is kept on and they are famous for that that is what it is why do they whiten paper paper is exactly pleasing to the eye. It is more than ever what they ask. It is by this time that they are asked to be gracious. Graciously if you must do do it graciously. When indeed they are likely to love when indeed they are likely to love. Made it a variety of differences of which vainly is just and various is first and variously is first and they may be by this time ready at once they are very much better very much heard from and very much out loud and very much a bother and very much did he ask did they like to have land chosen rather than butter. Land chosen rather than butter. He asked did he rather that they had chosen land rather than butter. This is what they might do. It is very much one at a time and free for all they were nearly allowing for it which is by the way why they were meaning to leave it alone as much as they did it is partly that at one time.

Bright colors are desirable.

Payable at once in order that they make theirs leave more than which there is in a likely placid relentlessness of the quality of the predisposition in alarm with not without in pearls that whenever it makes many abound without merely in choice of newly enlivening to pertaining more than count which when without mainly as precaution made in an-nouncement mainly because with bestowal predatory con-sidered amounting to a division of their integrity shortly fol-lowing nearly enlivening because recalling the moistened rejoining of the fresher painstaking leave it to more that is prevailing should without applicable needless round about come to calling it is violently as made share of this more justly in a space of intricacy that should annul be come to the endless annoying of the violence of their without it is not what they have that they fear but the most of the allowance of their establishing nearly enough to mostly consider why it is beamingly in that inundated temporarily fugitive made invalid announced candidly seen whenever it is made just mainly theirs as choice might more than increasing left mainly inches of it to the noise of their implanting the mag-niloquent individual indirection of their unity to magnify in the state of their rejection of it pointedly made meaning in ability that it is whichever delightfully more that it is prevail-ing in a cluster of which behind the inescapable left to the joint elasticity of their intervention benignly released as a plentiful result of the negligible hindrance of what is the weight of their willing to be as much of it as when might there become well endowed with their betrothal to the neg-ligence of their martyrising more than is without a portion of the mystification of their renewal of the primary peddling of the hindrance to an authentic withdrawal of independence in relation to the non use of changeable to be sure without it

as not blameable in the case of their intrusion made mostly
in the coiling of their willingness to be in ritualistic
parrallelism with needless betrayal of the rejoicing of their
singularity in redoubt of the mainly shared jump of a plaintive miracle of having how to do it a pleasure to their incite-
ment which candidly is a ministration to the ones having patently rendered it an obligation to the annoyance of have not
to be in the absurdity of their surrounding it without a wall of
their jumping up and down come to be sure that it is plainly
in referring combined as much as if in raised january of the
pressure of inspiring it mainly just as it was combined very
well done as much as when wherever made from the inundation of their tranquilly must it be flown come to the never
rejoiced made it be not as much as clearly it is what they
remember of arbitration which is why when there is insistence they say so made beneath when and foremost as it can
perhaps leaving it out made alone that it is in calamity of
their arrangement an origin of nearly theirs as they assert it is
not without an arrangement in delicacy to be matter of fact
as it can cloy that it is in amount by native conception of
their integrity integrally withstood clarified by the nearly ex-
posed retaliation of their witness of the calender of their made
finally choosing pointedly nearly in time of it in the place of
when it is not known as it can be cherished as manifestly left
to them unknown as merely as it is coming to be made a
parallel of why they are noted to be made suddenly and shared
as they can having it made a mother in two and they were by
the time that they were using that they were staring and en-
feebling the management of the troublesome essentially bridal
with a semblance of pasturage as they were presently concili-
ating in a regrettable infusion of their hesitation to be might
when they were checked as in the gaining of their explosion

of the resignation of the one who was there which is what
they like they must be when they are not at all more than can
be querulous because of it as it is not a diminishing consideration of their eventuality which they may do in that case because of it it is not what they think of it it is what when they
may join joining leave them one one of them then there and
they when they they do not condition it as consider nor when
it is a plentiful reminiscence they do fortunately leaving loudly
nearly by the main landing which has painfully made it chosen as a mistake they are mistaken they may be whatever it is
coming when they come and it is not what is made by the
pointing of it in the only place where they were to be liking it
as which when they were in authority considerably it pleases
me very much as it is.

Did I say Thurdsay I meant Wednesday middle class in
George George is in the middle class the end class the farther pasturage class the mind it whether they like it indifferently to their behavior pleasantly aroused precariously lasting resting without it in mediocre recognition of their inability to be left deniably to need as much as it indelibly left to
their annoyance of their chartering the pressure of their withdrawal of their previously admired needless to adorn that is
carry it about as much as when gratified in presumably made
defective measurably in redating it pointedly as much as when
they did they were mediocre in a relative influx to the
unauthorised rejection of their plentiful prevailing inestimable because without it it should be as when whether because unaccountably leaving the radical withstanding orderly
chosen jeopardy of their reliance because ineradicably with
an imitation of a stabling so that outwardly it was to be atro-
ciously further in annoyance making it be that they left foot-
steps in the sands of time whether or not it did happen that

they were not mentioning the renown of the real estate actively repointed more than is by an accidental orientation of their bewilderment if it is a paragraph that they were shouting as much as though they knew the day or two whichever has to be made because it is monday she knew that queens who were not now widows had been having the headdress as having the hair worn in that matter but if it was partly as if they could be boisterous it could be shut away from them in accordance pointedly with their reasonable willingness to be amounting to prevailing without their having nightly made it be whatever could there be in no advantage to their willingness to have wax be thought to be vulgar and so it was when they were not tired it is not only that they were fairly left to it in having identically allowed whichever by the way if could it be not more than coming to be strangely left to mutter without intrusion that they were colliding as if in their interpretation coming to be nearly half of it made surely to be naturally retaken as an avoidance of the ingenuity because of it in time and it is why they went that made it be an appointment they knew very well that they were liquidating whatever was palpably adjoining the failure of the reflection as to whether it is inevitable that they would be betraying the need of not liking it as much as they did it is properly speaking what they do they must be as they were tightly sought in the place of their disturbance that they were antagonistic but because remembering finally it is not by any means what they could it is a polite showing of their widening the pointed needles of when they were intimating baskets which is as separation into mainly that in disappointing it comes that nothing follows apart because when two and two and two and two come to be he can come to be made to be nicely in rattling where they were it is extra in the appointment of their churlishness made elegantly

left to be not behind with whatever they were intricately penetrating in the manner of their noisiness which can be as
prostrating as without plainly as it is made selfishly with soon
as that because by it it is more than they could be known
awfully in China making it be that it is very light it is without
doubt that they like it painted it makes it look mores like a
lamb and pasture and therefor they are not accustomed to
violation of the ordinance that they are prepared because by
it radically they must it is never what they said they were very
well known however and it is not because of it having come
so quickly that so much of it has been saved they have thrown
away what ever they had to leave behind them nobody came
to see them they saw everybody they say it was Wednesday
and not Thursday and they were always very politely refusing to need whatever it was that they came to say because
and because of it it was made deplorable that they could
have now been what they were it was a remarkable hope that
all of it is made to be partly what without calling they come
having it as very delicately made which whenever it is partly
that they made leaving it hardly more than could and should
and would and they might be annoying without at all left to
them as mainly as they are to glance that way which without
that as halting makes it maidenly in their allowance of one
two three it is indeed as we and they were wherever they
were theirs without number. It is manifestly that they were
accepting angels made of pudding. Very many tickle them
then. They are sticklers for right and justice. They are without price. They produce in great abundance. They have no
sorrow because they are noisy having with difficulty understood that they were to be known at that time for just what
they were they were very well pleased with their coming in.
It is by now not an allowance they were gradually arranging

that they were to mean it all the time and they were formidably interfering with not when they were anxious to be not made without which when they were in penalty of nearly bestowing when they were without distinction that is meant in elaboration because rightly or wrongly they would never be called that now not when without should and in preference which may care to be carried challenging that is a credit to them. What is it. They are all of them without partly joined to their installation of might it be genuinely left to it in a distance of when they were outside of within the pleasure of their just as it was because they were all of it as to be bought which makes that they have twice leaving it out make it be not only theirs as noise which is a name George Henry or Georgiana Jacqueline Wise. Thanks to them it is about time. When they do have to be accounting for the best that has been that they have been saying how do they like it. They do like it. So do they like it they do not do it because it is what they like they do it because it is reflective and they are meditative about whether it should be changed. It is not only that it is not nonsense that makes it be all of it a blame of by nearly leaving it where they had to trouble to be in kitchens. This is not like the name of planning nor may it be because of cutting it off. They were better able to like it just when it was there. Where is it when they are very well known to be adding it in the meantime where they are to like it very likely.

Admirably without which in the middle of never ending integrity with an allowance previously conditional to their withstanding shaving it partly in the methodical spending of their whether it is sheltered by the more heaving in plenty of elaboration of their willingness to be untidily left to not whether if without could they be orthodox to the enjoyment of why when it is widely nearer than that as they call made it

be in remembrance for the fairly authenticated renown made
by the chance of an undiluted renewal of poisonously nearly
without made to be suffering whenever it is left to them to
further collaborate in the jealousy of which without blue they
can and do not alloy the known made with chance because
it is ineradicable plainly as they will see because it is a maintenance of the newly plainly as it is a cause of their indicting
it made to be known could they mainly say that it is because
he has never known a good woman that he makes them all
so precisely a sacrifice to their initial begonia which when
flavored made it be that it is a despair of a desertion that will
welcome in renewal that it can be churned without leave
into without the more indefensible left to it by the time that
they were bearing it as a dual might it be without which they
can be courageous to the mile of intentional escaping finally
it is coming as it is more finished to the knowing of whether
without it at first they need to be mistaken undertaken in out
loud as they could certificately in ignorance of their without
an arranged enjoying of when it is without making it leave it
to the knowing of why do they rob and they must not be only
without the north and nearly much as it is to be rightly as it is
fairly without theirs in gain it can be not too tumult in the
enlivening of their cunning to disaster it is appointed for the
name of their mistake which has been coming to be combed
and in the bright when they are there it is not only very much
to do so which willing and they can it is more meant and if
coming having it to do it is without it remarkably in no time
which is very well shown yesterday as to be willing need it be
whatever they can be without a doubt of wherever it is just
made to be not only where they went it is as if not coming to
be without that they could as whenever now and then called
it is more than ever judicious to be plainly near to it coming

fortunately with without names that is what they do to be just as you and they can to tell and to like it it is more over just one just as that time that they might come to be fairly cautious of whether it is more or less can it be made to go farther in a way that without excellent interruption of the well shadowed mind of their particular do they mind when it is what they do not unusually declare because without it as a point it is very much whatever it is in innocent and left to be nearly half of it as one another which when whenever it is made coming to be sure that it is hearing that can fulfill with and all because they can have it as a joint and it is melodious because coming it can be just as well as ever where they were in the objection that they are interlaced without a plank of meritorious in connection to their otherwise whenever it is to be left without them they were very much and they were indifferent and in all of which when it is a current of their needing it not a cherry because without and bewail they can carve it as a fortune to be sure they must be nearly extremely in organisation in a methodical coming to be pliant it is more than they can in indication made it to be come whichever they can place it in and around it is more than partly a wish whichever it is that they please please do not come here alto-gether they are very well after all it it is not a great deal of trouble they can without doubt pray pray to be sure instead with which it is right when they can in place of shown it is shown to them just as they do to say they can be left after it it is more than ever this as they know in no case coming with-out partly at one time it is made whenever they can have a class of coming to be after which whenever made it be po-litely leaving it to an occasion it is not ever after all without a pleasure they could be what makes it have fairly in the case of what ever it is that it is as annointed with or with wherever which when making it be never in partly coming to be not more when is it that they fancy that they will like it very much which makes it their in once as much as they had it to doubt if they are not at all as likely which they do do it is a remarkable number of times wherein without and made it suffer as they very well do have without arouse coming which she does know that it is as much as ever which they please however much they can place twenty as women which is never to be shut in open making nicely what is not only known as when tomorrow they do allow it coming to say so it is not only why they are very much as they were all of it too to do it is very much where they have been saying every and whichever it is in the middle of it never to be stopped by them when coming in the most of the day at noon which is why they like whatever is to be not only nearly with because before them it is very much as why it is known without this to be sure to be certainly welcome as their allowance it is very fortunate that they are here. Is it very fortunate that they are here it is very fortunate it is very fortunate that they are here is it it is very fortunate that they are here is very fortunate very fortunate that they are here it is very it is very fortunate that they are here is very fortunate it is very they are here is very fortunate that is very fortunate it is very fortunate that they are here which it is which is very fortunate they are here it is very fortunate that they are here it is. Very fortunate that they are here it is. It is. Very fortunate that they are here which it is. It is very fortunate. That they are here.

Leaving lavender and faucet without a division of their eradicating that the passage of sheep makes fragrance and in told that they are meant to be violet and violence with them as attachment because whether welcome welcoming in so far that to be sorry because it is not applicable to the urgent foundation of multiplying carefully in their especial realisation of whether it is prepared that they tell them so it is very much better in an inescapable net-work of the pointed incessant left to it beside whenever in applicable to the noise of their bewailing why which and whenever it is admonishing to be not without their intentional around and surround as because with and in change becoming preciously after it at all they were made with them to be called where and making it fairly in by an accidental without a joining of their instance in plainly commencing a rest of it to be with and without fail as they allow it is not just as they do with a list of whether it is a major which makes it be that in all they can be a collusion of never to have it just be an allowance of which coming to have is estranged in their account of whether north is Africa and west is Australia and it is because of this that it is doubtful if they come to whistle boy remaining as much as if they could not double way laying as a straggle beneath their enlightenment which makes them just as much so as ever make it having that reliably it is not what is made perfectly that the origin of the adjoining with it now that is that it is celebrated with an exodus of their maltreatment of the nicety of which because in a plain estuary that it is not without a dimple of this which makes it become fact and the name of their that they have with it because because can never have it a sameness of the winning that it is if it is scolded to be known that they can shielding in a dog when it is that if there in an impass of their known house coming to be at work as when without wooden and rollers she well and new this in the critical combine to antedate a benevolent with and without some making that it cannot be true that they will turn if when a made to be share which it is not a renewal of remarkable coming to stare that is if it is seen first with a whichever they can in attribution it is not by merely coming in combination coming this is there now is in the next as a fashion of come to be a difference between a house rolling which when elevating which when when elevating which when when rolling and it is in the make of their plant that the cousin to the noon which is made an alternative to a band of gilded without the consolation consolation of not in a joining of their wistful in a clannish come to the never to have jumped a way to a way in an and if if there is surrounded rounded come coming it can be in tears and it is very much as soon as stopped that they which is she made more might have in a renown that the accordion with it will it may be come to be to be noon to be to when to when to be that it is not that she must must have wait waiting in a plaque of their with widening come to be in in attachment and they call that is that they can shove and sure it is an outer countenance in left to be and be as disappointment with a madrigal and made and much and when and madagascar that they shone. They like to ask will they do it again and will I like it then. This is what they do when after it is made an edge of between the portion without which solidly and sold it is not in and on account of the discipline of their withstood to be a portion of welcoming it can be handled with a better notch of when they do have it come to be nearly where they are it is not as it is a date of their flying away from figs which have been left it can never be a noise all called. This is what they are tempting. How can very many be what they are. How can very very many be what they are. She says that they can not do so if they do not believe in it. She says that they can not believe in it. She says that they can not do so. Do they believe in it. If they can do so. It is not what they ask but whether there is any difference between water boiling and rain.

Down and water boiling and down and rain is there any raising of what ever whichever they can be characteristic in a moment of when they with it without it they do not know that they care for it care to do it care to do it and care to do it for it they do not know that they do care to do it that they do care to do it for it because when they are actually in the withstood withstanding withdrawing of their wind and water plan water is much as much as by an instance of their vagary. If she sends another. It is very likely that they are difficult to understand if they talk slowly.

What is it. It is this. Once upon a time there was evolution. He made it. He made it he heard it he had it he and he meant it he meant it he is what they mean when they say it. That is done. Done and done. This is a wager.

Now they knew know that they have it having it having it come to be willing willing and welling welling is an oil an oil is a security security against so many so many have to have to should and would would and condition. Conditional. A place opposite is how many. How many is never on account. An account. In on on the bay on the bay after all they are not interested. It is humiliating who and you is how and with it a sanctioning of two bid. This is an auction and they are how how are they. How are they come to be Susan. How are they come to be clear clarity come to be an affectionate at all. They are all all to tall. This is an elegantly fed to them with and with and with a trifle to be can have it a change. It is this. What they do is to call it you. You are my life. This is the day that they can pay. They can pay it as a coming to the awry. It is a change. There is no Sodom and Gomorah. How do you do. And so forth. Please forgive twenty to two. Call it a place of their changing it to four and forty. Now and again. What is it. He admires that it is not why and when there were ribbons. There were no ribbons. Ribbons are not at all six or seven. They can be curly at the edges. This is why they differ. They differ as it is come to be sure. This is the way they sag. Come to be hum. Humming is a sign of discouragement. Resolution. Going to stay. Have it a way. They are proud to be known as when they sit.

Come to be as I explained it to him. Now.

Look and stuck it is a jelly when it is a wine jelly. They are artificial and not interested in fishing, fishing is always unfortunate and red fishes are not known as golden but as reds. They are like the name of sand and send her. She is at once why. They cannot have it known as coming. They are very well as they are. They are without doubt come to be sure. They are sure to like what ever is given to them. If it is given to them they must be must be very well to do all of it as it is very difficult to have crossed an ocean without an ocean of preparation.

There is a difference between quickly slowly and at once. We have been all three and this is an explanation. Everybody knows that I am right. Right right. Left left. Right foot left foot, hay foot straw foot, left left he had a good job and he left. Right right. Right right alright. Right alright.

Able to be all to the mend and made it be an unaccustomed shadow of their wondering because it is regrettable that it is an incredible day-light which makes it show that the only absolute antagonism between arousing and arising which they shade with their expenses as they must in the moment of the entanglement of their shown acting in the evidence of the anticipation of their what ever it is in desirability as a pointedly left to the cataloguing of their relishing of the jointedness of the indisposition to not collect the relative organisation of while without pink it is nearly made in possibly passing that where it is made as much because without blaming they can be admonished that it is playful in collected determination to be mystified by their judging finally how to in a passably making the annulling of their advantage that they had the incident that it is nightly with all and come to have not as a square wherein it is never had without the assisting coin of the as much as it can and call it the not to be committed to an allowance of their prevailing it is made a plentiful as much as shade that they drew be nearly compared to the naming of the gesture with which they did it is in time that they did it at all which whenever they might be the much that is calculating an effort that they did not come it is more than the submission of why it is politer than they were in the midst of their opposing that they could in and once in a while before they with a pleasure in not having this as a place where when it is not more behind in the calculation that they are an announcement and best as it is they will joining in the prevarication that it is a hope for them that they like to be not at all by the way by the way how do you do and does it behave as a collection of following when they came to be not why they were without dishes, which were given away for them. It is very much what they hoped for.

Letting it for half of it and it is right, it is better to be right than to be perfect and perfectly it is better to be perfectly right than after all to have a caller tell it in their name. And last and land. Land and a band a band of which it is in individual chosen to have theirs in the name of letting it have it as an indicating that it is made with a persistence of which it is not having letting and damaging in the nearly foundation of these in specially named admiring it for them to be with and patiently as not forever change this to the annoyance of their allowing joined the new which is new and been to the

name of their undeniably finding it an altitude that without
an annoyance of their being nervous with stairs which coming to be not without and widening it is more or less pointed
to pitiful that it is merchant and marine amounting to the
care without the bedewing and bestowal for this felicity in
the rounding coming indefatigable the challenge in the
mounting of the newly adjusted in the point that it is without
the interval mainly in the allowance made finally come to be
shared as the noninterference of their appointment which
they shadow in their conceding that more than it is in perpe-
tuity not motioned in the interval reliability that is because
made should without the pleasing of their weeding it in the
appointing of a plum tree which has been green in the same
hand where they were in originally following the situation of
their plainly sufficing to be in an established of the nonsuiting
of the mounting of which it is privately enjoined that they
may be in violence to the established of the known of the
wherever it can be trained that is if they like making it incon-
testably that without further in as an shown and made man-
fully the strain of the nicely playing indolence of whenever it
is in the attaching to it that is costlier more if in pouting that
the simultaneity of their shown is as left to the never to be
selected as to the settlement of when there is more than the
same whatever it is that they like that it is not by the alteration of the better shown to be plentifully so much as the
strain of the customary which it has as when it is not more
nervously come to the share which may left shining it for the
interval of the shadowing of the better instructed made in
their place that it is nine at a time to the never having loaned
it more than it is very nearly as the collecting of the habit of
their idealising the colleague made to the same without not
only to the having it behind and peculiar and perpendicular

to the building of their chain of wharves which is not made to be handled without the specification of their not having it higher as it is not made come to the same and as the frame which when with and remind makes it more that in the alignment of their rectangular choosing the point that it is in the violence of having plaster rising in the change of the passenger of the considerable restitution of the rehabilitation of the not known by the unique without the moistened of their retarding wherein they must falter without the change of their willingness to be boldly to them considerable as it is when felt as if in a difference beside most as they can find it should without a hall to be hold to not knowing it as weld which is in an amount of their endangering it as an appointment of when they can come more as it is in the spoiling of their unknown to them that it is by the time that they are very much as fortunately as that it is what is very well wanted when the most of it is allowed for as they are calling for it as a pleasure to them in the way of everything made to be thought about. It is whatever is known as best.

Prehaps it has something to do with her other arrangements because without any obstruction she has never received the impetus of their outlandish witnessing of a prevarication in resulting before indefinably shared antedating in the pressure of the endowment controlled by the uniting of the predicament of their pedestal if it should be suggestible in the noise of the pleasure of the bewilderment might and carelessly fanned in the joint of an aptitude meant redoubtably in the vacation of their willing to not correct as should in beside have for instance culling the fancy of what in by and without more as it could shown come to be this most as they made it fanciful to be certainly as the choice of winnowing as the asterisk of the change which can might in bestowal for the receipt of their enlightenment which named in the case of their freedom by the willingness of the and bountiful remorse of indelible as chosen considered may it in for having appointed as it was marble in the wood of the shallowness combined and combed to thrill about which have it make a splendor of the amount in the adjustment of the prevailing debate made intricately in the union of unification may find which amaze the calender of just as well as in the instance beside the management of without left to the between never as spoiled in the angle of the voyage intermittent kind lain to might well shown rested come to not send out of the whole wide world they chose him and it is best that it should be so because it can be developed as better than if it was not to have meant to like it as at all whatever they must not despise as wondering because it is an interval of all that it made it be known peculiarly with a better than adjustment of the pronouncing argument of when he went to go to the plainly delight of which it is not actual but presented made without stirs of the undiluted esteem of why it is wide in that sense pointed to be nicely administered to the better of the hope without it, can be clouded fortunately with winding established in the objection of the amount that it is not nearly along made to be neatly appraised in a shown as to come surely which it is whenever they make rudeness alone not in left to right as lonely as the pleasure of international as they use positively in the occasion of the analysis of the once upon a time shared without them as when it is by their behavior in the moment not in the nail of the shoe and maker in the habit of liking it very well so much in interruption to now go and partake with her if it is better which it is very likely as well continue to will with when estimated properly in the veteran plainly come to be at once as allowance interval abuse persistence connection inviolability combine shall and select in the avoidance of the resolute possibility of enchainment because with prevailing and a list come to not as soon in outward as shown it is might and for it as forget that the same as well as much as win in integral arouse come to finality as moon in the abidance of the renown with shall for the seen and sending have to be as come around in call when have it to do not might because may matter worthy for the taller of the two it is known as a non roaring but it is a jewel to be too.

Are bother acting before laterally made finally in permanence then to some appertaining without moments in calmness of chancing to have mentioned wells planting it primarily for the not without a plentiful exhuberance to absolutely treasure the residue of their change made pointedly in the making of it either way preferably as becoming with all of the nicely strewn shall the come to be lilies of the valley be wetted. I do not mind that they like me. Awfully and as at a amendment ability achieving absolutely an accidental apt are always at a amiably after all as allowing about asterisk account aimed angelically authority avoidance are actually abler apposite as a having made a price a well wisher as an arranger after an appointment and antedating all arbitration always amounting accordingly as an answer a better merited obliging well known as having a pleasure in renewal. So it was as an avoiding absurdly as aiming all addition are with it a bother whichever gets it. It is a division plainly to their cost which between halls plainly refused as in doubtful proximity made in claiming in case of the weeding without dots as to pay fairly elegantly reversing a renewal might when a vehement avoidance of their fairly pointing without which may come shadowed as they soon shall see. Because it is a round without a doubt that it is named that it is a preferably lost to them without a blame of sharing which ever abundantly after all arranged allowing actually are abandoned alright about all alone acceptably arranging among a better part of it that they have without this as they have thought about it arousing alike abruptly as affecting. It was noon to-day and there was hesitation in her walk. Sometimes they were wrong to name it as having been so and sold so abiding by it the arrangment that they had. It was often all of it in amount. How many fats are there in narcissus and also in lilies and also in hyacinths and also in crocuses. George makes no mistake. Lilacs lilies vases Voltaire and Basket. It would be easy to imagine a conversation.

When they have looked down because they are next door to one it is a plainly withstanding allowance of realisation adjusted appointing advantageously renowned completely announcing renewal as within a differently precisely justified adjournment left to it summing nearly when they were as if it had to be thought articulately however it is made to trade away my own. How do thanks go to whether utter purse very much left kindly to many indifferences of the perilously shouted reading if as wells to do to shine why they could bother about it remedially coupling just what ever it was plainly to an advantage as it were to place repeatedly the nice when after all a call might it make when shall it challenge in the spirits right to do so all to do so where they were often all as property to awaken it for them strangely when it was the right it was the left.

Better let her with her have her made to be a nicely with referring supper as a strong example of their individual resuming of allowance nearly should it come to be a nicely accelerated indisposed to join with partly representing for the nuisance of polite as shown for the occasional reversal beside in the completion pointedly might without reciprocally weathering rejoinder known tender come part readily planted which without welcome having amount not left to believe well should adherent with please or cause shed broken at an angle mind it for them which is a matter of the color yet or yellow this to blow conundrum of their incline which believe in years have heard in that made top and side and could it might a meal be with a footing that they were to behavior as an arbitration next in a colliding become shoulder whether Arthur butter or blotter made crude coupling reflect by beneath restitution coupling mingle to other I do. Come come it can they be their ball there bay there battle particular to an entirely just with an incomprehensible play fair join better an amalgam plain cut in counting please do not intermit this doll which is a fork made plain to the annullment consoled pages opposed pardonably interviewed as an appointment place and placed this when a man can have a suitable exodus respectively so called shoulder by the lain as astonishing place wither they moreover it is that they are particularly proud of nails which have but this little way to go wherever they are driven because it is a very great merriment possibly cared to know parlor and parlor which spreads guns they and the neck of land was why they knew more of bay shore. Forbearance with an appeal of where it is made by collaboration they can call twelfth of Sarah which should plan not at a very rest of it to a stupor that is an ineradicable play fair of the shoving what is it of this in that at all. Very well sir. How do they like theirs whether farther and farther. It is a very little more that they she helps play lilies of the valley in the winter. If it looks like spring is it winter. If it looks like it in there made a change. Fifteen days be a bother. Every morning they go and bring back whatever attracts them that they need but they all have oranges and bananas and brussels sprouts and salads and beets and celery roots and some winter pears and some winters a thousand apples or potatoes but not every year every day. Too late.

How many boxes make a crate or rather a pleasure of a horizontal grey wooden ladder too true to him and too to you. As repassing this is open to ironing which is not at all why they have shutters made of wood and iron. They do know how often they cause. Harbor and cause. Farther and because. Found about in walking. It is very much. Very likely. Wind and winding. How do they scare them to be and wave. It is a part of the way. They pay. I am so sorry. Why. Because of repetition. Five fifty there. Jackal. Tall. Doeskin and chinchilla. It is very much better so. Bestow. Cut and dried. Not to like like description deride wide better side may batter cut it in a next to that mentally sure of the have and what is it that they like. They like everything. There is all the difference in the world in refreshing. Better be a harvest. And it made no difference. Compel cake. Standard dresses. Butter as yellow. Flowers withstand. Should it be three. They will abide by the decision to apply for it as a place where they may withdraw in safety should it not apply to its use for the name of solace find let shawls be under over cut in half made might they be whatever with or varied as they do know the difference between simmering.

Really with a definite demand that a denial is a place of why they are as winning with on top so many do their duty come to see a choice of by the width made plan of acute as a noon of the prevision of wading loud as a shone of their vulnerability in excess of extravagance to the anointing made a predicate of cheerily by implication known as a joint of their splice to rest shall will amount recuperate too soon to sully the movement of invalidity chambers and the moaning of blocked and counted prevailing pushed bother nodding come to a feather in avoidance that restitution of inability coupled may be as went cone of the rear that is obligatory to the obliged why do they spread and apply forfeit for it come as if it is not a gulp to own to own and whether and restored pushing countless for the avoid whether ever told beady as a what the reversed appliance of the sheltering of their coupling of allowance of indivisibility of springing shut up powerfully shown cupped with and beneath because a radically mothered widened and may and made to be to all it was very good but it went bad. One made by the gulp in twine. It cushioned the pillow in a pillow slip of here. There to there. It is a doubtless why they do. Not to be returned to ought. Why should they suggest a departure. When they have pages which can in trains lay up the water which is to flow through the hose to water the garden.

It is with a palatial opportunity not to estrange the dilapidation of utter edge of outer egging it on in a best of when it is in desperation to be announcing left make for forfeiting that if it is made and made in change which when it is nearly edging in retrenching because called purpose made elongation to fraternity that it can have to have to care to become a meditatively octoroon for their family and assembly they were made desperately especially for the waiting without blenching to the curling of their negligence made for this as in an instance of preciously pleading that it is when they cry they must make cake with their how do you do they need to have a lake should it be such with while for their mercifully made practicing for the convinced and joined playing the rest of the carefulness of reaching the appointing of the abandoning of never let it having that as an invidiously chartered to be theirs soon as in flexibly irritating that without moon made it a care for them call hear should fortunately for and even have not what is in the precision of common to them as a ground of their complaint which whenever and an amount of open they please call tell will and bottom it with a new zeal of restitution as if have and with it it is what in an anoint-ment of the disposing of it about so when bereft of their sta-tioning in superior and in touches of the noun which made latter as at once the pressure of willing made in plenty of retribution that it is for the nicely modest of it not with as the noise of made which in about the vacancy of lining without their precision of useful to supposition made in declaration of the weeding amount of places named as yet.

The often richer top to not the table of their without want-ing for near as to be all this made of it as if theirs is not a shutting of the point of advantage advantages how it is but not as a mother to her one. Forgetting a mother to her one whether. Babies a pleasure. She says that it is what ever makes a difference. It is a trap and corrected for their after how is it in hours. It is not that once in and out comes to be shoved around to the wade and wading. They have forgotten weigh-ing.

Many articles fetter the mistaken rectitude of being shel-tered a blunder of the acknowledgment prevailed running in indivisibility this make left to them now which a blight that is perverted to the investing made should in the carriage of mounting that the division joined in the curiosity of rul-ing in the claim of their blanket of shown this do the collaps-ing precede agate and a double of the endowment whether measure it is a deliberation of frequently preyed not habit as the size made it is feasibly about the prevailing with and way of aspect in a test show come to side within a willing fort of this or to avoid more cut in half out of it in temperate as a pole without for this not a while back. Very sorry that it will never do.

Bay with abate a nuisance to be predicted in nomenclature for fortunately better than however should it be claimed about the whether it is find and found made the prevarication of two knew in but plainly in the intermittent of the power that can have just without it point of embroidered collared as a freshness of the utilitarian cover of a needle better regular wended as met believe that new should calculate finely theirs in response none messed with pale in consultation minimising for the forest imperilled collaboration utility mournful at most rain is and must the polite feeling remain provided just as much known this in through the having printed woe begone south and brushed with special shown a glance adaptable come in a closed rented fabrication just in endowment as they please easily only without doubt plaited as a cooling of the interval combed as the point without which prudence comes to before whatever politically rather for that as nice and made a plate of to dare say in justificating what inland makes dolls have feet and tidies when ought it or laugh to-day gone in restless toned it mellow of balloon in so more with wending partial to highly bade known restoring escape for the choice could when weather loved in truly rusted channel of their biting it in consequence of double which is change for that and hurled believe come copper in the just able presiding fairly interval to best of it said without a blow they were worth while in the hope of it may to gallop in the season because straddling could it amount when but for it as a to do pardonably a gold and coin with a vase last as a point of departure which is why they are interminable out of the whole wide world I chose to do good which is what they own of him he has been met by their helping it to come about.

It is a pleasure to converse without an answer and as to that having a part of the time in which to bother about it as in case that it is predetermined to be fancifully all of it in spite of the surroundings with which they are so nevertheless renewed equitably to do the not at all as if it is a politeness chequered be whether it is blooming as an antidote beside the bother of this with and worried let her be thought less than it is a kind of neatness in the blend of lubricant as whenever coming right away as can forget the more of it when is it that it is more then ever what they had rather have when it is about due.

In attended violently ability if two see which in elaborate readily cress and avoided there alarm which indirectly for that in seen considerable made it prefer their chance with polite shattering of the widening of which it is not that a pleasure in pairs for that as within collided obviously a copy refer just as chosen to not lonely in a minute thereby the understatement of advantage perfectly balancing not by chief with it at a point that there is in elaboration for there nearly please which is a prevailing colored in the point of their betrothed to the as soon as when it is an occupation for the appointing of lots of the well being of lighten to be rest of it as there was made to choice come to elaboration mixed finally as relentless in the reach of when might it in the avoidance of meticulous as which is dawn to be declaration of arose made as with it for the next instance adroitly shut it in the correction of weakness in the out put of meditation made away come to be please there accurately in radius of their soon having fathomed should next be named there is waning for the reach out in a plating of the inelastic just as a door

to be conveniently rest as whether in bestowed rushed to be
soon for this in the election of their while it is best for them
to like it at all as much as they could which is by their nearly
with a better industry for it formidable should without welcome rushed as an avoidance of minor principally called it
having made a point of their rather having richness in the
partly without close as they many in a time for this is complaint of not prevailing partly for this in a tether that change
it made merely with all in entirely it is made from fanciful in
rest to the renouncement of their with it shown as made which
because individual should choose same the same as all droll
that it is in might when with it for the nuisance of the allowance of whether it is integral in reliable fast plain and a twice
as once they could for gather summary collect renew collide
race and might for the best of it as predicted come to the
claim of their revelling in shall which it is best when there
can be cover to hover let it down to an obliged to be severed
from the very much whatever it is that is at all like it the rest
of the believe it or not as they like it makes no difference
whichever they like it to have it to do it in a way which is the
one that is not only all of it nearly come to be thought that it
is very well known and not mistaken in liking to rely with
which is it in the after all that it is more than that which
makes it to and fro a much better than it is blankly a rest of it
in the meantime because it is in inclusion that it is called
highly presentable to the resistance of their welfare and willingness an appointment restfully allowed by their being willing not by half of the interruption that they color as the better than it is without a draw of which it may shall form in the
care of their responsibility such when and select the remainder of the disappointment of the hardness of reversing it in
change to be all called within and for their rights as they can

be and draw determined come meant and renounce to do it
as mainly which is in rehabilitation for their chance which
is why they must be very careful made to be allowed vacantly
in be wide and side of the better wished for relatively thought
about the same that is all of it a kind as kind in the new better
than called when they gain what ever they have of it it is
news to them they like it they must miss it they will be better
than at any time whenever it is not what is when they are
obliging in the honorable discharge of their husbanding their
effort which is what is what even call it in indigo that it is a
positively ardently marvelling that they could which can when
made a name to be on account which way they went there
where leaves are loaned by the avoidance of having it a loss
that they might come to be whether whichever collaboration in intrusion indicated should it have remembered up to
fifty that is allowed for the shoulder of mutton that is very
well beside the agreeable round about when it is needless as
they may boast of why they were called cherry which can
make intermittent have finely bestowal jump come to soon
as how they were beside on the way which is very much
whichever they wished and likely to do as well for them whenever it is a fatigue to have proper papers in the day-time for
the same which is what is it in the rightly loving angel as they
may whenever it could and said it once in a while in accord
with it in a denial of rain could it be about the time they said
which is why they always like it better which is very well for
them whenever they will be alternately adjusted to it not a
partly chosen with why should and come to see about it whenever they are there where it is a pleasure to have it known as
having been done by them which it is as is very well known
whenever they care to have an influence which makes them
leave it alone very much in the way they like as is very much

better for them and which they do do whenever they have the chance and it is just as well to know it even better as coming to be relieved it is not known as a burden not as a relief but as a pleasure which it is just at this time all of it as light as a feather in a part of the day which it could be had as whatever they liked that is what they never like more than they do this all in a way of revolting in the selection of does it happen to do made in time to be exciting and a convenience and an estimation of this in two which is not a change to rest in it alike from it in the correction of better than stained glass too which is it as they have with all found come rested in a colliding with tall and vegetables close to the best of it in a winding restlessness of why do they come within made to order whenever it is done that they like they made it clear for it is just what they must do to call as allowed be with this reading made easy by plenty of time and to be sure with which it is please not to meddle in the advice of why they went with all to do with every once in a while which is made to be lost with respiration as to duty calls not hopping come to their care made without as to their plan to shave it down it is too bad and they must be known as a part of it as at all they could be thought to have it about twinkling refuse a bedewing in a star of shut it to destiny that it could dwindle in the taking it away where they went in about that time there too in a cause of remounting the statues on a pedestal which had been used as a flower garden being filled with earth like that to do thought it actually an adjunct to the garden.

It makes no difference within right about what collecting from ferns shall be mislaid by fuller had by mine fasten the lent for whichever can doubly have passed behind netting conditionally roused when by the stand in which confidence to be enclosed for the allowance of past rationing for the finality

of upper condition of eventually tranquility of unified indubitable should glance without that washing for the shown
without mere provocative establishment of having met with
called that they will fasten in restiveness combined in the
moistening of the peculiar for which it is in equity that it can
shoulder join this prevailing as the sum put which ever the
appointment in apples of the sheen of their popularity for
this intricacy that it shall illuminating the fastening of the
pealed in stability of their allowance for it for a fortune of
known sensibility of when wedding it must in the interval of
the restiveness of why is it that to come again makes it a
change and it does with or without symptoms they have to
be as allowed for the funicular of respectability of their
whether it is chance that belies it for the much as in a point
to make it do made without explanation for the reiteration of
the endowment of withering exclamation shortly to have fi-
nance actively in retarding the ministering of abundantly for
them in shine of not cut shall and be in two for season that it
is law that makes it made to have it speech that for the renown meant but to for to add made with a call it is at all that
they can share and share alike letting it undo the more than
twenty five that they have in the house more under moreover in the undeniability of wrecking it shut in before the
best of it in intent come by more than it is in that in because
of an article of close which made a neglect of chosen for the
amount of whatever it is left to call that it is a share of that it
is shared in the narrowing of the conditional interposition of
the adjoinment of when they are laughing it is not to be believed that it is come together with well very much better
known made easily in plane it is a disappointment to not do
whatever is what they must be sure to share that they like
that they say that they are particularly to go away. What does

make a difference. It is in plenty of time that they are in plenty with venom and a complaint of inundation of better to judge others as at once that they cannot be said to have butter too in the name of Jerusalem which makes it dreaded and mended as towering and she needs signatures. It is out of a better left to the period of attenuating this in season for the approach of resting of the bewidening of their popularity because it can be that a dome in ignoring of advantage is precluded from the justified attempt to dove in the bother alone of their consigning made to shut in two in a claim of allowing adjutant of the precision of middle of the room of when it is in a choice of faintly have had hand heavily attract in the rectangular bewilderment of what it is as though. It is why they have this. Left to them. At all. It is better not to do too much if you are bewildered. Not in a way of championing the considerable divulging of it is present. That more entitled. For the renewal. Come to be shining. In a way to not left it over in the progression of entitled made in time that they do bent in the way related.

With a wedding. He is not in the event of their closing not as much as will intermittent of a change to below with on account of their relative bewilderment as just when it is more than it is ever in the interval of their occasional having known much at a time to spare that is that after every spoon they shall be clouded with a better than a half of their impression that it is a politeness of predilection in the arrangement of their delegating it to them from them as to how are halves made deplorably with an edifice of their mediocrity in the violence of which it is remembered that in the indication of annoyance they without a drama of appurtenances which shall a shawl choose a repetition of their fabrication of whether it is well to do the more that they could should and had in interpretation as a resemblance to whether it is yet at once their praise and she can in chicanery be anointed to an indirect restfulness of plenty of their realisation of whether it is in gentler form of why it is whatever it can show the amount of this as a girl of admirable tendencies in the amount which it is by most of them to call that they allow is intermediate in an hourly shown which it is in planned for the consumption of their repercussion of in violence which they may cut in there for them when it is an abjectly restored in this as a considerable interval of the nicely after three months one every week at home and so they shall with and can change made mean and fairly that it is with soap in indeterminate for the champion of their inequality of reading it from them and they must sing with all be short from having as might with could laugh in as as estimable that it is whatever with a holier because it can without refrain she must be just as careful as ever made to fasten it in a more than resting for it in amount. There is this about forgetting they can be once up. She may come to be here just whenever it suits her to like to have it made into an astonishment that it is allowed. For that as it is. For a time to be known. In case of climbing. She should be there. Just as well as they are told. In time to go. There is a use in crying stop from going and there is a use in reproduction of a work of art. That is what it is. To follow he can to follow he can to follow a better lost to him. And he is awfully rude and impolite and they may make mountains as it has been said out of this as it has to be foremost in the thunder and storm and snow and not snow and ice with what they had it is as absolutely for them with at all as is in shattered made commit in all reliance for the fun of the new color of it as a plenty of the escape of theirs around she does have it all. How do they do.

Having made a mistake about composition they interrupt begin again. It is why they crowd. Authentically. Has nothing to do with it.

With me. An allowance made in less than ever of there partly shown to have had it in as a predilection for the ungoverning rejoinder of mislaying should it be a difference of one and a half in arrangement parallel to the contraction of their joining that it is a favor that they do them to be indicated in a troublesome heavily arbitrated in the reunion not precisely coming to be held for alone as they accept that in a new light shut it must in whether attempted in the exchange which because rested should in our allowance of when they call bother it for them a precisely worded exceptional inelastic appointment of which chosen they must without brief love of not a partly raised machination completed by delectation of made of white and egg color just the same in delicacy and precisely ordered for the admission of when it is too much to take alone of the prevailing that it is as ever sympathetic coming to the known forever as a joining of the million of the soothing of ushered from the mean of in between the failing of it in climax of shone that it is selling as made letting it be all this is as much this is as much as a plain reflection in a glass that is a mirror and the quinces which have value to be outlined in attempted winding much as is frightfully left to the soon to have just as it came without welling from and about upon the announcement of it is just yet when loaned around the whichever it is a light of their rest of it come to the able to take and after all this is as soon that it is come to be not shouted in the eluding as they say two and to make whether they ever remember to have lost it as they did with them which cordiality it makes no difference to like why they know them make it a door a day although a great many more and it is when they like that they can have their favorite in with as a spoon as soon as a liability to the each of which ever could make it if it is a worry to them that they are always to like it in the behavior of their exactly in a part of the circular as a fair of which it is meditatively theirs too in a mistake as no more they than when if it is no more this than they make with it did it it is a crowd of whether they like acting as they go and made a very prevailing incident in it as well come to be hated as a challenge to a colonial if at all a welfare to the necessity of crying why do they have to hover as it is much of it just like a little girl who went. A little girl who went. And why are there eight in forty-two because two are a behavior that has everything for them in in diminishing a better time than they could see it for the whichever it is not very likely that it is knew in known. It is peculiar that if one thing is called white mountain everything not everything but something is called white mountain. They are able to if they have to be aware of sixes and sevens.

It is very pretty to love a pretty person and to think of her when she is sleeping very pretty. It is a thing which gives great pleasure it is thought that they might not be only just as they are about to copy that they say so and a little of it may make a tease a little of it they may be how can it be but known that it is an edge without which they forget to gulp. Some people when they eat make food disappear. That is strange. And obviously near the beginning of edifice in extension for the judgment of the winding of the wading without it as a prevention of why they went. How do they leave it as a message how do they leave it as a weight. How do they leave it as a loss how do they leave it out with it. Now how do they accomodate themselves to the all around feeling that it is better to be right than carefully.

If a little girl is in an aeroplane alone how long is it that she has forgotten what what is it it is not a part of of it not a different part for it with a grass that is should it be more that a cup of this that is a precluding of rather she than thought of how to go about it with a preclusion of the rest of what is born to be come becoming and looks like is it a fair to me. She likes hats. Who has whose. It is fair to me to be as well as they can be. It is a method of construction. Did she.

Be very careful of what you do think carefully do not be very anxious to have it begun but be very good about it and have it already to wait so that if you hear about it you will be there already and that makes no difference by the right of way waiting is partly a favor to them that it is a prevailing joining of indication of which it is combined with arbiter of their destiny to a satisfactory degree need not be mine.

If we must part let us go together.

Never remember that a letter can be read that another can read that whether there is whether regret aigrette which they do not know is the name.

Not to have behavior alter crushed without strawberry or alignment of violet or premeditated behavior in extension of vehement or forsooth or lightness or color or politeness she could know that grass is as moss without seeds and just as well shell peas in early fast as soon they dislike with it or provision not a resume what for. Come and cut. It is not what away with it an early train trained to be through.

Just with him just with him one two one two one two through.

Did he forgot that they can be all three very much better than they were.

A astrakan borrow with all a day that is not to be seen if it looks as if it was through.

Why will martin not a name will nicely ready to be jumped a garment in about before come be wearing is as wainright for the exclusion remind come to be new. Excuse me.

If in bees known never see what is said.

One two three should be as in a refer to it all inclosed that it is a gain of from sand which in where could in especial fortunately extra they may faintly as conditional in retribution it is made of particular for this an instance of their in kind to betray what is it if it is a noon of an extremely exploited unification of bewildering it fancifully just as a delight of when in a chance that it is that there for them all the name of when it is a cloud of their region as a glorious of a not entailing there in time should it for the variety of perpendicular should it come too in decision of a change plan there at another could with a combined of inegality as a prevailing rest that they will do which is why they could in a vertical beam of letting it have twenty to their date it is at once for the best.

Finally I in a let her sell it as a table come to an annoyance for the untied shelf of a hindrance that it is copied in an accounting could it indicative combed shall name coupled resounding accomplishing vertical latterly in avoidable just faintly made on account of the noise in remaining particle of well seasoned hour object restitution only color come in on account made really with ownership to an indelicate invite notional completion be an anointing of caligraphy in bestowal with chunks remained let in to union of appointment considerably with a predicting invariable cushion forty angel just appointment to in vogue that it is representative consignment able in remarked this one to four a plain management of beware to indubitable rest of the announcing partially joined make with a tendency more renowned for

the value as a plate of by joining it is currency to be shunted
for the bewailing indictment of their bother without shrine
of twenty in accomodation knelt for the collusion of reset-
tling the manner of when a tail should not as it is rented by
like a mean aspect of an object to in doubt of felicity custom
of the rendition of in an aspect continue like relative a plain
distance that they can know made to tell a day apart that it is
whether a whisper is what to call them roses in a very good
light it is easy to see that it is more than they can think in
tearing it in to pieces for the vermillion that they call chain
and she is just what she should be she can be always ready to
come. It is very much whatever they will have as a perfect
succession of why they are establishing theirs in evidence of
not in an account of it by the time that it is made very much
better than it is in the receptacle of the shame of a partly
divided reward of being asked to come two days before that it
is not called all of it as bouncing of the though fullness of a
just as much as when they were after it as on account of done
which it is by the prevailing wish to be very much finished in
the elegance of their having an extra waste of a predicament
of how can they flounder because it is all to all in a conditional revisal of a prevalent estimated in an account of which
is it in the variety of their delicate best of the more which it is
calculated that they shall bigger than at drawn in a better
way to make it happen to have it as uniquely left to the
whether it is just added in rather that it is plush in a custom
of which for it as most that a colliding in reality of the more
estimated that it is come to the shadowed in able attitude in
collide with a bell of fortunately come to be three it is not a
very known ably to be mixed as a considerable custodian of
why rush and rule away and so and kind and it is making it a
fuss of them that it is a very much whenever it is shutting up

the daily bust of bread which is why they can aim to be all of known whether it is called glorification and a more why will it be that it is not whatever they can like to do for them when they are here in time to ask just what it was that they were made to do when it was at a time that it could not be known as like when it is a faint and rested choice of coming to the umbrella that is not used for a very good reason as they say appointedly to the fabrication of yellow in a sense so to do what is not that it is as a welcome should in a plant of which eight in the sense of the six be the thrown that to five is a chance made instead of a bed of wall flowers alright.

It is a very agreeable thing to have drawn work made of thread and sheets made of linen and pillow slips made of linen and anything made of pink thread and white linen a very nice thing to like it all at once a very nice to like linen and a thread drawn and everything everything to like everything all at once to like everything as linen as everything to like everything it is a very nice thing.

If any one dreams of the ocean they will dream of little waves.

Very soon frantically at a time when it is not as needed from a knock to anticipate in haste they united in absently furnishing a restless foundation of interval precluding an emerging then in the rest of the undesirable should it with a could have it now. So much intelligence in telling because of inventiveness they come tell well and cream of is it a wedding for the shone upon inverse from a letter box they knew.

It is it one hundred many eaten for the in hand baby should with clarity count now bow and for this is old name could rear let own to not readaptable made have part with will co-incidence made a particle come to do to not immense out lying restitution in ability come climb for they have called with a meandering rest it of them that they have known not to dislike the repeal shown committed cardinally left to have it owned with might for it a share of peculiarly constructed as a hat for them. It is a very great weakness. Who can be told to like wire and a business commenced with a time for them fortunately no more as they were made to be crying yes yes with a dear little just as much could with which it reft from the notable as best that it is not just by the time with all it guessed for them make made do do the dividing not all that just with by come wait for now leave there going advisably with a distinct in to the readjusting with whom make it devoted out now they will be a stretch of country. This is what happened. We were going along and we were looking in at the windows and just ahead of us was a side walk and a number of ones which had a furnishing for coming in and there possibly was if afterwards there was to be uncertainty just like that suddenly. What is the use of interesting any one as to who it was when it might be wrong as to him. And so there is no pleasure except sitting.

Very who not a perilous way of having it is very well to own a dear little box that was new a way wading just a change realise adaptable to choose a placate for now a direction which taken it is fanciful a durable annex called lightly remainder plant from a prefix justification merrily with this non ray of light who can misconstrue knew they dove tail a moisten do fix just as much they need can adroit belabor not fulfilling but west in delight which it is for them to have it as they can they must be known as elegant they will not do what ever they are told is to the daily danger of covering it so all do for this sacred of which it is issue that near by if there have been called horses and dogs so are they painting painting how do you do it is called have it as well and as now it is now to

recuperate individually are just whenever it can have a relaxation of their being a widow it is now that he has managed
not to tell as well as that. It has been said that those con-
cerned with it do not desire to have to go to whether they
like adroit or come to say which is it alright all the time to to
know to deploy notably in caution their vertically an ingredient to catching a pinnacle of additional release conspicuous
to theirs in turn that they must mind in kind to be very serviceable for fortunately reissued known carpet as asiatic do
so that is what I do not fear a resemblance but it is often after
it is possibly to known with with who is in tears for the main
part of which it is not at all that it is what is not very much
what they have both with having that it is just mine because
with a readiness to be planting it for the best of all like when
they do need a very tender shut of the veil of near by come to
be is it in dustiness of the shawl shall sent jacket of course
near when it is a doubt of where will it find the name of
Pendleton always a best to say double to collapse an inhibition of ingredient made a remarkable just as a press of their
sending an appointment of what was it that they looked at as
they were very much as willing as a sound they believe that
they are going to have it. And so do I.

How can it be made to have no identity with having half.
Separate. It does not but pearls. Just like that.

There is no connection in a separation. Connection separation. Flounder. Leather. He is younger than it is of importance to gather that it does not need seven hyacinths instead
of the eight. That is by the way so to speak do they hear let it
be what they have as they need all alike for the place in the
sense not at home on account of the flower which is replacing ahead of time callously in a hurry of needing a little
moving just like in and out in went reminding parsimonious

with a state of at her boy touch it a little way more than ever presumably.

Indifferent to whether to recognise a brother's choice in a picture.

Just as a credibility that a poise and a poison is a part symphony of extension of implacability just gently too suitable judge of no connection. Study connection. A study connection. How splendid. Nobody eats pearls. Smiling. Nobody eats heats does arose piles of dates which are frezeing in the summer able to state it. No combustible hours.

Begin frames.

Ahead wed.

Hour our.

Out she went in and came out.

How do you feel. About it. This way that there is no connection. Between it and just why just in as an ending that there is a fix to be sent to leave or be sent. Say well. Well.

It is to be a study of how to say they were asking if it is what they said. It makes no difference. Longer louder. All in all. Bother and other. Oh the heavenly scent.

It must be known.

But what difference does it make in the little while after that that they in all install in distribution of the anticipation of their address which they share. Come one come all in as a place and plan to have that.

Partly meant just as soon as they have it as a call that they share with a hat of not shone when they must too for the nucleus with a withdrawal of nicely come to have it as a purpose of the inhibition of the recklessness of not being mistaken that it sounded all or a quarrel of the knowing it as all of it alike.

Alike like a patient they mean all a tune attuned an angle

periodic of a kind to be selfish just whenever they are disposed to vindicate out of it now that they must be a way of holding their hand so that the dimple shows by bending in and out not by the placing of it in equality roughened an angle of the meant as firm should it now it would be to ask about it more can be shown in whispering that they were alright. It is why she must be asking one her two eyes alright alike or should they be different. Are her two eyes alright alike. Or should they be different as they are alright. Are they alright alike. Or should they be different. As they are are alike alright or should they be different.

Whether perilous or a curl or radiography or change or attributing it to the better of there out lasting shown to the nicely implicated of the soon as to be avoiding lent come to an integral shadowing of shown name named alike plenty of plainly have it a custom of the vehicle of interposition know which beside an imprudence for the languid knot cog of lent nor the prevailing just as compared near irregular reliance purchase govern not sorely as a condition pardoning various only known painstaking joined leave restitution by waylaid motionless does it reckon as one of two by dumping illighted most a predicament supple as to thirds named net of time that is so why needless come rest accidental join place mention are attributable less ankylose not dispelled just as a presently cause to announce large exact prearrangement of according them that lopped in the early just aspect close to nothing of a chance violently recalled as cause benighted of the soon will she be the best of the known fancying it pleasantly remarkable aspect of a quarter of a million it is just only that a culled from a stock near that in by a torn in inimical like that large prevented about the welcoming of come suitable reappointed just as they need never be in doubt like that at all tell to not a past dish of a stilled just as much as when nobody makes it a too to do not merely a planting of every day a daisy it is attributable in the region of a ground that they are dented which makes two new calls it accustomed to why they are willing as ever theirs to make it be twice at announce called when arrangement furtively parsimony in a gallop of a bewildering shutter of an allowance captiously readjust goes to forward in an agglomeration get it without wedding for the out loud of just change gain what they do do love it above all nearly alike to appoint read more arrange violet as it.

A mistake to think that it is what they have to have as in an hour.

Gently gotten for some such behavior alight ably to copy loose opposite charge join article call remind too affectionate as ready are agreeable announce happen as state.

How do better for a coat leave regular beneath a line of pails which in why they are spilled mountain of how what in once are for this lightly slightly remainder prevail a course to jump a guerdon of rope that they like two to three and is a business.

Porter all ought or a acting a group does twine outlined harping glean got at all rope there square but as it is a gone conclusion that is as in to own a just as it got it here very willing to be thought all right a cow in allowance radiography come to conclusion if it is my wish in a collection do more that is why and a dot for the clover for a rather collaborate two ninety handsomely in aggregate just when when at her floor in willing do must about they now do the search advance are this come to be with all a but will her. Did not do it.

How can it not be not be one be at her vainly a boy so now

they must be a hair on their head too such in wind and ought to her.

Water boy sheets which have told not to be mended for a whole water well which have been told to have it a peculiar character letting it let it fall.

Coincident planet couple of cup camille planet rectangle age of yet follow the employment crushed elucidation there in particularly mean offensive come collect touching genuinely dismay lain for the for instance accustomed customary long while engendered inch aim less category way farer way and land nut pain incredible letting combined fugitive have neighborly reissued determine named the peculiar as an establish main of the have it habit to call there.

What was it that it was a place could loan the still after ready shall to explain not but known come careful daily settle banded cover variably and shell this to hour as pass cut it around. How can you love what you tell what you tell where you tell that you tell all to tell a great deal of it to the arrangement of a plenty of bother.

Neatly a page well what is it when there is a better thought of in a better have it that it is enchained as a perpendicular in rest of agreeable nestle with nettled to be certain of renting in collaboration they make mistaken in a rest of the ability to annoy charge of believing this is out to cry that they made a poise of the chandler of a regard to the invitation of a chance to be authentic in the retribution of a custom to customary in the ground of a fanatic in the willow of a refectory should it be charged in place.

Leave a brown coiled alone for the nearly withdrew to be called why will it with a soon to have just as a planting of with and in a Paris that makes that standard standardised in glorious glow with a spurn it in a blanket of with wish plainly colored Willie in advise to call should a plantation of their soon.

Each one suffering and sun each one to be jelly and follow a prediction of whether it can be to tell her how very well it is better than being to begin to be pink and yellow and then a clarification of settling a precarious reiteration of why if in case of delightfully they arithmetical in a fellowship of their preparing it unaccountably just as amelioration of the intricacy coming to perfect at noon this is which if they go to be for just made and couple of the readjustment come to be clerical in their in union that it is just what they do to say come to the rapid wish and very merry make it do in inevitably they chance in a chance of their going with it might without a just to be he knew that he admired most why they were awaiting in the mixing of a joint rest established for the colliding of integral able to be not a considerable guess could too in maidenly maidenly count a countess obliges a well coming stamping not lightly but one two one two in a feat and they it in coming having the felt of a shelter in a considered with it as highly shyly she is at all to let a pair breathe too new to new to me to be a complaint theirs in periodical engine of a combine with it may they tell without them. Without them.

How owls read towels made for tea a sample of a tumble to the justly never couple of a done to the made that is she knew she was sad.

How have Hubbard Hubert and Bandol mandoline in a refreshed colored come a page need a wary rained purpose inchoate loud to a current of two she must be dead anyway without a horse or a blanket as it is what makes it have up and down a presiding they if an all went to the shutter they make had an answer just as well that they are a preparation for the reason that they never stock it in a white avoid whatever water couple radiant town. He went in town in town. It is very curious that they have all of the addresses so far apart where they live with their parents.

Who likes her.

Added to extra extras extraneous to be please.

Funerals are added to ministrations.

In time.

They made need pointed just as sewn faintly very pointed fair just made Williamson place pass please higher rightly for this they call must it be spangled in the corner of their blaming just as well when it is calculated in the best that it can be to come to save they do. To think about who means.

It was why they remembered they did for them just as will in a minute that is to reconsider faintly a joint pleasure in a irremediable point of color of the winding they must change is made integrity they will call close who can in replace joined made a cost of the plant of their around in obliging they shall be filled with a recondite curling of left to them to a large and in unavoidable rendition of the pleasing that it is a circumstance to make it for nearly polite in the eradication of a joint measure of their believing not behind in especially should without theirs always as cause to not only laying the absurd with a just as most to be conniving in just the reference referring in customed to the contrary called in force for the in an appointment melodious in eradication of the presence of allowed just as much in politeness come to be not as a kind of the inherent let it be called the not unsightly should with without near the most when noon come to be made as if it is too plain the making of a farm for the nuisance of a reliable does it when they can. It is a mistake to say does it.

Pine a table had to have its surface rubbed to pine to have a table to be a host in himself to have to have a relief when a new and old and frightened and as alike a part of the told this to the elaborated made a matter of their just as well that it is not counted as a nice foil to the laying of the just to it by near and nearly come to follow fellow fallow nearer this in climb with gay cost a does chance should and tell make a fasten fine in cost that it is market marketable grand in callow seen as ostracism extract for should to the new last and laid a time in which it is for the new because a light of how do they despair when it is what they like weighed instead patting a bed they have at and a point tumble this near if a wall is caught just goes to plenty in allusion named a call to face beseech with demean lain a padding for the going slightly ready near best and my faintly leave as gone makes a preparation to the test testing a will it go to the just now in plan for the occasion to be heard a plain accidentally up and down for the union in which there is may they be of assistance just as jointly they go well well at a well easter is Monday thanks to very much to-day.

It is very difficult to grow blue hyacinths while white ones are very large and as for lillies of the valley there is a difficulty they dry if they take too long and are not the right green for this in distress they make a remarkable difference in whether the table is higher than before in consequence of not being ready to-day in the best of this which is in amount of their peculiarly resembling for the sake in an intermission that they make they do distaste for partly in a restitive foreboding of their inelegance in just as an ointment of their selection with a with as sheltered to the touch their unknown for the point of where they were as blindly in their in name to be sure specially for this as known. How is poetry as cured let it alone for the behavior of a buoyant panting in a regular justification of individual declamation of without proof that it is an permissible to jump with a pointing of their in nine that it is what wither whether in allowance must it for the appointment radically just as soon as fold their appointment to not to leave in allocation of exploits to the notion of pondering without in relieve they can must it be for not the object that it is not more than it is counted combined they can see with season for the joint to ratify the pleasure of pondering in offense they told because in with just shade it lower as in guessing persist in raise for them now this which is it for alike told with a latterly to bequeath in in appropriation call it like new that it is gone without not for the existence of best letting rather gratify in soon come to this for in deliver later just made for the reference custom to it with a belittling of a region do and other of the are there for it lamentably guessed as to with a whether they can pay do not do gone for the day made rain light nor the guess are there lain with them they may do very much to make it matter for the rest that it is a part of the bather will they go in rest for coal more consider.

Are made ardently cause of line in amiable business for the thin dishes namely denied to be carpeted in the adjoining they or careless dear made leave the resultant in or just finely they cause with it as always to in tears may cost their inexhaustible for them to do which is a gross flattery. It is very difficult not to make an explanation. How does George avoid it. George avoids it by being an example of a life among better than left to it primarily just when they foreseen to be at all like it.

Bay and be patient they note their plainly very seen as a half in and on on account may shaft in retain do for it a right in a fan and Jaffa is his name Merton Jaffa is the name of the

one named as plainly as they can sign two there how or hardly
for the after avoidance do as told cutting part of the by light
charles Charles or one hours. Think of one thing do another.
How or how hardly.

All about it part reliable justify just if Kate they draw.

Hours and hours of these.

Pay less of the rest of the just as well as for the rest of the
just meant to be won partially in the realisable for the made
in careless joined correctly need because remained vindicate naturally leave reliable with act actually vacation notably remain politely that it is more of the calling there most
are with change for the to be sweetly this is the rejoinder of
let alone come with it too all of not possibly leaning for
changes remain best with all their various rusted color object of the fair that it is marketable leaning with a perversity
of prevailing that it is located with such mainly panting come
to the disappointment of an actual lighter model come to a
slip of a caught to be splinter this is what they call very much
as they have readily consecrated just as it is with a comfort of
their willing not nor in the justification like made around
with it as gone for the mocking does it just why they full and
fell left the prediction of not a adjustable left of leaving
mended by with soothing not for likely rested in rest about
comfort come in a widening does it left will will test test to
throw throw in about above getting freshly they need dining
room in the house with a known come to poise just as a welcoming does it double that it shows refrain near obstacle to
grace shatter because withal a gust of winding terrifically that
it will do rest of it not very strong forgive the share.

Much too much not much too much.

Hours and hours ours and ours bears and bears bear and

bear she had no children of her own and when she inherited she inherited nothing in comparison with what she had.

No not necessary a bay is placid and a behavior which makes it be all in all to always a prize around where they can be held capable of restlessly advising rapid delight in joining the very nearly paid and very likely what they knew are a partly considerable double widening of the inevitable bothering of them to be called why they went away just as it was might then be found near to the appointment of which could be thought left to them theirs made beside tooth as a went over plenty in tumbling reach for it out plead recall but need how known as it is.

Practically with a grow in growing dividing diversion paler gotten appointed verbally pained as a grace for the rally to this which goes gas in a court by merely an anchor in a burst does displace to an bewilder fairly cup in a heartily lain where they were arthur in wishes trimmed care with making tens made without wholly a funny tried an able render come truly for just pending theirs a furl of a hold how about it does well maid choose a ferry door and dug out bell benighted just as they wish it is does come too sore to be believed be calm blame.

In a bargain which is made allow best to be instead.

If axle accident a president pressing in a course of does ankle angle in disappoint meant may marry casement lend a line own cover just William willing for jumped for nightly they call mind minded gall splinter does it tarry Gus guess Gustave dear does able made in maple may bit a bit for narrow pistol day and wedding we will with verbal pay pained did most spare shall all might lean collect do adjoin play and elbow to a noon of cape to the toxic bone of count went more a glow grown with a wished pull it call they can reach remedial does plan amiable cut or trinket let after noon re-adjusting their same portended willow model from a throw them sent do drop it is an intended past left without in privately doubling a crowd to narrow their abandonment of a circle near by at all real way a way should it be not an announcement of a dismissal ascent dissent attention in might without call collect they if at least it is about about they know they will be seen all away not at twice as much familiarly in remainder in spoken for tease please bay obey they forget restitution a calender pine in two pines in refine a mistake in an indifferent reclamation let alone they why as if not minding minded readily the rest all but to go come where it is a predicament canary cannery allowance in an end blame emblem got to analysis of remaining postively call who change they must be folded with a mischance rebuttal of a tarpaulin realised terrace act article are artificial position in a coat rather more anticipated they can know, is he apt to be with them as a wait. He thinks of him as a admire but at best as better in bitter come to rain with a polite to readily to do call fairly provision it is what they meant.

Arbiter arbitrary arbitrarily Arthur are this are the result a claim for the renewal extra guess joined namely in a prevision of attribute does needless pained in persuaded finally finish finely named near which is manned precisely a plain with a call that it is mined custom a customarily they may need a large open darkening reference with and to allow not minding a persistence raised in position of a prevailing with main leave readjust do nor behave in behalf perfectly copied in a bother of a withering joined placidly does in collision rested merely a pleasure for the difference complacently made in a minor respect would and might a plan disturb mean like a renting powerfully this a providing dismay spent to fairly perfect a way to have maps maple a tree if thin and thank the moist play plain in according a please a pleasure stop a little.

Name names familiar famish a trump he is a triumph of the James is an even invented cordially a loosen loosening a grown growing give obstinate with her with an appointing it is about time cousin decent deceive deserve district displace deserve does and delight they will ask if it is whatever they may have to have for themselves perceiving in shown goes a near glance plainly take but with expenditure really classed fair to an disappoint love more they love disappoint love more goes as in share stainlessly a collect why they do render it fairly well as it were so much more or so which is why it is not their in an end a bit of it if it will is it quarreling in double restriction joined in a whether it is partly mere for in it partly come there banking upon it.

In the day-light blue is bright.

Disturbed because of details in plainly and at once in quantity that it is for and forest jumped perhaps willingly they may come to not land and but for the request of does with adjusted peculiaity ready to make it continue just alike this is highly desirable and in every which is away it is definitely definitely aroused deliberate part of part of the called with it in any particular just as an eradicate for the nodding peculiarity of a blame they must be offended and financially pleasure and a pleasure so that it is plentiful when they are best of it as known that it is with it as a wish they made made brightly in does it if it is difficult they could regain a pointedly left to them reference just as yielding in cloth that is made behind meticulous in rejoining the distance privately left to them in as soon in union causing it just as a friendly the announcement in repeal detailing the quantity of not aggressive as much as delusion in for and meant to shut in it unaccountably laid measure does and was nearly behind in the collusion not with it as at all near by the considerable named to the pressure of in resting for the announcement does when collect left just and made and tall the coming nearly for it as an article blamed mainly this which whether a pressure to be strive and left to not by the quintessence of reverberating jumped with an access of possibly which is does and make because tempted to define lain that the most counted in rectification marble that known akin and bow the fairly whether it is sustained just and nearly considerable for the negligence reliable confined namely pointed in doubt-fully legacy does near nearly fanned just with it as having ahead out this is made of with by and near for lain do be handed it as it is in precisely better than with a kind of rest-ing just as nearly to be candidly for a next to the just when-ever a dislike is privately arranged to be not at most consider-ably with a farther than it is merrily does with a going for it in joined mainly left to the resistance of an established dearly with it as it if caught not just to be doubled reasonably come to be politely diminish theirs as a standard of delightful and very sweetly thought and trusted entrusted not a consider-able distinguish it from mainly left to the disturbance with a jointly named accustomed robin known to them to leave a dearly formed essential rained in their with it is never an astonishment to leave to do to consider making fortune is a partly there that it is refrained hour our lay tumbled martin may farther reverberation in a glance with a place bar and a gust from which do mainly mingle in thin and define what is whatever just a considerable in a repetition founded in ex-cuse they we this dear in use a double leave train to tumble but in wind and is it naturally disdained with a point that is

mainly a provoking esteem just a terrific without settle leave
out leave and why it is recorded a diminish does a main and
mantle come to perfection deny double two and doubtful
they region and regain diverse possibly leave around makes
it about about this jumped indubitably with a credit of record
in allowance prevailed nicely in harrangue they may estimate and wheat is which for long need renewal cordial lain
protect annoy develop lightly in restitution does and there
having does very much well leave demand legacy surely
tyranical in a rush change a division into five and three they
and alike is a sound of a wonder whether it repeats just as he
said he was willing to go and come but he did not come he
was there every afternoon and he watched the workmen and
they were finished and then they were capitally added by
reason that it could be in a blame of the account of why it is
better than just if it is a very satisfactory went and garden
because a tree many at a time is not a garden but to call so
reflecting that it is not an advice an an advice change retain
retained ask and do behind beneath polite intricate higher
than a double hole in a terrace too won wondering under
join it at once once by theirs at in time which is why it is after
that by beneath a trunk a trunk of a tree is what is left when
the branches have been cut off and a tree is blooming. And
now come.

Sacramento felt with it cut a call of benches which when
ever the surrounding plainly near the attraction of undeniable beware of making it do that it is reclaimed their certainty be like the multiplying really in the candor of ulti-
mately bedewing carefully their contestation considerably just
as plainly for it in inclined comparative named graceful in
planting their perplexity of precarious just as agreeable to an
allowance perform perforate land again to many armored

come with justice contribute allowance prevail custom account to amount blame leave just to many ate renewable double render fairly less attribute come with about clearly arthur does make rain rainable manifest bother double wind to much kindle for the asset tumble leave a rather be for article of wane dear family lame bewilder does as best of it which more this in cruelty polish for more there as they said about it to visible appoint do appoint made with a point theirs clearly as finely paid remarkable admit to a considerable running because with a practicable adjoining only agreeable revision not as men attend shone rebewilder calm as to do squarely their poison for and minding when they say spoken. It is useless to be a mother. A little while Danny. Arthur. A little while Danny. Danny. Arthur. A part from here edge but as it is as flannel well attend at a tiring with a side and needle to be in when end then better mere for a capable abrupt lose for the coil of their as a sold all right come to it by nearly what is feel felt at a boat so that it is colliding they in supper and pacing made a wrinkle with as soon double rose in riding this in collected temper with at all make a pretty as pretty the adder with it a polite nearly offer juniper with no doubt a berry. That is whether made a market in resembling their recall minded with a pair made just as soon by this with them. Must it be attended.

There is this great difference between going and their promise in respect to following a passage where there without white they call able for an attachment to doubling dear to matter that it does date made in a proper just just made.

Whenever they have thought.

A very easy way to think. Come and pay may way to a dove wave shove lay allow does carry read remain but a lamentable do this about with a credit for which ardent light making both other amount when winding if it is asked to send for more a distinct liking for whether it washes as well as flannel as flannel as flannel. The kind of thinking that they carry Carry Ross Carry came to be all as if John as if John as if it is very be winding that they like a spoon. A spoon is full of gravy taken as soup. Which is which do you think. To think to think a think to and think. What is the difference between vocabulary and thought. He thought.

About a meant to take care. Having forgotten a wind of course. To be sure.

How has hours a day arbitrary lain dexterous riding carefully break this with diffficult namely relieve are there changes does it make a difference for their care double losing cried call labor not a highly interested without made prevailing cost rather a division excused seen see at all bother polite deliberate with our glass come to custom accustomed felicity does venturesome tally include as rather with about daily lamed a motion disability dislike for them that it is whatever made it be to heave they like. To whom toward a present that they give when asked for as a way not to take a liberty with a pleasant rest of the proper leaving namely to be to all entirely closed leave with whether does more not a change come highly with a peril that it is a kind might decide ream collect gone giving an as to send shone considerable beside with gone this is to with it a call lain fair near bustle this is to account given near within a place dotted considerably a disappoint when them they way where alright. It is very diffficult to talk talk chalk toward how a withstand does mainly leave with a willow which is an early thing early. In general. The general the general of the name.

Which is inelegant trying useful bewilder need copy used as a program theirs beside indolent neglect plainly there because furnish and planted practically named politeness for this carefully just in domination plainly their care for the nicely reminded but this which is making a pronouncement of laming it for this as a doubt if at a willingness there especially might refuting whenever latterly done bewildering are made rested a point this which left of then there placid for which raft because where ever lined as appointment weighed plainly leave it a circumstance of generally refuse are but her with lame last plentifully known custom of the handling peculiar in fact temporarily noon just as might without pass passively laid dexterous ramification known with a please what ever it is as a justifiable return to their abounding out loud made to differentiate because terminated colliding refer does and soon letting plenty spend toss without fail leave at last made jointly to shine might whichever comply they not unroofing a claim rested by nearly offering it to this as shown for the wondering if it is catapult to the difficulty lie near became wherever it is just as reference positively taken renounce bequeath in united panting clearly they must entangle account bestow ready granted likely shutting make for an instance do fortunately repeated integral left to the announcement marked once a place of theirs that it is at all opportunely leave in when wherever marketable this to be sure in an hour around the made it a behavior collect do nicely letter blown for a chattering bother that it is next.

It is very kind of Helen to be sorry that so told so with many visitors they must stay a very little while shortly and whatever they do.

Old older stuff as which when it is a kind of making partly once in a week remain doubt fully now known that he can having a certificate.

What is a difference between a vocabulary. A dictionary.

A vocabulary outlines the capable district of rendering it a count of however it is carelessly sentenced shattered record near this in sees. He sees a vocabulary that is article for article in a trough though amiable counting deferred knock before the door they will largely bother for it it is win fringes couple does differently farther indelible leaning clandestinely variety in sorts of liking a training leave moderately regarded apart restless that it is jeopardised in three that forsook considerable mailing partially riotous does deliver classify hoes and theirs that two and four in a claim regarded abandon dispatch recollected leaving rapid to mainly came well formerly readjust does care like namely regret oblige nodded to disable like line where end found fast to considerable alike the magnified to a time that is our a lane where it is what ever does it to how much they do after all agreement comb collar lest it should be happier for it yet.

That is not what is meant by indiscretion indiscreet indistructible interred interlined interpreted ineradicable may two.

Fifty fifty may too.

About what is it that they will not be very often right about what after it is put away where there needs to be plainly a called have it apart they carpet as to be particularly joined accident prolonged write merrily does appear apply go strong alike the nodding to a close play with it should it counting couple comply verbally does having a kitty across however it is probably is a toned and trick that they saw to in a beam forsake couple of collapse however used to definite in precluding as far as fixture preferable in occasion that it is soluble made in case for this which committed done as a just without this that they must do call in a blame where wherever gather exact manifest establish lain with cross crossly alike this is very after at all make their admit with see see and they call capable a couple dear does delay so that it is why when and wherever wherever are shut to be and which referred to dedicate in gathering allowance they made half of double be their share. This is why they occasionally to like repasts which is what fairly enjoins to cast it in a way theirs a pressure which makes it very much without whenever liked it confident to noon that it is done to an attend to resend here there considerable left to right have it as true truly just shut that is whenever like it they without around around at all a ball. Not very happen to be seize seven sort a sort of at all. This is without any doubt a number. Fifty fifty may too. The could be as would as they like come at a dish a table, at able at able a dish at a dish at a dish a dish add which they whichever they cause as like as like as whichever it is consequence consequence to.

There is a very great difference between a vocabulary a dictionary and Arthur Arthur and Ernest becoming George. Danny becoming a very increased produce a prosody. This is what a vocabulary is. What is a vocabulary. Settling the North Pole little by alike and never not liking a distinct layer of their repeal. The way to have a grammar is to learn diagram. A belief in right away they may, they may be following me up. Up cup culpable custard culpable account occupied and their tell. I see though a part of their say so. The next is more vocabulary and some grammar or more grammar or more grammar. Arthur or more grammar after Finally George a Vocabulary.

Forensics

THEY WILL HAVE NOTHING to do with still. They will
had that they have head of the skill with which they divided
them until they knew what they were doing without it.

A dog who has been washed has been washed clean with
our aid in our absence.

After a long decision they will wait for what she does.

She chose to be helped by their coming here.

No distress in elegance.

Quarrels may wear out wives but they help babies.

We will hope they will not wear out wives.

It is an appointment that he will keep in singing for them
and they keep an appointment.

They say it would have been better.

To invite.

Would it have been better.

To say.

Would it have been better

To show

Them this.

Forensics are a plan by which they will never pardon. They
will call butter yellow. Which it is. He is. They will call birds
attractive. Which they are. They are. They will also oblige
girls to be women that is a round is a kind of hovering for
instance.

Forensics may be because of having given.

They made all walk.

They say is it better to follow than to presume. Shown as shutters.

Now what is forensics. Forensics is eloquence and reduction.

It is they who were in a hurry.

She made Caesar leave it to Caesars.

What is forensics.

Forensics is a taught paragraph.

Paragraphs.

Will they cause more as the middle classes.

Does it make any difference to her that he has taken it. Of course it does although as she was considerate of me she did not manage it. This is forensics.

Everything makes spaces.

I agreed to everything.

This was not my business.

And yet I am not puzzled.

Because I was obedient.

Now think of forensics.

What are forensics establishing.

Forensics. I say I will obey her.

Forensics. She will reveal him.

Forensics. And they will come at them.

With him.

Now think of forensics as an argument.

Does he mind forensics if it is edited.

I can see that she can see to change one for three.

Now is this forensics for me.

When she can see she can cease to pursue how do you do. What is forensics forensics is an argument to be fought.

Ask for him. Do not ask for him.

Ask this for him.

It is very patient to ask this for him   Patient.

Forensics. How are and will she finish one before the other. If she does it will be satisfactory. There is no argument in forensics.

Just about why they asked her she bought it.

What is forensics. Did you meet Bruce yes but I did not mention it. If there had been a cause.

Shall we. A necessity.

Having been nervous was anticipated.

They might be and have spilt syrup.

What are forensics. Forensics are elaborated argument. Mister Bruce.

Elaborate argument.

There is a difference between a date and dreary.

Snow at an angle can fall.

But will she.

They may go.

At a certain gate.

For them to call.

Will she need a title.

Must they copy a matter.

Or would they call a cloth annul.

Categoric or a thought.

Heavenly just as bought.

Forensics are double.

They dispute a title and they dispute their trouble.

A title is made for defense. It did not defend him nor did I. I always do.

PART TWO.

Partly a defense.
Have you come in.
Yes I have but I am not in which is a pity.

PART THREE.

Just why does she mean me.
What are forensics.
Do not be persuaded that you have heard something that has caused you not to come. Theodore can give in to at least one.
That is not forensics because there are not two. He made forty thousand in two.
Yes which they did.
Forensics are the words which they like. They must be careful.
Once who was through.
Should think with you.
Which once she was through.
With it.
Enlightenment.
Forensics is an argument.
Does it make any difference if they are alike. That is an argument.
Forensics leads to reputation.
How about forensics.
It is farther which is for mixed happy in better.
Hear me.
She should be worthy of being careful.
And must it be felt.

They admire in the sense of lose that they thought.
With her.
She may be called amiable in fancy.
All this interests him with forensics.
What is the difference between him and his friend.
It is all alike forensics disposes of that.
Should he.
By their advice should he.
If he followed their advice.

That is not forensics forensics has nothing to do with advice and why. Now forensics has only to do with the difference between inconvenience and disgrace. There is no chance to better gather. It is able and beneficial. She made an argument do and after all she did frame. No pleasure in an accusation. Did I say she would go.

All this is conclusion.
What is forensics.
They need pleasure singly.

PART II

A parlor is a place.
Who knows why they feel that they had rather not gather there.

PART III

Will he ask them why she chose this. If they do he will be disappointed in her being so withdrawn and reminded and when will two meet one. The necessity. Further. Should hurry be advantageous more in coming than in going in adding and following. Should he be they worship welling. Their emotion welled up but admittedly they were admiring.

Forensics are plainly a determination.

Does and do all include obstinacy.

Particularly for pleasure in clarity.

She makes hours.

Well what do you believe. Do you believe in ease in understanding. Do you believe in favors in accomplishment. Do you believe that they regard with forbearance their increase of rectification nor do they they bewilder and but whether in fancy they charge them and consistently they are better without followers. They should be charity without call. No noise makes tranquility a burden with help and a trouble to them to end well. Very well I thank you is why they were generous. Think forensically. How I doubt.

It is more than a pleasure to dream more than a pleasure. To dream.

Were he to manage to whom would there be an obligation to oblige.

PART IV

If they think well of selling and they do who do they refuse for you of whom. Which they do.

An argument is sustained.

Has he meant to call out loud for his mother and not in disuse married or rather meant to marry. Should it be that with which they are startled. All arguments are helped with no insistence and she says. I will not positively deny, why. Better than they have the privilege of decrying them.

What is an argument. What are forensics. What are master

pieces. What are their hopes. An argument is this. I have it. They reserve it. They do not answer at once. Forensics is this. Better come when it rains, better come when it rains, and rains, better come and puzzle that they have been within and it rains who have all by the time and not also to go.

They had no argument without doubt.

What are master pieces. Master pieces are when he has been cold and has been softly so and now has turned over.

Forensics are a remedy in time. So have thousands. A master piece of strategy. An argument of their deliberation. The forensics of abuse which has not been written. No thought of their search.

PART V

She said I should be ready she was. I reply she was ready I was ready and we both went. Forensically this leads to establishment of a difference I beg to differ. Rather more than I beg to differ.

Our tower.

That is a fault

Forensics may bestow what they ought.

Shall judgments be perfect.

She came and bought one. Oh thank you. This makes a subject for forensics. She came and bought one. Oh thank you. And then they rest. She came. And bought one. Oh thank you. And then they rest. Forensics is in the state. They do feel that they are included in a state. In a state. A state is a piece of a part. Which they make added. Forensics is so true.

A state apart.

Will they content will they contend. Milk. Will they think

that they meant made an instance of shut her for them a time.

It is very easy to make forensics. Anxious.

At last I am writing a popular novel. Popular with whom. They may be popular with them. Or more ferociously.

Forensics consists not in hoping to have this destroyed. As much as why not.

Partly why not. Forensics is an adaption of trilogy. She is useful therefor she is not martyred. And they are correct or why do they so.

Forensics consists in disposing of violence by placating irony.

For that there is this use. Follow for mean. To mean to cover following by they mean to be at one and then they mean to follow with following their meaning.

She reads passionately for him in means. And they invite partly for him in means and so they ask appointments for him in means to carry on their pleasure in usage. How are ours entangled. Nobody can be declared for them formerly. Forensics reside in the power to receive many more often in use.

If I asked if it were so would the answer make them know that answering with intuition is what forensics are in vanishing. And have they vanished or been vanishing. Which they do not do. Because some are still doing something in answering.

Hurry hurry him do. This is not forensics because it is not added. Forensics establishes which is that they will rather than linger and so they establish. Follow me first they went there after they had been with him. This is forensics made into a certainty.

It is very extraordinary in forensics that they can be right which they are as they mean they add to compare. And so they win in fusion that so they oblige pleasure in advancement. Think of forensics, think placidly of forensics.

Who can come to this in pleasure and believe that they will have their certainty. When they leave they must betow this on and with them which they relish. In which way they resolve to abolish devastation for them as planned. It is made more nearly eaten which is very close to his watching. And so they know that they are patient in progress. This makes forensics independent. It is very easy to see that he has been bowed by constraint because he waits. This is forensics illuminated.

What is a forensic bird. A bird considered forensically is very close to admiration. In consequence to have it said leave and carry, a bird leaves and a bird carries. Birds leave and carry. And gradually as if in indifference. Birds leave and birds carry. As if in indifference. Forensics chooses that they conclude. In carrying and in choosing and in leaving birds leave birds carry birds choose, birds in leaving birds in choosing, birds in carrying conclude the carrying the choosing and the leaving. As reasonably. And so forensics begins again.

Make it be mine partly can not enter into forensics.

If she is sitting quietly and it is known will they correct this in explaining. Forensics as we are told are always bold.

No no indeed not they and forensics can be held at bay.

This is a forensic sentence. She meant not to think of what would be the use to which that which was done would be put. She refused to think of the use to which that which was done would be put. And in the struggle because preparatorily there need not be a struggle in the meantime and with significance a struggle is separated irremediably with outburst. And yet it is all occasionally. For them it is and might. For instance forensics does not use nor deny nor imply it refuses to curve. In that way there is abundance.

She said she liked it best and did she like it best or did she change her mind upon seeing the other. This is a question and answer and forensics will gather that they were familiar with the answer. Yes they would think very well of them both. And she would be very happy in having accounted for it. This is forensics mildly. And yet it can be recognised.

She knew that they could care to leave forty more there. Forensics is in use when calling further they arouse misuse of their action as having appealed to it for them to requite them. It is better to have it lost than if it had remained two. So she says in her pleasure of their detention. And then. It will be changed to their advantage. This is the way that they do not need pleasure in forensics. Pleasure is their capacity to choose well known rings. And they covet a brooch and love a brook and neglect broods and all of it will measure theirs as much. Retain them. Follow another. And but whether. They could continue. To countenance them.

Should it be reasoned that they will plan their trophy in winter. She made such light as there was fatter.

A climax is better than farther. And so forensics choose. And never. To differ. Forensics asserts that calm in time is their remedy. Just as is an obligation to reinforce presence of their protection.

How can they use policy of persuasion. Listen to hints. Forensics begins with union and organisation. After that. Advance in volume.

They shall stretch. Their conclusions. From here. To there. They will. Prepare. Efficaciously. Just as much. As they have been. In the habit. Of anticipating. Melodiously. In reference. To their analysis. In a garden. Admire forensics.

If in the meaning of their connection. They disturb. Without it. As much. As they generously instil. Into them. In their allowance. Of whether. They will partly fail.

Forensics is a distribution unequally.

Explain why it matters. That they must bewilder. With whatever. They could crowd. As treasure. And so they fastened. Window curtains. Forensics makes regaining wholly a feather in meditation.

Just when they please.

Forensics is established.

Just why they met. They will bemoan, they will excuse they will reverse they will comply with them as a cause. And wealth, they will use energy in very much with which they will have caused their ought, ought they to comply, made it as predetermined, vouchsafed, or with the cause of their relief, that they once knew. It is a gradual cause. They will be perfectly in love with doves and woods. And very much what they had hoped. In singing.

Forensics can be so delicately heard.

What did she do with fire. She almost put fire to forensics. As useful. As usual. As vagrant. As appointed. As veiled. And as welcome. In their plenty. This may be there. And they will dwell upon it.

This may not be there and they will not venture not to dwell in this way more upon it. They may be very able to cover it without a change of leading it from this to that in violence. In which. They may encounter. All that they. May trust.

For them there is no escape. Forensics may pale. It often does. And such as it. Is more than very often their return. Do not be cautious in readiness.

Just why. They like. What they do.

Forensics is richly in a hurry.

They fasten the best ways on their detachment.

A detachment of troops. Who can. Be careful. Of a. Detachment. Of troops. And if they are. What is it. That they leave there. As they leave alike. It. Alike. As a bother.

To them. This can show. That they. Must. Accept. A denial. They have authority. For all. That they want. As their. Treasure. And. Do they. Hope. To show. Something. For it. Without. An appointment. Just when they went. Usefully. In their. Destruction. In. Enjoyment.

Such forensics can lately take shape.

Just plan their use. Then carry it out in principle. Find it a favorable moment. To advance. Their interests. Moreover. Just at once. Which is. By their account. That they will have it as a blemish. In theirs. In unison. An advantage to forsake. Which they will. As they may glean. More facts. For which. By their ordinary values. They will be practically. As far apart. Forenscis may be athirst for gold. It may with them battle and die. It can as much bequeath and condole. For them. To merit. That they. Should console. Them.

Afternote

The Plain Edition of 1931 of Gertrude Stein's *How to Write* was published in Paris in a limited edition of 1,000 copies. Perhaps because of its French typographers and printers, the edition—from which the Something Else Press edition of 1973 and the Dover edition of 1975 were reprinted—contains what appear to be several typographical errors. Some of these apparent "errors" are quite obviously just that, typographical mistakes. However, given Stein's penchant for word play and punning in this particular book, it is nearly impossible to know the authorial intention of a great many ostensible errata. For example, in her list of "ways to welcome painters," Stein interrupts a catalogue of nationalities with "Urugayen painters." Although it might be tempting for the stonedeaf proofreader to correct this to "Uruguayan," the original animates a sexual pun demonstrating another way to welcome some painters. Similarly, Stein's preference for a "Buic" car may insinuate her desire for a French-sounding automobile over the American Buick. Her sudden revelation that the name Harold Acton might be "useful altogether" as "Hatold Acton," clearly makes more "sense" than repeating the original name. In short, it would be a mistake to normalize Stein's writing which, consistently throughout her career, toys with odd punctuation and, together with an almost Dadaist sophistication of structure and syntax, often reflects a healthy disregard of Eighteenth-century rooted grammatical principles. Hers is a language of the ear as much as it is represented by a standardized "text."

Accordingly, my editorial assistant, Jawad Ali, and I made only six alterations in the entire text. Rather than make arbitrary changes in the Plain Edition, we retained the remaining "errors." To help future scholars, however, we thought it would be useful to list the most obvious misspellings and neologisms. The number in parentheses represents the Plain Edition page number, while the number appearing after the word or phrase represents the Sun & Moon Press page number. We have also noted the changes we agreed upon.

—DOUGLAS MESSERLI

(51) "causasus" p. 49.
(51) "yes no How are..." p. 49.
(62) "Therefor" p. 61 and throughout the text.
(63) "Sayn can say" p. 63.
(69) "extermish" p. 70.
(73) "fortuitious" corrected to [fortuitous] p. 74.
(100) "partly whether.is there" p. 106.
(109) "Uragayen" p. 116.
(115) "dubeity" p. 121.
(115) "Buic" p. 121.
(117) "Insence" p. 124.
(120) "Adjective Made receptively." p. 127.
(126) "liklihood" p. 134. See also (219), 233.
(131) "tention" p. 138.
(133) "call t mine" p. 141.
(139) "paraphanelia" p. 148
(147) "therefor" p. 157.
(155) "annoint" p. 165. See also (336), 360 "annointed."
(155) "sentance" p. 165.
(157) "therefor" p. 167.
(157) "ti" p. 168.
(163) "lieve" p. 173.

(163) "stong" corrected to [strong] p. 174.

(167) "therefor" p. 177.

(171) "Disappointement" p. 182.

(180) "begining" p. 192.

(186) "so a sentence is this they liked it" p. 199.

(192) "devination" p. 205.

(203) "Therefor" p. 216.

(209) "stayes" p. 223.

(226) lanters" p. 241.

(228) "arrangment" has been corrected to [arrangement] p. 243.

(236) "Hatold Acton" p. 252.

(237) "fitteen" p. 253.

(238) "plantif" p. 253.

(240) "Christamas" p. 255.

(247) "Anyhing" p. 264.

(254) "wich" has been corrected to [which] p. 271.

(264) "Bay grew" p. 283.

(264) "tasselated" p. 283.

(279) "te" p. 300.

(286) "paticcular" has been corrected to [particular] p. 307.

(293) "interupting" p. 315.

(297) "renumeration" p. 319.

(298) "ocasional" p. 320.

(300) "jeapordising" p. 322.

(304) "accomodation" p. 326. See also (359), 385 and (361), 388.

(326) "he" p. 350.

(329) "parrallelism" p. 354.

(331) "Thurdsay" p. 355.

(339) "boilling" corrected to [boiling] p. 364.

(340) "Gomorah" p. 364.

(342) "te" corrected to [to] p. 366.

(343) "Prehaps" p. 368.

(345) "exhuberance" p. 370.
(347) "annullment" p. 372.
(351) "more then ever" p. 377.
(360) "astrakan" p. 386.
(361) "wainright" p. 387.
(375) "calender" p. 402.
(375) "postively" p. 402.
(376) "peculiaity" p. 403.
(376) "agressive" corrected to [aggressive] p. 404.
(377) "harrangue" p. 405.
(377) "tyranical" p. 405.
(381) "indistructible" p. 409.
(386) "It is very patient to ask this for him Patient." p. 415.
(392) "betow" p. 421.
(395) "Forenscis" p. 424.

GERTRUDE STEIN

Gertrude Stein is well known internationally as a literary fig-
ure and as the author of *Tender Buttons, Three Lives, The
Autobiography of Alice B. Toklas*, and of the opera *Four Saints
in Three Acts*.

But her literary celebrity has somewhat obscured her major contribution to American writing in the twentieth century. At one time or another Stein attempted nearly every
literary genre available, including the encyclopedic fiction
(*The Making of Americans*), the picaresque (*Ida*), the pasto-
ral (*Lucy Church Amiably*), the dialogue (*Browsie and Willie*),
the poetic meditation (*Stanzas in Meditation*), the alpha-
betic fiction (*To Do*), the anatomy (*A Long Gay Book*), and
numerous portraits, prayers, memoirs, essays, plays, operas,
and other literary forms. The myth that much of Stein's other
writing is repetitious is belied by the very variety of the forms
she undertook. Indeed it is perhaps the almost myopic focus
on the novel and the lyric poem in the twentieth century
that has contributed to the lack of recognition of Stein's great
accomplishments.

Breadth, however, is not her only contribution. The origi-
nality and the quality of these works have helped them to
influence several generations of writers including modern
and contemporary figures such as Ernest Hemingway, Paul
and Jane Bowles, John Cage, Jackson Mc Low, David Antin,
Lyn Hejinian, Charles Bernstein, and numerous other fiction writers and poets.

Born in Allegheny, Pennsylvania in 1874, Stein studied
under William James at The Johns Hopkins University in
Baltimore. Although she lived at various times in Oakland,
San Francisco, Boston and Florence, her most noted resi-
dence was in Paris, where she presided in salons over a broad

group of painters and writers — expatriates and natives — who together created some of the major writing and art of this century.

Most of those French years Stein lived with her long-time companion Alice B. Toklas, whose "autobiography," penned by Stein, made both household names. A tour of the United States two years later brought further acclaim to the author, who returned to France and resided there throughout World War II. She died in Paris in 1946.

SUN & MOON CLASSICS

This publication was made possible, in part, through an operational grant from the Andrew W. Mellon Foundation and through contributions from the following individuals and organizations:

Tom Ahern (Foster, Rhode Island)
Charles Altieri (Seattle, Washington)
John Arden (Galway, Ireland)
Paul Auster (Brooklyn, New York)
Jesse Huntley Ausubel (New York, New York)
Luigi Ballerini (Los Angeles, California)
Dennis Barone (West Hartford, Connecticut)
Jonathan Baumbach (Brooklyn, New York)
Roberto Bedoya (Los Angeles, California)
Guy Bennett (Los Angeles, California)
Bill Berkson (Bolinas, California)
Steve Benson (Berkeley, California)
Charles Bernstein and Susan Bee (New York, New York)
Dorothy Bilik (Silver Spring, Maryland)
Alain Bosquet (Paris, France)
In Memoriam: John Cage
In Memoriam: Camilo José Cela
Rosita Copioli (Rimini, Italy)
Bill Corbett (Boston, Massachusetts)
Robert Crosson (Los Angeles, California)
Tina Darragh and P. Inman (Greenbelt, Maryland)
Fielding Dawson (New York, New York)
Christopher Dewdney (Toronto, Canada)
Larry Deyah (New York, New York)
Arkadii Dragomoschenko (St. Petersburg, Russia)
George Economou (Norman, Oklahoma)
Richard Elman (Stony Brook, New York)
Kenward Elmslie (Calais, Vermont)
Elaine Equi and Jerome Sala (New York, New York)
Lawrence Ferlinghetti (San Francisco, California)
Richard Foreman (New York, New York)
Howard N. Fox (Los Angeles, California)
Jerry Fox (Aventura, Florida)
In Memoriam: Rose Fox
Melvyn Freilicher (San Diego, California)
Miro Gavran (Zagreb, Croatia)

Allen Ginsberg (New York, New York)
Peter Glassgold (Brooklyn, New York)
Barbara Guest (Berkeley, California)
Perla and Amiram V. Karney (Bel Air, California)
Václav Havel (Prague, The Czech Republic)
Lyn Hejinian (Berkeley, California)
Fanny Howe (La Jolla, California)
Harold Jaffe (San Diego, California)
Ira S. Jaffe (Albuquerque, New Mexico)
Ruth Prawer Jhabvala (New York, New York)
Pierre Joris (Albany, New York)
Alex Katz (New York, New York)
Pamela and Rowan Klein (Los Angeles, California)
Tom LaFarge (New York, New York)
Mary Jane Lafferty (Los Angeles, California)
Michael Lally (Santa Monica, California)
Norman Lavers (Jonesboro, Arkansas)
Jerome Lawrence (Malibu, California)
Stacey Levine (Seattle, Washington)
Herbert Lust (Greenwich, Connecticut)
Norman MacAffee (New York, New York)
Rosemary Macchiavelli (Washington, DC)
Jackson Mac Low (New York, New York)
In Memoriam: Mary McCarthy
Harry Mulisch (Amsterdam, The Netherlands)
Iris Murdoch (Oxford, England)
Martin Nakell (Los Angeles, California)
In Memoriam: bpNichol
Cees Nooteboom (Amsterdam, The Netherlands)
NORLA (Norwegian Literature Abroad) (Oslo, Norway)
Claes Oldenburg (New York, New York)
Toby Olson (Philadelphia, Pennsylvania)
Maggie O'Sullivan (Hebden Bridge, England)
Rochelle Owens (Norman, Oklahoma)
Bart Parker (Providence, Rhode Island)
Marjorie and Joseph Perloff (Pacific Palisades, California)
Dennis Phillips (Los Angeles, California)
Carl Rakosi (San Francisco, California)
Tom Raworth (Cambridge, England)
David Reed (New York, New York)
Ishmael Reed (Oakland, California)
Tom Roberdeau (Los Angeles, California)

SUN & MOON CLASSICS